THE CAMPAIGNS OF WORLD WAR II

THE FALL OF THE REICH

Dr. Duncan Anderson

MBI Publishing Company

940
.5421
AND

This edition first published in 2000 by
MBI Publishing Company,
729 Prospect Avenue, PO Box 1, Osceola, WI 54020-0001 USA

MBI Publishing Company books are also available at discounts in bulk quantity
for industrial or sales-promotional use. For details write to Special Sales Manager
at Motorbooks International Wholesalers & Distributors, 729 Prospect Avenue,
PO Box 1, Osceola, WI 54020-0001 USA.

Library of Congress Cataloging-in-Publication Data Available.

ISBN 0-7603-0922-1

Editorial and design: Amber Books Ltd
Bradley's Close, 74-77 White Lion Street,
London N1 9PF

Chapters 10 and 11 in this volume were written by Lloyd Clark

Project Editor: Charles Catton
Editor: Stuart McReady
Design: Neil Rigby at Stylus Design, www.stylus-design.com
Picture Research: Ken Botham at TRH Pictures

Picture credits
TRH Pictures: 6 (US Dept of Defense), 8, 9, 11, 12, 13, 14, 14-15, 16 (US National Archives), 17, 18, (IWM), 19, 20 (US Air Force), 22, 24, 25, 26, 27 (US National Archives), 28-29 (US Army), 29, 30 (IWM), 31 (IWM), 32 (IWM), 33, 35 (t) (US Dept of Defense), 35 (b) (IWM), 36 (IWM), 37 (US Army), 38 (US Army), 40 (IWM), 41 (t) (US National Archives), 41 (b), 42, 44 (US Navy), 45 (US Dept of Defense), 46 (IWM), 47 (t), 48 (t) (IWM), 49 (US National Archives), 50 (b), 51, 52 (both), 53 (US Dept of Defense), 54 (IWM), 55, 56, 57 (b), 59 (t), 60 (t) (IWM), 60, 61, 62, 64, 65 (both), 66 (t) (IWM), 67 (both), 68 (both) (IWM), 69 (US National Archives), 70 (t) (US Army), 70 (b), 71 (t), 72, 73 (t) (US National Archives), 73 (b) (IWM), 74 (t), 75, 76 (both), 77, 78, 81, 82, 83 (m), 83 (b) (US Army), 84, 86 (both), 87, 88 (b), 89, 90 (IWM), 91 (both), 92, 93 (t), 94 (t) (IWM), 94 (b) (US National Archives), 95, 96, 97 (both), 98 (both), 99, 100 (IWM), 100-101, 102, 103 (both), 104 (both), 105 (t), 106 (IWM), 106-107, 108, 110, 111 (IWM), 112 (both), 113, 114, 115, 116, 117 (US National Archives), 118 (IWM), 119 (t) (US National Archives), 119, 120, 121 (US Dept. of Defense), 122 (US National Archives), 123, 124 (both), 125, 126, 128, 129, 130, 132 (IWM), 133, 134, 135, 136, 137, 138, 130 (IWM), 140, 141, 142, 144 (US Army), 145, 146, 147, 148, 149, 150 (IWM), 151 (US National Archives), 152, 153, 154, 155 (IWM), 156 (IWM), 157 (IWM), 158 (IWM), 159, 161, 162 (IWM), 163 (t) (Bundesarchiv), 163, 164, 166, 167 (t), 168, 169 (IWM), 170, 171, 172, 173, 174, 175 (IWM), 176 177 (b), 178, 180 (both), 181, 182 (IWM), 184 (both), 185 (both), 186, 187 (b), 188, 189 (both), 190 (US Dept of Defense), 191 (IWM), 192 (both), 193 (US National Archives), 194 (US National Archives), 195 (t) (IWM), 195 (b) (US Army), 196 (both), 197, 198 (US Army), 200 (t) (IWM), 200 (b) (US Army), 201 (IWM), 202, 203 (both), 204 (US Army), 206-207, 208, 209 (b), 210 (both), 211, 212 (both), 213 (both), 214 (t), 215 (both), 216 (both), 217, 218 (t), 219 (b), 220, 221 (both), 222, 223, 224 (b), 224-225, 226 (b), 226-227, 228, 229, 230, 231 (both), 232 (US National Archives), 233 (US National Archives).

Artwork credits
Aerospace Publishing: 21, 47 (b), 50 (t), 57 (t), 66 (b), 80, 153 (t), 167 (b), 181 (t), 187 (t), 209.
De Agostini UK: 10, 23, 34, 43, 48 (b), 58, 59 (b), 71(b), 74 (b), 79, 88 (t), 93 (b), 105 (b) 117 (b), 131, 160, 177 (t), 183 (both), 199, 206, 210 (b), 218 (b), 219 (t), 225 (b), 226 (t).

Printed and bound in Italy

*Page 2: Three American GIs walk up a road in shortly after Operation Anvil, the landings in southern France.
By late summer 1944, the German Reich found itself being squeezed on all fronts. (TRH Pictures)*

CONTENTS

CHAPTER ONE

PREPARATIONS FOR D-DAY

The long-anticipated invasion of France was a huge gamble for the Allies, and mounting the largest amphibious operation yet seen would require a great deal of planning and preparation.

During the winter of 1941–42 the *Oberkommando der Wehrmacht* (OKW, the German armed forces high command) came to accept that the war was going to last years rather than months. The completely unexpected Soviet counter-offensive of 5 December 1941 had been followed two days later by the Japanese attack on Pearl Harbor, which had triggered a German declaration of war against the United States on 10 December. Although it had a large navy, the army of the United States was minuscule, and OKW reasoned that it would be at least 18 months before substantial American forces could be established in Britain, and perhaps even longer if the German navy's submarine campaign maintained its so far successful campaign against Allied shipping. In these circumstances the most logical strategy for Germany was to concentrate on the defeat of the USSR, while establishing a defensive system which would delay any Allied attempt to land on the coasts of western Europe. On 23 March 1942 Adolf Hitler issued Directive No 40, an order to begin the construction of fortifications along the coastline of the continent, from Norway's North Cape to the Franco-Spanish frontier.

At first construction proceeded at an almost leisurely pace. The apparent lack of urgency was reflected in the appointment of 67-year-old Field Marshal Gerd von Rundstedt as commander-in-chief in the west. Hitler, obsessed that the British would attempt a landing in Norway to protect their convoys to the Soviet port of Murmansk, ordered that priority be given to defending the coastline from Narvik to Bergen. By the autumn of 1943, the harbours and fjords of Norway bristled with 350 batteries, with guns ranging from 88mm (3.49in) to 406mm (16in), making the Norwegian coast the most heavily fortified in the world. The French coast, by contrast, had been relatively neglected, construction being confined to ports and submarine bases. On 18 August 1942 the still-unfinished Dieppe defences, manned initially by only 200 over-age reservists, managed to defeat a landing attempt by 5000 Canadian and British troops. Hitler now ordered that the construction of fortifications along the French coast, similar to the Siegfried Line along the Franco-German border, should proceed with 'fanatic energy'. However, the real effect of the victory at Dieppe was to lull OKW into complacency. It was only after the success of Allied landings against opposition in Sicily in July 1943 and at Salerno in September 1943, that Hitler issued Directive 51, ordering a crash programme to create a system of fortifications from Antwerp to Biarritz which would ensure 'the collapse of the enemy attack before, if possible, but at the latest upon the actual landing'.

In order to accelerate the work, on 5 November Hitler ordered Field Marshal Erwin Rommel on a tour of inspection of the Atlantic Wall, and on 1 January 1944 appointed him to operational command of Army Group B, the 7th and 15th armies, responsible for the north coast of France from the Pas de Calais to Brittany. Almost immediately, Rommel was in dispute with commander-in-chief von Rundstedt, who very much resented Germany's most famous soldier interfering with his command. In addition, the two men disagreed fundamentally on the best way to resist an Allied landing. Having served in the victorious campaigns in France in 1940 and Russia in 1941, von Rundstedt was loathe to adopt a purely defensive attitude, and had been pressing hard for the stationing of first-line field divisions in

France. By early 1944 he had 24, including 10 panzer divisions. Von Rundstedt wanted to wait until the Allies were in the process of establishing a beachhead and then hit them with a large panzer group of 6 divisions, which he was keeping in reserve around Paris under the command of General Leo Freiherr Geyr von Schweppenberg. Rommel, who had fought in North Africa between October 1942 and May 1943 against Allied forces who who enjoyed ever-increasing air superiority, believed Geyr von Schweppenberg's panzers would be obliterated by a combination of Allied bombers and naval gunfire while they were still miles from the beachhead. The only solution, Rommel argued, was to destroy Allied landing forces while they were coming ashore, a position which was supported by Admiral Theodor Krancke, commander-in-chief of Naval Group Command West. Rommel and Krancke urged a massive and rapid expansion of the Atlantic Wall defences, with the stationing of Geyr von Schweppenberg's armour close to the coast behind the more likely landing beaches.

German preparations continue

In January 1944, in an interview for a special edition of the Wehrmacht's *Signal* magazine covering the construction of the Atlantic Wall, von Rundstedt launched a covert attack on Rommel, stating that 'we Germans do not indulge in the tired Maginot spirit.' Rommel responded with a scathing report to OKW on the Atlantic Wall, warning that unless his policy was adopted, 'the enemy will probably succeed in creating bridgeheads at several different points and in achieving a major penetration of our coastal defences.' The row between the field marshals soon involved the inspector general of panzers, Heinz Guderian, and finally Hitler himself, who suggested the face-saving compromise that the panzer reserve should be placed under his command, and not be moved without his authority. Thus a third layer of command was imposed on a structure which had already caused friction.

In the meantime, largely thanks to Rommel's exertions, the Atlantic Wall defences were beginning to become a reality. By the spring the Todt Organisation (an organisation of noncombatant Nazi party construction brigades, named after Hitler's minister for munitions and construction, 1940-42, Dr Fritz Todt) and the *Reichsarbeitsdienst* (the compulsory labour

BELOW

Field Marshal Erwin Rommel inspecting the defences of the Atlantic Wall. Rommel was appointed to the operational command of Army Group B on 1 January 1944, and at once ordered the strengthening of the Atlantic coastal defences.

Some of the Organisation Todt's concrete mixers churning out the necessary ingredients for the Atlantic Wall's defences under Rommel's crash construction programme. Much of the equipment Rommel asked for never actually made it to Normandy.

service) were engaged in the largest construction project in European history, with 260,000 men pouring 13 million tons of concrete and using 1.2 million tons of steel to create a planned 15,000 strong points. Albert Speer, now minister of munitions and head of the Todt Organisation, recalled that Hitler, a frustrated architect, took a close personal interest in the design of the installations, remarking that 'his plans met all the requirements of the front-line soldier.' For once he was right.

In order to speed production, the Germans concentrated on three basic types of position: the *Verteidigungsbereich*, a fortress capable of protecting several battalions, the *Stutzpunkt*, a position occupied by a unit from company up to battalion size, and the *Widerstandsnest*, which could hold a unit from section to platoon size. Because the Allies now had virtual control of the air, these positions were skilfully camouflaged, but could, in any event, survive a considerable bombardment by either aerial bombs or naval gunfire.

The Germans armed these positions by stripping guns from the Czech Sudeten defences, the Maginot Line, and the Stalin Line. In March 1944 German forces in the west had been supplied with nearly 4000 guns of foreign manufacture, comprising 61 different types, a nightmare for logisticians, though only about a quarter of these had actually been positioned in emplacements. The heaviest concentrations were around the Pas de Calais, in and around ports and U-boat bases, and in the Channel Islands, where 32,000 workers had installed 32 heavy guns, though by June 1944 all parts of the coast could be brought under gun fire. The German navy provided a communication system of land lines linked to teletype machines, which could not be listened in on, and a chain of radar stations, which could give early warning of an attack and help direct fire.

Rommel's minefields

At El Alamein in October 1942 Rommel had placed about half a million mines – many of them constructed from captured British bombs and shells – in the densest minefield yet seen, and had prevented Montgomery's numerically superior forces from breaking through for nearly two weeks. Rommel now drew up plans for laying 60 million mines in broad belts along the coast, though only 6 million were in place by the beginning of June. On the more likely landing beaches mines were combined with artificial obstacles.

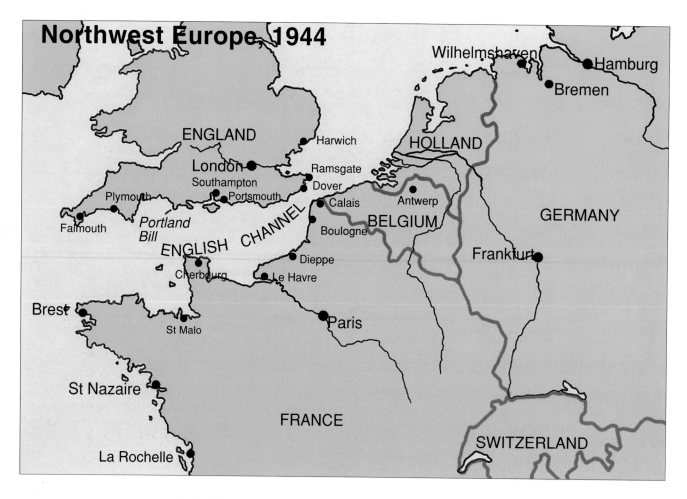

Northwest Europe 1944

At the low-water mark wooden or concrete stakes were driven into the sand and angled outward, usually with an explosive device attached, designed to rip the bottom out of a landing craft. Closer to the high-water mark, engineers utilised rows of tetrahedra – pyramids composed of five steel stakes – which had originally formed part of the Czech anti-tank defences in the Sudetenland. Closer still to the shoreline the Germans implanted rows of curved-rail obstacles with sharp ends, which could hole a landing craft or hold it in position while artillery zeroed in.

Anti-paratroop defences

Rommel was well aware that the Allies now had large airborne formations, and that any invasion would involve gliders and paratroops as well as landing craft. During the winter a specialist battalion of geologists and geographers had surveyed the northern coast of France, and with the help of engineers and the the Todt Organisation had flooded river valleys and estuaries from the Somme to the Loire, converting water meadows to swamps, and swamps to lakes, which in some places, particularly in the south-east of the

Contentin Peninsula, were deep enough to drown paratroops. In drier areas German pioneers drove sharpened wooden stakes into fields and linked them with a lattice work of wire so that they resembled gigantic bird nets. By the beginning of June, 5 million stakes were in place in northern France, and another 45 million were scheduled. On 5 May Rommel rejected a proposal from 15th Army to have the Luftwaffe inspect these obstacles. He was only too well aware that they were of doubtful effectiveness, and he admitted to his aide Speidel that the effect was largely psychological, in that they improved the morale of the defenders.

The Atlantic Wall was of little use without troops to man it, and during the course of 1943 the Germans had been deploying static divisions as coastal defence divisions, composed of men too old for service in field divisions. The 711th, for example, which was deployed at the mouth of the Orne River in Normandy, was largely composed of Class II reservists, men born in 1901 who had undergone no military training prior to the outbreak of war. As the likelihood of invasion rose, the static divisions were supplemented by the so-called 'stomach divisions', men whose physical disabilities debarred them from other forms of service. The most famous, the 70th division, consisted entirely of men suffering from stomach ulcers, who, because they were concentrated in their own formation, could receive special acid-free rations. In the winter of 1943-44 the coastal-defence divisions were reinforced by battalions of *Osttruppen*, volunteers from amongst Soviet prisoners. The 709th divisions, which was stationed on the eastern shore of the Cotentin Peninsula, received eight battalions of Georgians, while the 275th division contained eight different national groups, mainly from the Caucasus and Central Asia, but including a handful of disoriented Tibetans who had been press-ganged into the Soviet army while grazing their herds near the Khazak border in 1941. Some of the *Osttruppen* were clearly of indifferent quality, but not all. On 18 May 1944, during an inspection of the 77th Division on the south-western coast of the Cotentin Peninsula, Rommel had been favourably impressed with a battalion of Tartars who had been trained

and were commanded 'in an exemplary fashion'. By May 1944, 34 static divisions had been formed and were manning the Atlantic Wall between Calais and Biarritz.

Rather than waiting for an Allied invasion fleet to arrive, Rommel would have preferred to have had naval and air forces attack it in mid-Channel. By June 1944 the German navy on the Atlantic and Channel coast had been reduced to just four destroyers, four large torpedo boats, 35 'E-boats' (Motor Torpedo Boats), 50 submarines, and about 450 smaller craft – armed trawlers, coasters and the like – but although massively outclassed by Allied forces there was still much that it could do. In the winter of 1943-44 the German navy laid 16 minefields in the Channel between Boulogne and Cherbourg, with a number of smaller fields closer to shore. Most mines were fitted with a time mechanism which deactivated them after 80 days, however, so that by June they had been inert for more than two months. Once the invasion force had been detected the German navy intended to use its 'E-boats' to lay *Blitzsperren* (lightning fields) of 'oyster' mines

BELOW
German gunners in late 1943, building up defensive earthworks around their artillery piece, which has been camouflaged to hide it from air attack.

in the path of the Allies, devices which were detonated by the change in water pressure caused by ships passing over them. Submarines, destroyers and torpedo boats were to conduct attacks on the flanks of the Allied convoys.

The Germans' most serious deficiency was in the air. On 1 April 1944 Hitler had promised Field Marshal Hugo Sperrle, commander of the 3rd Air Force, which had responsibility for north-west Europe, that the arrival of the first of 1000 new Messerschmitt Me 262 jet fighters was imminent. In June Sperrle was still waiting, his nominal strength down to 500 aircraft, of which only 160 (90 bombers and 70 fighters) were operational. Despite this much reduced capacity, Sperrle still commanded over 300,000 men, of whom 100,000 were serving in the Luftwaffe's powerful III Flak Corps, a much more potent threat to enemy aircraft than the hapless fighter squadrons. In addition, Sperrle commanded a new strategic offensive force, the *Vergeltunsgwaffen* I (VI) pilotless aircraft, the launchers for which were being built in the area between Calais and Le Have, and on the

northern coast of the Cotentin Peninsula. They were originally intended for use on 20 April 1944, (Hitler's birthday), but delays in production caused the postponement of the first attacks until 13 June.

German confidence

Though they had been slow to mature, German plans for the defence of the west were well advanced by the early summer of 1944. If he could concentrate his forces quickly, Rommel was confident he could smash any invasion on the beaches, but the problem lay in not knowing where the invasion would hit. Rommel and his naval counterparts at first thought the Allies would land at the mouth of the Somme, but von Rundstedt and Sperrle were sure that it would come in the Pas de Calais, in part because of the concentration of V1 sites in this region, in part because it was closer to Germany, but mainly because this is where German agents in Britain said the attack was going to come. After the war, admirers of Rommel claimed near miraculous powers of divination for their hero. On 9 May, during a visit to the 1716th Artillery Regiment dug in at Ouistreham in Normandy, the seaport for Caen, Rommel reportedly called the officers together, stood for a long time with his back to them staring out to sea, and turning slowly said, 'Gentlemen, if they come they will come here.' But Rommel was not alone at this stage in predicting a landing in Normandy, for the following day an OKW intelligence summary stated tersely 'Point of concentration first and foremost: Normandy; secondly, Brittany'. Over the next few days Rommel and the rest of the German high command again changed their minds, and in a conversation with Major General Kramer at von Rundstedt's head-quarters on 3 June, Rommel was now fairly certain that the landings would come at the mouth of the Somme. The simple truth is that the Germans did not know where or when the blow would fall, and their predictions oscillated back and forth along the northern coast of France, just occasionally getting it

right. But there was one thing Rommel did get right, and that was the circumstances in which the Allies would attack. Addressing the crew of a gun battery on 17 May, Rommel told them 'not to expect the enemy during good weather or during the day. They would have to be prepared for the enemy to come with clouds and storm, and after midnight.' It seems extraordinary, then, that on 4 June, when the weather changed from a warm early summer calm to rain and stormy westerlies, Rommel left for Germany to celebrate his wife's 50th birthday.

British reluctance

Since 1945 British historians have been at pains to prove that Britain was preparing to return to Europe with a cross-Channel invasion almost as soon as the evacuation of Dunkirk was completed. The prime mover of a British invasion, these historians argue, was the prime minister, Winston Churchill.

BELOW
A machine gunner mans his weapon in a bunker on the Atlantic Wall. Many of the soldiers responsible for Rommel's defences were Ostruppen, soldiers who had gone over to the German side after Hitler's invasion of the Soviet Union in 1941.

Unfortunately, the basis of this argument depends on taking a few scattered references out of context, and ignoring a mass of evidence to the contrary. The simple fact was that the British high command were not at all happy about a cross-Channel invasion, and would have preferred almost any other means of attacking Germany.

There were several reasons for this reluctance. The British had relatively recent experience of a major amphibious operation going terribly wrong. On 25 April 1915 British and Dominion troops, hoping that they could take Istanbul and knock Turkey out of the war, had landed on Gallipoli. The result had been a fiasco, in which the Turks pinned the British down in narrow

BELOW

A German artillery bunker on the Atlantic Wall. Defensive works originally built by the French were often strengthened and upgraded by the Germans. At St Malo, for example, 19.4cm (7.6 inch) guns of French manufacture commanded the harbour.

bridgeheads, inflicted some 250,000 casualties upon them, and forced their evacuation at the end of the year. As First Lord of the Admiralty, Churchill had been one of the architects of the landings, and had been forced to resign. In addition, Churchill, most of his cabinet, and all senior officers were haunted by the losses suffered in the various frontal assaults on the Western Front during World War I, particularly the Somme in July 1916 and Passchendaele in October 1917. In *The World Crisis*, Churchill's analysis of World War I published in 1928, he had made scathing references to the generalship of Sir Douglas Haig – the overall British commander – and other senior generals, who seemed to lack the

ABOVE

SS troops being inspected by Rommel in Normandy. Behind them is the workhorse of the German Army's transport units throughout World War II, the Opel Blitz truck.

ability to think in terms other than striking at the enemy in the most obvious place.

The indirect strategy

Now that Churchill was running his own war, his instinct was that Britain should follow an indirect strategy, using the Royal Navy's preponderance at sea to hit at Germany and her allies in peripheral theatres, while Bomber Command of the RAF brought the war directly to German cities. Thus in 1942, when the Germans began work on the Atlantic Wall, four of Britain's eight armoured divisions and 14 of her 25 infantry divisions were employed in the Middle or the Far East, defending the Suez Canal against the Italians and the Indian empire against the Japanese. The British had formed a Combined Operations command in 1940, tasked with planning amphibious and airborne operations against the German occupied coast of north-west Europe, but its aim was to conduct raids, not a full-scale invasion of the continent.

Hitler's and Mussolini's declaration of war on 11 December 1941 brought the United States into the European conflict. Seizing the moment, on 22 December Churchill and the British chiefs of staff arrived in Washington, and stayed until 14 January 1942 for what would become known as the Arcadia Conference. The British managed to secure

British Prime Minister Winston S. Churchill addressing American troops at a location somewhere in England. To mislead the Germans, the Allies created a 'phantom army' in the south-east, diverting attention away from the main build-up in southern England.

the American high command's agreement to give priority to the war against Germany, though this caused difficulties for Roosevelt. While the Pearl Harbor attack had incensed popular feeling in the United States against Japan, feelings towards Germany and Italy were more ambivalent. This was not merely because a high proportion of the American population were of German or Italian descent, but because there was a genuine suspicion that Britain would seek to use US power largely to further its own ends. To a certain extent this popular apprehension was shared by members of the high command, particularly the chief of staff of the US Navy,

Admiral Ernest J. King, and chief of staff of the US Army, General George C. Marshall. For the rest of the war King headed a faction which wanted to concentrate efforts against Japan, and gave Roosevelt a powerful bargaining chip in his dealings with Churchill. Marshall disagreed with King, but argued that the only legitimate use of American forces in the European theatre would be for the earliest possible cross-Channel invasion.

Sitting behind Marshall during the Arcadia meetings was a bald officer in his early fifties, Major General Dwight D. Eisenhower, the head of the military planning department. A little over two years earlier, Eisenhower had been a 'passed-over' major, serving as chief of staff in the Philippines to the imperious and increasingly erratic General Douglas MacArthur. In late 1939 Eisenhower had managed to secure himself a transfer back to the United States, and eventually to Washington, where Marshall found his advice on managing MacArthur, a man he personally loathed, invaluable. Eisenhower's promotion had been rapid, even by the standards of wartime, and the diary he kept during the Arcadia conference traced the evolution of the major into a global strategist. On 5 January Eisenhower wrote, 'The conversations with the British grow wearisome. They're difficult to talk to, apparently afraid someone is trying to tell them what to do and how to do it. Their practice of war is dilatory.' By the end of the conference, later in the month, his views had crystallised. 'We've got to build up air and land forces in England and when we're strong enough, go after Germany's vitals, and we've got to do it while Russia is still in the war.'

At Marshall's instruction, by late March 1942 Eisenhower and his staff had prepared an invasion plan, code-named Round Up. By 1 April 1943 he wanted to be able to land six British and American divisions on the French coast somewhere between Boulogne and Le Havre. Reinforcements would follow at the rate of 100,000 men a week, until a force of 30 American and 18 British divisions was in Europe. The invasion would require 7000 landing craft (yet to be built), 3000 American and 2500 British aircraft, few of which had yet left the factory.

British doubts

Such was the scheme which Marshall, accompanied by Roosevelt's aide Harry Hopkins, took to London on 8 April 1942. The British, desperate for American aid, paid lip service to it, and on the evening of 14 April Marshall expressed before Churchill his relief that 'agreement has been reached on the basic for a frontal assault on the enemy in northern France in 1943.' In reality there was nothing

BELOW
General Dwight D. Eisenhower chats with American troops on the eve of the invasion. Eisenhower had never commanded troops until he was put in charge of the Anglo-American 'Torch' landings in North Africa in November 1942. There was a good deal of opposition to his appointment as Supreme Commander Allied Forces in Europe, but he had many qualities that made him a good leader.

about it that the British liked. The prime minister, always conscious of the power of words, was appalled by the code name, but felt he was stuck with it. He minuted, 'I fear that to change the name "Round Up" would make the Americans think there was some change of purpose. Therefore we must stick to this boastful, ill-chosen name, and hope it does not bring us bad luck.' The chief of the imperial general staff, General Alan Brooke, confided to his diary: 'These plans are fraught with the gravest dangers. The prospects of success are small and dependent on a mass of unknowns, while the chances of disaster are great and dependent on a mass of well-established military facts.'

Sledgehammer

The British high command had an additional problem, for in the autumn of 1941 its planning staff had drawn up an operation code-named Sledgehammer. This involved landing 8-10 British divisions on the coast of France, possibly in Brittany or on the Cotentin Peninsula, in the event that a Soviet collapse appeared imminent. It was, in fact, no more than a contingency plan, which would involve the almost certain loss of most of the forces involved. Unfortunately, Eisenhower was taken with the idea, offered to add two American divisions to the landing forces, and set a target date of 15 September 1942. Like the British, he regarded it as little more than a suicide operation, estimated that the chances of getting the lead division ashore were about one in two, while the chances of establishing a six-division beachhead were about one in five, but argued that it should nevertheless go ahead because 'the prize we seek is to keep 8,000,000 Russians in the war.'

When the British received Eisenhower's version of Sledgehammer on 20 July, they were aghast. Brooke argued that only the diversion of dozens of German divisions, not the few which they would require to eliminate Sledgehammer, would help the Russians, and on 22 July Churchill informed Roosevelt that 'no responsible British general,

BELOW
Watching and waiting: a German gunner at his position on the Atlantic Wall. Allied deception tactics kept the Germans guessing about where the invasion would take place.

LEFT
A knocked-out Churchill tank on the beach at Dieppe after the disastrous raid. Although the attack was a dreadful failure, it did teach the Allies valuable lessons on how to conduct amphibious landings.

admiral, or air marshal is prepared to recommend "Sledgehammer" as a practicable operation in 1942.' They proposed instead landings in French North Africa, which Roosevelt and Marshall accepted as all that could be accomplished in 1942. A deeply depressed Eisenhower confided to a friend, 'Well, I hardly know where to start the day.' He wrote in his diary that Wednesday 22 July 1942 could well go down as the 'blackest day in history'.

The problem with the Americans, the British told each other, was that they were too enthusiastic, and had not been involved in an amphibious operation since 1898, a landing against demoralised Spanish forces in Cuba. They believed that modern, armoured, engine-powered landing craft and radio communications had obviated many of the difficulties which had bedevilled the British at Gallipoli, and this was something the British knew was not true. In the early hours of 19 August 1942 a joint force – 5000 Canadians, 1100 British Commandos, and 50 American Rangers – went ashore at Dieppe. The highly-trained, experienced Commandos, tasked with attacking German coastal defence guns to the east and west of Dieppe, conducted a successful operation. The flamboyant Lieutenant Colonel Lord Lovat led No. 4 Commando in a ferocious attack against the battery at Berneval, 6km (3.7 miles) east of Dieppe, and virtually wiped out the German

defenders. Meanwhile, No 3 Commando, reduced to one landing craft and 20 men after a battle in the English Channel with German 'E-boats', put ashore at the Varengeville battery, 6km (3.7 miles) to the west of the town. Major Peter Young, the surviving senior officer, led his small command into a furious assault which pinned down the German gunners for the next three hours.

The main attack at Dieppe

With the flanking defence batteries out of action, the bulk of the inexperienced Canadians came ashore at Dieppe. Since the town was defended by only 200 over-age reservists, the attack should have been a foregone conclusion, but it turned into a disaster. The firing to the east and west alerted the Germans, who immediately occupied strong positions, setting up their machine guns in newly constructed cliff-side pillboxes, and in the upper rooms of houses with a clear view of the beach. The handful of Germans poured a stream of fire into the landing craft, cutting swathes through the Canadians as they struggled out of the water.

With the Canadians held on the beach, the Germans rushed reserves to Dieppe. The result was a massacre. By late afternoon von Rundstedt could report to Hitler the satisfying news that 'no armed Englishman remains on the continent.' The British and Canadians left behind 3648 dead and wounded men and

Douglas Boston (A-20) light bombers en route to attack targets on the Channel coast. By the first week of June 1944 air attack had knocked out some 80 per cent of the enemy's coastal radar capability. This view illustrates clearly the wide sandy beaches of the Normandy coast, one of the reasons this area was chosen for the invasion.

prisoners at Dieppe. Some 500 of those who made it back to England were very badly wounded, whereas the Germans took comparatively few casualties. There was no coordination between air, sea and land forces, and when air and naval gunfire support finally arrived, it proved woefully inadequate. Worse still, the Allies' Churchill tanks had handled the beach conditions very badly – they either dug into the shale, or shed tracks when trying to climb the sea wall.

Churchill's response

It was fortunate for the commander of Combined Operations, Lord Louis Mountbatten, that Churchill was in Egypt on 19 August, and was well pleased with Mountbatten's overly optimistic account of the impact of the raid. But on his return to Britain he read detailed reports, and minuted to his chief of staff, General 'Pug' Ismay: 'I must be informed more precisely about the

military plans. Who made them? Who approved them?' As details of the fiasco slowly emerged, Churchill consoled himself that Dieppe had 'shed revealing light on many shortcomings in our outlook.' It had revealed yet again 'that team work was the secret of success. This could only be provided by trained and organised amphibious formations.' Above all, Dieppe shocked the Americans out of their naive optimism about the ease with which major amphibious operations could be conducted, and a new and more sombre mood characterised discussions.

In January 1943 Roosevelt, Churchill and the Combined Chiefs of Staff met at Casablanca. They agreed to press ahead with Operation Round Up, and also to establish an Anglo-American planing staff. Eight weeks later, British logistics specialist General Sir Frederick Morgan was appointed chief of staff to the supreme Allied commander (COSSAC), and given the task of planning the invasion.

Morgan's offices, in Norfolk House in London's St James' Square, were soon filled with the best staff which the British and American armies could provide, their numbers swollen by transfers from Lord Louis Mountbatten's combined operations headquarters, the organisation which had planned many commando raids. The size of Morgan's staff was unprecedented, but so too was the complexity of the operation it had to plan. Two months later Morgan learned that Churchill and Roosevelt, meeting at the Trident Conference in Washington, had decided that the landings should take place on 1 May 1944, code-named D-Day. Fully aware of the operation's portentous historical significance, they had replaced the code name Round Up with the new code name Overlord, a name resonant with implications of great deeds.

One of the first problems with which COSSAC had to deal was deciding where to land. The overriding lesson from Dieppe was that a landing force could not take even a weakly-defended port without suffering unacceptable casualties, and that consequently troops would have to come ashore on open beaches well away from fortified harbours. Combined operations staff had already analysed the French coast and had narrowed down the possibilities to three: the Pas de Calais, Brittany and Normandy. The Pas de Calais offered the shortest route across the English Channel, meaning that the navy could land more men and materiel in less time than elsewhere, and the air forces could keep their fighters in the air longer and provide increased protection for an invasion fleet. The Pas de Calais also offered land forces the most direct route to Germany's industrial heartland, the Ruhr, which would minimise logistic difficulties.

But the advantages the Pas de Calais offered an invader were equally obvious to the Germans, who were heavily fortifying the region. In addition, the area's high cliffs and narrow shingle beaches with restricted exits posed enormous problems for heavy tracked vehicles. This problem meant that any beachhead would have to be extended either eastwards to include Belgian ports or westwards, to include the ports in the Seine estuary, all of which were heavily defended. Moreover, the ports on the Kent coast were too small to accommodate the thousands of ships which would comprise the invasion fleet. The bulk of them would still have to be based in the vast anchorages of the Portsmouth-Southampton complex. Much of the invasion fleet would therefore have to sail eastwards up the Channel for more than 100 miles under the fire of German shore batteries, before depositing landing forces in harbours which were now more strongly defended than Dieppe had been at the time of the raid in August 1942.

Brittany

One largely American group in COSSAC argued hard instead for a Brittany landing. Brittany's long, heavily-indented coastline with a number of good beaches offered obvious advantages. A successful landing might also lead to the capture of one of Brittany's large ports from the landward side; but the great distance between Brittany and Germany would enormously increase Allied logistical difficulties. It was also too far from England for Allied fighter aircraft to provide constant and effective air cover and support. In addition, the beaches of Brittany were exposed to the south-west winds of the Atlantic. The storms on this coast were savage and unpredictable, and the coast itself was studded with potentially dangerous islets and reefs. Royal Navy officers attached to COSSAC were horrified by the prospect of a Brittany landing. They persisted in reminding their American

BELOW
The Landing Craft, Tank (Rocket) was a British adaptation of the standard LCT designed to give extra fire support to the troops as they went ashore. It carried over a thousand 127mm (5 inch) rockets, released in 24 salvoes. Although they could not penetrate concrete bunkers, they were spectacular morale boosters.

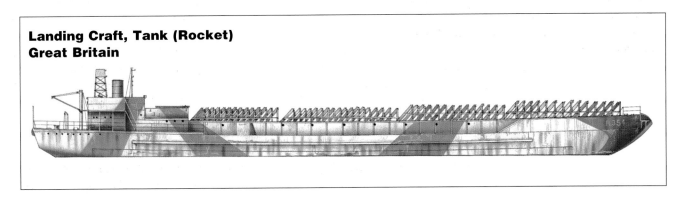

Landing Craft, Tank (Rocket)
Great Britain

colleagues of the numerous disasters suffered along this coast by both British and French fleets in previous centuries.

That left only two stretches of the Atlantic and Channel coasts; from the Gironde to the Spanish border (too far away), and from the estuary of the Seine to the Cotentin Peninsula, the coast of Normandy. The Normandy coast featured long, wide sandy beaches, backed by dunes and low cliffs. It presented none of the difficulties of the Pas de Calais or Brittany. Moreover, the Cotentin Peninsula, jutting north into the Channel, protected the beaches from the storms that almost invariably came in from the south-west. The beaches were also midway between two heavily defended major ports, Le Havre and Cherbourg. Once ashore, the Allied armies would have the option of capturing either or both from the landward side. All the

LIFE-LINE OF FREEDOM
THE MERCHANT MARINE

arguments were weighed up and assessed at the Rattle Conference, convened by Mount-batten's Combined Operations Headquarters in Scotland on 28 June 1943. Normandy emerged as the only real possible landing site.

The Normandy defences

COSSAC already had considerable information about German defences in the Normandy region, thanks to the work of the French Resistance. In 1940 the French film-maker Gilbert Renault-Roulier had been one of the first to offer his services to General Charles de Gaulle's embryonic forces. Adopting the name Colonel Rémy, he had returned to France, established an intelligence network, the *Confrérie Notre Dame*, which soon covered most of the northern coast. Norman and Breton fishermen proved a useful source, because they knew the coast well and were able to work out, thanks to the restrictions the Germans sometimes placed on fishing, the location of many of the gun emplacements. Some of Rémy's men, posing as real estate agents, toured the coastal towns of Normandy openly photographing desirable holiday cottages with panoramic views. A particular coup was provided by René Duchez, a house painter in Caen, who while painting the Todt Organisation's headquarters in the city, simply walked off with a 6m-square (7yd-square) blueprint of part of the Atlantic Wall defences. By the summer of 1943 COSSAC was receiving some 500 detailed reports from Free French intelligence each month, though as the Germans' lax ways of 1942 gave way to increased security in 1943, it was gathered at a price which was becoming ever heavier, with agents arrested and executed.

All this information was forwarded to the Inter-Services Topographical Unit, based in Oxford. In offices along St Giles a staff, made up of geography dons and Royal Navy offi-cers, recorded and sifted every piece of information, the composition of the beaches, the nature of the currents, and the times of the tides. This was all incorporated in a minutely detailed scale model of the Normandy coast in the basement of the city's Ashmolean Museum. The Inter-Services Topographical Unit insisted that the facts be checked again and again. To supplement the work of the Resistance, reconnaissance aircraft took millions of high- and low-level photographs, while boats and miniature

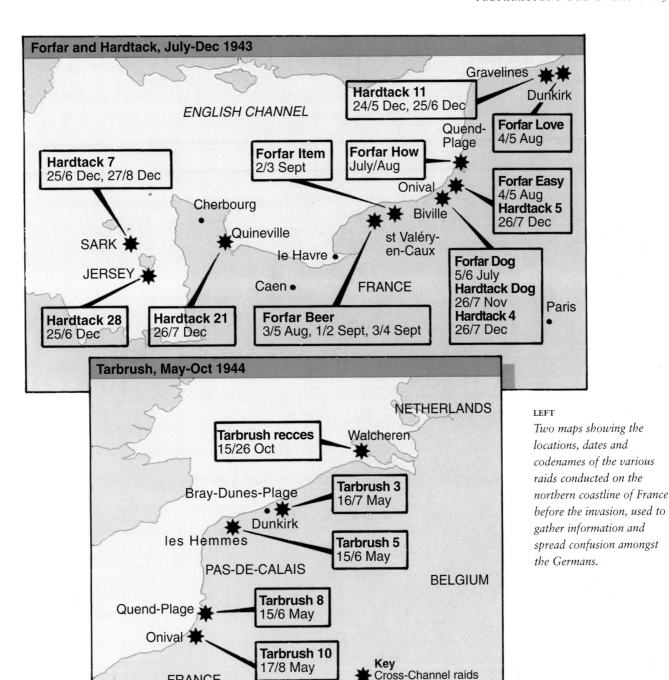

Forfar and Hardtack, July-Dec 1943

ENGLISH CHANNEL

Gravelines
Dunkirk

Hardtack 11
24/5 Dec, 25/6 Dec

Quend-Plage

Forfar Love
4/5 Aug

Hardtack 7
25/6 Dec, 27/8 Dec

Forfar Item
2/3 Sept

Forfar How
July/Aug

Onival

Forfar Easy
4/5 Aug
Hardtack 5
26/7 Dec

Cherbourg

Quineville

Biville

st Valéry-en-Caux

SARK

le Havre

JERSEY

Caen

FRANCE

Forfar Dog
5/6 July
Hardtack Dog
26/7 Nov
Hardtack 4
26/7 Dec

Paris

Hardtack 28
25/6 Dec

Hardtack 21
26/7 Dec

Forfar Beer
3/5 Aug, 1/2 Sept, 3/4 Sept

Tarbrush, May-Oct 1944

NETHERLANDS

Tarbrush recces
15/26 Oct

Walcheren

Bray-Dunes-Plage

Tarbrush 3
16/7 May

Dunkirk

Tarbrush 5
15/6 May

les Hemmes

PAS-DE-CALAIS

BELGIUM

Quend-Plage

Tarbrush 8
15/6 May

Onival

Tarbrush 10
17/8 May

FRANCE

Key
Cross-Channel raids

LEFT
Two maps showing the locations, dates and codenames of the various raids conducted on the northern coastline of France before the invasion, used to gather information and spread confusion amongst the Germans.

submarines took swimmers to within a few hundred metres of the shore. From here they swam onto the beaches to test the composition of the sand with augers. The work was desperately dangerous, for the likelihood of capture was high, and under the terms of Hitler's Commando Order of November 1942 they were liable to be executed as terrorists. (Two of the more fortunate, captured on 20 May 1944, were taken to Rommel, interviewed in person by the field marshal, and then sent direct to a POW camp, rather than to the *Sicherheitsdienst*, the SS Security Service.) On the basis of this hard-won information, the Topographical Unit was able to prepare accurate and detailed maps of enemy-

occupied territory. In all, 170 million individual maps were printed, of which 40,000 were top-secret maps of the invasion beaches, detailing German defences right down to barbed-wire entanglements and tetrahedra.

New landing craft

Deciding where to land was only one of the problems COSSAC had to solve. At Dieppe the Canadians and Commandos had used landing craft manufactured by Andrew Higgins, a New Orleans boat builder. Higgins' craft had considerable power for their size and were highly manoeuvrable, but they were made of wood with lightly armoured sides, and offered virtually no

A Sherman flail tank in action during exercises in southwest England, with another tank emerging from an LST. The rapidly-rotating chains would set off any mines in the tank's path.

protection in a major assault landing, when the craft would have to sail at a constant speed and on rigidly determined routes. In 1940 the Royal Navy had designed steel boats, Landing Craft Assault (LCA), which could be carried aboard troop transports and lowered from davits. The navy also had on its drawing boards the Landing Craft Tank, a steel barge which could carry from three to five tanks, and Landing Ship Tanks (LSTs), large ocean-going shallow-bottomed ships which could ground themselves on gently sloping beaches and disgorge as many as 60 tanks. Unfortunately, British shipbuilding capacity was already pushed to the limit, and by the end of 1942 they had manufactured just over 900 craft, of which nearly 650 were the small LCAs.

At the Arcadia Conference in January 1942 the Americans had agreed to construct ships and craft to British specifications, both for their own use and to hand over to their ally as part of Lend Lease. In 1942 alone American yards built nearly 7000 amphibious warfare vessels, including 62 of the large LSTs, and it seemed for a time that a landing would be possible. But at the Casablanca Conference in January 1943, the Anglo-American leadership decided that, because the Battle of the Atlantic was entering a critical phase, shipbuilding capacity should be devoted to destroyers and destroyer escorts. For a time the production of amphibious vessels plunged, but picked up again in the latter months of 1943, when British yards produced an astonishing 442 major landing craft, almost as many as the USA.

Rocket-equipped LCTs

Another lesson the British (though not the Americans) learned from Dieppe was that assault forces needed supporting fire alongside them on the beach. The Royal Navy's solution to this was to fit LCTs with banks of five-inch (127mm) rockets. A single LCT could fire 1080 rockets in just 30 seconds, which the propaganda of the time claimed was more than the combined firepower of all the cruisers of the Royal Navy firing simultaneously. In fact, the rockets could not penetrate bunkers, but the 36 LCTs eventually fitted out in this manner made an impressive noise, were very good for morale, and would certainly kill any German soldier who was unwise enough to be caught out in the open.

Once ashore, of course, the value of support from even a flat-bottomed rocket-firing LCT rapidly diminished. COSSAC dusted off plans for a cancelled amphibious operation against the German-occupied Belgian coast in 1917, and discovered designs for a variety of armoured assault vehicles which would have made Dieppe a more even match. In March 1943 Brooke ordered the conversion of 79th Armoured Division into an engineer assault division, and placed in command one of the great pioneers of armoured warfare, Major General Percy Hobart. Less than two years earlier he had been serving as a private in the Home Guard, his career as a regular soldier having been terminated prematurely in 1939 by his more conventionally-minded superiors.

Hobart's 'funnies'

Within weeks Hobart had assembled around him some of Britain's finest engineers, who came up with an extraordinary variety of machines, nicknamed 'funnies' by the British Army. The most conventional was the 'DD' (Duplex Drive) or swimming tank, a Sherman fitted with propellers driven by its main engine, and a canvas skirt and air bags to give it buoyancy. These tanks would land either before or with the infantry. Minefields were to be destroyed by 'crabs', tanks fitted with rotary drums which flailed the ground with steel chains. The walls of even the strongest bunkers were to be cracked by an 18kg (40-pound) bomb lobbed from a petard, a large mortar, mounted on a Churchill tank, which was designated an

BELOW
A gunner sits astride the business end of a Churchill Mk III AVRE (Armoured Vehicle Royal Engineers), whose petard mortar fired a 'flying dustbin' 11.3kg (25lb) heavy mortar bomb designed to knock out pillboxes and blockhouses at close range.

AVRE (Armoured Vehicle Royal Engineers) Mk III. And with the walls of a bunker cracked, Mark VII Crocodile tanks equipped with flame-throwers would shoot in high-pressure jets of liquid fire. To help the AVREs negotiate walls and trenches, Churchill tanks were fitted with 9m (30-foot) box-girder bridges, and carried 2.5m-wide (8-foot) fascines of chestnut palings or lengths of pipe, designed to be tipped into anti-tank ditches. In effect, 79th Division fulfilled the same function as a medieval siege train. Much effort was devoted to design and construction, and the division did not receive its first AVREs until the beginning of April 1944.

The Mulberry harbours

The ingenuity applied to getting the troops ashore was also applied to the problem of sustaining them over open beaches. The fate of the Dieppe operation had ruled out an early attempt on a port, and COSSAC's most optimistic assessment estimated a two-week period between the first landings and the capture of Cherbourg, and a further two to three months to clear the mines and repair the damage left by the Germans. Once again, COSSAC found a solution in the files of the cancelled landing of 1917, the plans of a pre-fabricated floating harbour. The COSSAC naval commander, Admiral John Hughes Hallet, brought the plans up to date, and incorporated into them suggestions from the prime minister, who remembered the original scheme of 1917. There were to be two artificial harbours, code-named Mulberry A and Mulberry B. Mulberry A, designed to supply the Americans, was to be towed to the east of Pointe du Hoc, while Mulberry B, to support the British, was to be towed into position off Arromanches 15km (9.3 miles) to the east, operations which would require the use of 150 very powerful tugboats. To protect

the harbours, COSSAC planned two great artificial reefs, made by sinking some 74 old cargo vessels and obsolete warships, which would be supplemented by specially-constructed steel and concrete caissons, which were given the code name Phoenix.

In October 1943 orders were placed with shipyards from the Clyde to the Tyne for the construction of more than 200 steel and concrete caissons, some as much as 60m (65 yards) long, 18m (20 yards) high, and displacing 6000 tons. There were also to be floating pierheads, 16km (10 miles) of steel roadway, and 93 steel and concrete floats each weighing 2000 tons. As soon as the yards launched the component parts, they were to be sunk immediately in the Tyne, the Clyde and a hundred other rivers, estuaries, and sea lochs. Here they could be hidden from German reconnaissance until needed, when the water would be pumped out and the Phoenix caissons would re-emerge from the depths.

All the ingenuity displayed by the British would have been of little use without Operation Bolero, the code name for the American build-up. American industrial production had exceeded even the most optimistic predictions of 1942. The 15 American fighter and bomber groups based in Britain at the end of 1942 had grown to 86 groups, more than half of the entire US air force, by June 1944, with large tracts of East Anglia virtually a preserve of the American air bases. The south-west of England, too, had been transformed, as the 36,000 American soldiers present in May 1942 grew to 1.5 million by May 1944. The American flow of materiel for the invasion was even more striking. In the 24 months between April 1942 and April 1944, five million tons of military freight flowed through British ports, 10 per cent of the total tonnage of all goods imported into Britain during this time.

Bolero was an impressive achievement and it was far from easy. America's chief logistician, General Brehon B. Somervell, devoted much energy to matching ships and cargoes, and there were times, particularly in the summer of 1943 when the focus of attention was the Mediterranean, that the schedule fell dangerously low. By early 1944 Somervell was trying to shift an enormous backlog of cargo which had built up in New York, but there was simply not the shipping to move it in time for the projected date of the invasion. Responding to a request from Roosevelt,

BELOW

Pre-fabricated artificial harbours were vital to the success of the invasion, as they allowed the smooth unloading of logistics. They were made up of 'Phoenix' caissons like the one shown below; 146 of them had to be towed across the Channel and sunk in exactly the right position.

Churchill ordered that imports for British civilian consumption be cut further, thereby imposing increasingly severe rationing on an already exhausted population, but also making available the shipping space which would make Overlord possible. By the end of May 1944 Somervell had moved to England 50,000 tanks and armoured vehicles, 450,000 trucks and 450,000 tons of ammunition, transforming the country, in Eisenhower's words, into 'the greatest operating military base of all time'.

The build-up continues

The American build-up was the most impressive, but other countries were also sending men and equipment. By May 1944 the Canadian army had nearly 200,000 troops in Britain, and the Royal Canadian Air Force had 54,000 personnel flying in 37 Canadian squadrons, or serving with the RAF. There were also more than 40,000 Australians and New Zealanders, either serving in national air squadrons, in the RAF, or with the Royal Navy. The occupied nations of Europe, too, made a contribution, with the Poles and Free French together fielding 40,000, and the Belgians, Dutch, Norwegians and Czechs accounting for perhaps another 10,000. But the largest army, at least initially, was the British: by spring 1944 it stood at 1.75 million men within the British Isles. All told, the Allies had three million men waiting in southern England, while another one million Americans would come directly from the USA, and nearly 100,000 Canadians would arrive both from Canada and from Canadian forces in Italy.

As late as the autumn of 1943 this steadily growing host had no overall commander. Churchill had assumed that the job would go to a British general and had half promised it to the chief of the imperial general staff, General Alan Brooke. But Roosevelt felt that,

ABOVE

American Waco Hadrian gliders being uncrated and assembled at a British airfield. Gliders formed an important part of the invasion plan, carrying the paratroops' heavy weapons and jeeps.

given the increasing preponderance of American materiel and manpower, the commander should be an American, and had sounded out US army chief of staff General Marshall. Realising there was likely to be a clash, both prime minister and president were content to let the matter lie. The Russians, however, were increasingly unhappy with this state of affairs, interpreting the Anglo-American reluctance to appoint an overall commander as an Anglo-American reluctance to launch a second front. Things came to a head at the Teheran Conference in November 1943, when Stalin asked the Western leaders to appoint a commander immediately as a token of good faith.

Eisenhower becomes commander

Churchill did his best to push Brooke's claims, but Roosevelt made it clear that American public opinion would react very badly to the appointment of a British commander, and that 1944 was an election year. The Anglo-American alliance functioned as smoothly as it did because of the close personal understanding between prime minister and president, and in order to help Roosevelt Churchill withdrew his favoured candidate. Roosevelt prevaricated until 7 December, and then decided not upon Marshall, who could not be spared from Washington, but on General Eisenhower. Since drafting Round Up Eisenhower had been appointed to lead

and complemented the affable Eisenhower perfectly. When he arrived in London in January 1944, Eisenhower found that Smith already had the formation of SHAEF well under way. Set up in Bushey Park by the Thames, it assimilated COSSAC staff, and by May 1944 had grown to some 7000 personnel.

Eisenhower spent the first months of 1944 constructing a team of subordinate commanders. He chose as his deputy Air Chief Marshal Arthur Tedder, former commander-in-chief of Allied air forces in the Mediterranean. Eisenhower had first met him in December 1942. A graduate of Cambridge, the scholarly, introspective, pipe-smoking Tedder looked more like a university don than a man of action. Churchill, who tended at least initially to judge men by superficial appearance, dismissed him as of no consequence, but Eisenhower had quickly learned to value the sharpness of his brain. Tedder was a firm advocate of air, land and sea cooperation; quite unlike many airmen, who seemed convinced that their bomber fleets could win the war by themselves. So important did Tedder regard air-ground cooperation that he ensured that Air Marshal Trafford Leigh-Mallory, who shared his beliefs, was appointed

BELOW
American soldiers practising the use of a 'Bangalore Torpedo'. This device, which was a simple tube filled with explosive, was extremely effective in blasting a path through barbed wire defences.

the Torch landings in North Africa in November 1942, and had then been given command of the Mediterranean theatre. He had very little experience of commanding men in combat, but had already proved his worth as an administrator and had a growing reputation as a diplomat, enormously enhanced by his dealings with the French in North Africa. When he was selected to command Overlord, Eisenhower sent his chief of staff, Major General Walter Bedell Smith, to London to organise the Supreme Headquarters Allied Expeditionary Force (SHAEF). Irascible, brutal in manner, impatient and fiercely demanding, Smith had been promoted from the ranks during World War I, to command the new Allied Tactical Air Force, despite the fact that Leigh-Mallory was known to be abrasive and difficult. Naval forces would obviously play a vital role, and Eisenhower agreed to Churchill's suggestion of Admiral Bertram Ramsay for the commanding post. Ramsay's skill, both at getting forces ashore and back to sea, was unmatched; he had commanded both the Dunkirk evacuation in 1940 and the Allied landings in North Africa in 1942. Churchill may have pressed for Ramsay's appointment with the unspoken thought that were things to go badly wrong on D-Day, he would be an ideal admiral to take control.

Montgomery's appointment

Eisenhower had more difficulty choosing a general to command ground forces. In North Africa, he had been very impressed by General Harold Alexander, an impeccably dressed, ramrod straight, stiff-upper-lipped officer of the Irish Guards who looked just like the Hollywood stereotype of the British general. Churchill, too, thought very highly of Alexander, but many of his British colleagues, while acknowledging his near suicidal bravery and diplomatic skills, had a much lower opinion of his abilities in most

other respects. The chief of the imperial general staff, General Alan Brooke, pushed hard to appoint his protégé, General Bernard Montgomery, who had commanded a division under him at Dunkirk. Montgomery was now Britain's most successful general, but he was egotistical and acerbic, and in North Africa had patronised Eisenhower and other American commanders unmercifully. Eisenhower's misgivings about Montgomery had not yet hardened into hatred, but he accepted Montgomery's appointment with reluctance. He had no such doubts about accepting the appointment of General Omar Bradley to command US First Army. Bradley, an old and close friend, was the very antithesis of Montgomery – modest, quiet and unassuming. The commander of Third Army, General George Patton, was another old friend, whose flamboyant behaviour was occasionally to drive Eisenhower to the point of dismissing him, but who, like Eisenhower, had already developed a deep ambivalence towards Montgomery.

This team probably represented the best possible from the senior commanders available in early 1944. Eisenhower proved himself an excellent 'chairman of the board'. Having served as executive officer to General

BELOW

General Dwight D. Eisenhower, the Supreme Allied Commander, with his subordinate commanders: Admiral Sir Bertram Ramsay, Air Chief Marshal Sir Trafford Leigh-Mallory, Air Chief Marshal Sir Arthur Tedder and General Sir Bernard Montgomery.

Douglas MacArthur, he was used to dealing with prima donnas and egocentrics. On many occasions over the next few months, Eisenhower's tact and charm kept the complicated human machinery of SHAEF working. He put up with Montgomery's patronising behaviour and vented his frustrations in private, but never in public.

One of Eisenhower's first major problems was to get the 'bomber barons', Air Chief Marshal Arthur Harris of RAF Bomber Command and General Carl Spaatz of US Eighth Air Force, to agree to divert their squadrons from the bombing of Germany to the disruption of the transport system of northern France. At the beginning of 1944 Professor Solly Zuckerman, Tedder's chief scientific advisor, presented a scheme for the destruction of more than 100 railway centres throughout northern France, which he claimed would bring movement of German forces and supplies to a virtual standstill. The Transportation Plan, as it became known, quickly won the support of Tedder and Leigh Mallory, but was anathema to Harris and Spaatz, both of whom believed they were winning the war by concentrating on the strategic bombing of Germany. Churchill,

too, concerned about the civilian casualties which were certain to be inflicted in France, was reluctant to support the Transportation Plan, until assured by De Gaulle that the French people would be dishonoured if they, too, did not pay the price of their liberation.

Eisenhower's first victory

Harris and Spaatz remained obdurate, coming up with ingeniously oblique alternatives, such as the bombing of synthetic oil plants and motor factories, which were, in fact, a continuation of existing bombing policy. On 25 March Eisenhower had his first major victory as supreme commander. In a hostile and confrontational meeting with the bomber barons at SHAEF headquarters, Eisenhower threatened to resign unless they agreed to devote their forces to bombing the French railway system. Faced with the prospect of being branded as the men who disrupted the Anglo-American alliance and delayed Overlord, Harris and Spaatz capitulated.

The bombing began in earnest in early April. Over the next nine weeks Allied aircraft dropped 71,000 tons of bombs on 80 railway centres. Beginning on 10 May, targets were expanded to include all the major

ABOVE

General Montgomery flanked by General Omar Bradley (US 1st Army) and Lieutenant General Miles Dempsey (British 2nd Army). Bradley and Dempsey commanded the American and Commonwealth forces respectively, with Montgomery in charge of all ground forces in France, a position he held until 1 September 1944, when Eisenhower took over.

ABOVE
British infantry practising their assault from a Landing Craft Infantry (LCI). This particular craft was built by Curtis of Looe, Cornwall – one of dozens involved in the construction of these vital vessels, without which the invasion could never have taken place.

bridges over the rivers of north-western France and 10 days later Allied fighter-bombers began strafing trains all over northern France. The effect on the Germans was increasingly pronounced. On 9 May, for example, Admiral Friedrich Ruge, Rommel's naval commander, recorded in his diary that the Todt Organisation in the Houlgate area had not received deliveries of cement since 1 May. On 11 May the Todt Organisation estimated that it had diverted 65,000 men from the construction of defences to the repair of railways. And on the afternoon of 30 May Field Marshal Rommel on a tour of inspection had to speed across the Seine bridge at Gallion, as bombs fell all around. An hour later the bridge was gone. 'Numerous aircraft were above us, none of them German,' was Ruge's pithy comment. By 5 June Allied air forces had flown more than 200,000 sorties and dropped nearly 200,000 tons of bombs. Lancasters and B-17s had pulverised rail centres and marshalling yards, and had reduced

rail traffic in northern France by 60 per cent. They had then turned their attention to the fortresses of the Atlantic Wall, destroying 74 of the 92 German radar stations, considerably reducing the ability of the Germans to monitor movement on and over the English Channel. But Allied losses had been heavy – 2000 aircraft and 12,000 aircrew – the first casualties of Overlord.

Allied precautions

While the Transportation Plan was under way, Allied forces conducted their last pre-invasion exercises. For many troops it could not come too soon. Efficiency had peaked, and over-training had started to set in, the jadedness which comes when exercises become well-rehearsed rituals bearing no apparent relationship to reality. Most American divisions, with the exception of a few such as the 29th Infantry, stationed in England since 1942, were far more recent arrivals in the theatre, and though inexperienced and anxious, were enthusiastic soldiers. Other troops had already seen too much action. Famous British formations like the 51st Highland and 7th Armoured Divisions had fought from Egypt to Italy, via Libya, Tunisia and Sicily. They remembered battles like El Alamein, the Mareth Line and Salerno. They had suffered heavy casualties and, knowing what to expect, were not looking forward to storming the Atlantic Wall.

Churchill's concerns

The prime minister shared their apprehension. One evening in February while discussing Overlord with his personal staff, he suddenly said 'Why are we trying to do this? Why do we not land instead in a friendly territory, the territory of our oldest ally? Why do we not land in Portugal?' A minute was sent to the Chiefs of Staff that it should be discussed the following morning, and all through the night planners worked on a paper outlining the possibilities of an advance through Spain and across the Pyrenees.

When he found the plan lying on his desk the following morning, Alan Brooke exploded with rage. He had spent his

childhood in France, knew the Pyrenees well, and at the subsequent meeting with Churchill was trenchant in his criticism. On reflection Churchill realised it had been a foolish proposal which had wasted valuable time, but it was also an indication of Churchill's acute awareness of the dangers inherent in Overlord. Just two months later during Operation Fabius, realistic amphibious training exercises on several areas of the British coast which resembled Normandy, officers and men were shocked out of complacency by malfunctioning equipment, traffic jams, collisions at sea and general confusion. On the night of 27 April off Slapton Sands in Dorset, nine German 'E-boats' attacked a convoy of American landing craft, sinking three with torpedoes. More than 750 Americans lost their lives, and for days afterwards bodies were being washed up along the Dorset coast, a salutary reminder of the enemy's military capability.

On 15 May 1944, in the model room of London's St Paul's School, Montgomery unfolded Overlord in all its complexity before a select audience, including the prime minister, the king, the supreme Allied

BELOW
Caen railway station pictured in the wake of Allied air attacks designed to inhibit the Germans' ability to transport men and materiel around the invasion area. In the case of this town, rubble caused by bombing seriously impeded the Anglo-Canadian advance during the invasion itself.

An officer of the Canadian Regiment de Levis seen during the build-up in 1943. His uniform is identical to that of a British officer except for the distinctive headgear – although this is winter wear. The Canadians, who had suffered heavy losses at Dieppe two years earlier, fought with great courage in Normandy.

commander, the chief of the imperial general staff and scores of admirals, generals and air marshals. On D-Day, now set for 5 June, eight divisions were to land in Normandy, three from the air and five from the sea. Two American airborne divisions, the 82nd and 101st, were to drop at night along the eastern coast of the Cotentin Peninsula to secure the western flank of the beachhead. Meanwhile the British 6th Airborne Division was to land east of the River Orne. The other five divisions were to land on five different beaches – code-named respectively Utah, Omaha, Gold, Juno and Sword – running from west to east between the areas secured by the airborne forces. The US 4th Infantry Division was to land on Utah, the westernmost beach at the base of the Cotentin Peninsula; the US 1st Infantry Division and elements of the US 29th Division on Omaha, the area roughly between the heavily defended Pointe du Hoc and Port en Bessin; the British 50th Division on Gold, the area from Arromanches to La Rivière; the Canadian 3rd Infantry on Juno, which lay between La Rivière and Luc; and the British 3rd Infantry Division on Sword.

D-Day objectives

By the end of D-Day the Allies planned to control a stretch of the Normandy coast 80km (50 miles) long and some 16km (10 miles) deep. The British would have secured Caen and Bayeux, important communication centres. Meanwhile the Americans would be on the point of pivoting to the north-west to take the port of Cherbourg from the landward side. Once ashore, there was to be a rapid and massive build-up, to be made possible by the arrival of the Mulberry harbours from D+3 onward. The 17 divisions in Normandy would expand rapidly to 39 divisions by D+90. By that time, the bulk of Allied forces would have broken out and would be well across the Seine, heading for the Low Countries and the Siegfried Line.

As D-Day came closer, the number of officers who had to know the details of the invasion steadily increased, so that security became ever more rigorous. There was always the possibility of a chance remark at a dinner or a party, particularly amongst London's diplomatic community, being relayed back to Germany. The British imposed a ban on privileged diplomatic correspondence leaving the United Kingdom, but there were numerous

close calls. In April, for example, Major General Henry J. Miller, a West Point classmate of Eisenhower's and an old friend, went to a cocktail party at Claridges Hotel, drank too much, talked freely about D-Day, and even mentioned the date. Eisenhower responded ruthlessly, reducing Miller to his permanent rank of colonel and sending him back to the United States in disgrace. He wrote to Marshall, 'I get so angry at the occurrence of such needless and additional hazards that I could cheerfully shoot the offender myself.'

Allied precautions

Secrecy alone was not enough to guard the details of D-Day from the enemy. The Allies had an active as well as a passive security stratagem, one that would mislead and deceive the Germans into concentrating their forces in the wrong areas before D-Day. During the course of 1943 various plans had been devised – 'Cockade', 'Jael', 'Bodyguard' – and on 23 February 1944 these were amalgamated into an over-arching scheme code-named Fortitude. One part of the operation, Fortitude North, was designed to mislead the Germans into believing that the Allies would land in the Pas de Calais. The Normandy landing, even after it had taken place, had to look like a mere diversionary tactic for the 'real' invasion, and this meant creating a phantom army in Kent. All genuine radio traffic generated by 21st Army Group in south-central and south-west England was sent over land lines to the south-east and rebroadcast. Meanwhile, the fields of Essex and Suffolk blossomed with huge encampments crammed with rubber blow-up tanks and airfields packed with mock-up transports made from wooden three-ply. Former German agents, who had been 'turned' and were now managed by MI5, broadcast plausibly accurate reports of the vast extent of these encampments.

The Transportation Plan bombing which began in April had knocked out German telephone and telegraph communications for long periods, so that the army once again began to use radio as the primary form of communication. Ultra signals intelligence at Bletchley Park was soon reading enemy traffic, which showed that at the beginning of May the Germans believed that the Allies had 79 divisions, whereas the actual number was 52, and that while there might

LEFT
Heavy equipment being loaded at a British port. Tractors and bulldozers were as vital to the success of the invasion as tanks and guns.

be diversionary landings in Brittany and Normandy, the main landing would come in the Pas de Calais. Ultra learned that the Germans had even divined the name of the invasion force commander, General George Patton, who, according to intercepted German signal traffic, had been assessed by the German high command as the Allies' best general. On seeing the report, Eisenhower commented wryly that 'George is sure to agree,' and then confirmed German preconceptions by issuing an order which placed Patton in command of the phantom army.

Final preparations

During May last-minute preparations got under way. At the start of the month Admiral Ramsay warned Eisenhower of an impending delay: not all the LSTs had yet arrived from America; however, Eisenhower's naval staff advised him that best-possible tidal conditions would occur during the week beginning Monday 5 June. This was the date set for D-Day. May 1944 proved to be a beautiful month over southern England – the skies were blue and cloudless, the temperature well above average, and the English Channel was like a mill-pond.

All over England the roads to the south-coast ports were choked with military convoys, some over 160km (100 miles) long. The coastal zone of the south and south-west was now closed to civilians: once the troops entered this area they were out of contact.

The gigantic machine was at last in motion, an avalanche of men and materiel.

But the English weather is mercurial. As the south coast continued to bask under a near tropical sun, the commanders became anxious. On 30 May Churchill asked the First

BELOW
An American tank commander practises throwing a grenade from his cupola during exercises on the south coast of England.

Sea Lord: 'How does this hot spell fit in with our dates? Does it tend to bring about a violent reaction or is it all clear ahead? Let me have the best your meteorologists can do.' Eisenhower grew obsessed by weather reports, but by the evening of 31 May he was beginning to relax.

Deteriorating weather

A few hours later the weather broke – rain and wind gusting to gale force swept over the English Channel, accompanied by heavy, scudding cloud. Over the next 72 hours the weather continued to deteriorate. On Saturday 3 June Eisenhower reiterated preparation orders for a 5 June landing, but at 0415 on Sunday 4 June the forecast for the next 24 hours was for mounting seas, poor visibility, and low cloud over the Normandy beaches. The Supreme Commander had no choice – he brought the huge invasion machine grinding to a halt.

Unfortunately, American convoys destined for Utah Beach were already at sea off Cornwall observing radio silence, and RAF Coastal Command had to send out aircraft to ensure their return. Conditions on the crowded transports became appalling. Even in the Solent's sheltered waters they rolled and

lurched, causing violent sea sickness among the troops. Those crammed below decks could barely cope with the overwhelming stench of vomit. Eisenhower knew that if he cancelled Overlord, it would take at least a month before conditions would be right again, a month in which morale would drop and the edge go from the men's training, a month in which the Germans might manage to penetrate Operation Fortitude and redeploy their forces. But if he made the decision to go ahead, the result might be the greatest disaster in maritime history.

At 0400, on 5 June, meteorologists predicted a 24-hour abatement in the bad weather, beginning in the early hours of Tuesday 6 June. Admiral Ramsay and General

BELOW
US Rangers practising unarmed combat. The task of the Rangers and their British counterparts, the Commandos, was to destroy German bunkers and then push rapidly inland to link up with their respective airborne forces ahead of the main advance.

Montgomery, also present, were convinced that the operation should go ahead. Eisenhower now gave the most momentous order of World War II. He simply said, 'OK, let's go.'

Overlord launched

That evening Eisenhower drove from his advance headquarters at Southwick House near Southampton to Greenham Common near Newbury, where the 101st Airborne were loading for the flight to Normandy. A week earlier Leigh Mallory, worried by reports that the Germans were reinforcing units in the drop zones, told Eisenhower that the airborne operations would be a useless slaughter of fine divisions, and begged the supreme commander to cancel them. Eisenhower had refused, but he now went to say good-bye to men he was certain he was sending to their deaths. The photographs taken that evening capture the strain under which he was labouring. As the last of the aircraft flew off Eisenhower's shoulders sagged and he walked back to his staff car in tears.

The same night Churchill, who had been prevented from sailing with the landing forces only by the direct intervention of the king himself, said to his wife as she went to bed, 'Do you realise that by the time you wake up in the morning, 20,000 men may have been killed?' In headquarters throughout England, the Anglo-American commanders settled down for their longest night.

ABOVE
General Eisenhower addressing men of the 101st Airborne Division prior to their departure for Normandy, the strain of his responsibilty clearly showing on his face.

CHAPTER TWO

D-DAY

In the early hours of 6 June 1944, the German defenders of the Normandy coast were wakened by a massive bombardment, to find that the long-prophesied invasion had finally begun.

As was its custom, on the evening of 5 June 1944 the BBC's French-language service broadcast personal messages after the news. This evening there was an unusually large number – 325 – and it took more than an hour to get through all of them. One message – 'I will bring the eglantine' – was particularly significant. It was the order to the Resistance throughout northern France to implement Operation Vert, the scheme for rail sabotage. As the broadcast continued, other announcements activated Operation Tortue, the destruction of bridges and highways, Operation Bleu, the disruption of the electricity supply system, and Operation Violet, the cutting of telephone and telegraph links. Before midnight teams of the French Forces of the Interior (FFI) were moving into action. In the area of the Normandy beachheads, FFI intelligence chief Guilloum Mercader, a nationally famous cyclist who had come close to winning the Tour de France, pedalled at breakneck speed along coastal roads carrying orders from team to team. In Caen, stationmaster Albert Auge and his men set about disabling the locomotives in the city's marshalling yards.

Farther west, teams commanded by a café proprietor, André Farine, cut the telephone cables leading out of Cherbourg. Meanwhile other teams led by Yves Gresslin, a Cherbourg grocer, were dynamiting the railway lines linking Cherbourg, St Lo and Paris. In Brittany, small teams of the *Deuxième Régiment des Chasseurs Parachutistes* (RCP), the Free French equivalent of the British SAS, parachuted down to join more than 3500 Resistance activists. Before the night was out they had carved a swathe of destruction through eastern Brittany. They wrecked bridges and railway tracks, demolished electricity pylons, and established roadblocks covered by machine-gun and bazooka teams. They took every step to stop the 150,000 German troops in Brittany from reinforcing the beachhead quickly. Some 600km (375 miles) away, large sections of the lines radiating from Dijon, the hub of the railway network in eastern France, erupted in explosions; in all 37 cuts were made. Across the whole of France the first few hours of FFI operations succeeded in cutting the rail network in 950 places, causing the derailment of 180 trains.

Aerial armada

Meanwhile wave upon wave of transport aircraft, many towing gliders, had been taking off from airfields in England. Around midnight, a stream of some 1270 aircraft, C-47s and old converted bombers like the Stirling and the Albermarle, and about 850 British Horsa and

OPPOSITE
An American paratrooper of the 101st Airborne Division, festooned with equipment that includes an anti-tank projector, boards a C-47 transport. Some 1270 aircraft and 850 gliders took 17,000 British and American airborne troops to Normandy.

Hamilcar and American Waco gliders carrying 17,000 men, stretched from southern England to the coasts of Normandy. The first phase of the air landings, Operation Titanic, was under way just after midnight, as small groups of the SAS accompanied by some 500 dummy paratroops dropped behind Omaha, Gold and Juno beaches, well away from the actual landing zones. At Le Molay Littry, 10km (6 miles) behind Omaha Beach, the headquarters of the 352nd Division, the divisional commander, Major General Dietrich Kraiss, took fright and had his reserve regiment up and searching the woods south-east of Isigny.

At about the same time, American and British pathfinder aircraft, guided by skilled crews with sophisticated navigational equipment, were dropping paratroops equipped with flares and powerful lamps onto the landing zones. Twenty minutes later the aircraft and gliders of the American IX Troop Carrier Command carrying the 101st and 82nd Airborne banked to the south-east just north of the Channel Islands and passed over the western coast of the Cotentin Peninsula, climbing from 150 to 450m (500 to 1500

feet). They were detected by the radar of the 243rd Artillery Regiment, and a stream of anti-aircraft fire suddenly hit the transports, bringing down several C-47s. The pilots took evasive action, ducking, diving and disappearing into cloud banks, and within minutes the formations had broken up. Pilots, uncertain of their bearings, nevertheless gave the paratroops the order to jump. Some dropped directly into streams of tracer; others, weighed down by equipment and tangled in their parachutes, plummeted into flooded fields and drowned. Those who made it down unscathed blundered around in the dark trying to form their units. Brigadier General Maxwell Taylor, commander of the 101st, landed alone in a field and scouted around before he found some men. By the end of the day only about 2500 of the 6600 men who had jumped had assembled in the drop zones. Some of the 101st had landed on the outskirts of Cherbourg, while three paratroops had come down on Pointe du Hoc, just to the west of Omaha Beach.

With a drop zone just to the north of the 101st, the 82nd also suffered heavy casualties

BELOW

Into the unknown: officers of the British 6th Airborne Division synchronise their watches before setting off for their drop zone in Normandy. The engine in the background belongs to an Armstrong Whitworth Albemarle troop transport.

LEFT

US paratroops en route to Normandy in their C-47 troop carrier. Two American airborne divisions, the 82nd and 101st, were involved in the invasion of Normandy; in both cases, the drops were badly scattered, making it hard to secure the planned objectives.

in the jump, with 272 men killed or seriously injured, and some landed more than 32km (20 miles) from the drop zone. About 30 paratroops did land right on top of their primary objective, the town of Ste Mère Eglise, part of which had been set on fire by a bombing raid earlier in the day. The German garrison had little difficulty picking off most of the paratroops as they descended, silhouetted against the flames, although one man's parachute became snagged on the church steeple and he hung there for two hours, deafened by the ringing of the church bells before he was taken prisoner. Another 100 or so, landing on the outskirts of the town, were rapidly organised by Lieutenant Colonel Edward Krause. Fighting their way into the town, they quickly killed or captured the garrison and then spent the rest of the day fighting off German counter-attacks.

Chaos on the ground

The divisional commander, Major General Matthew B. Ridgeway, managed to get control over about 2000 of the 6396 men who had jumped by the end of the day, and, like the 101st's Maxwell Taylor, he felt that he was presiding over chaos. In fact, although nothing had gone as planned, the scattered bands of highly trained, well-armed paratroops posed serious problems for the German defenders, the 709th and 91st Divisions. They were so widely scattered that the Germans found it

impossible to focus on any single target, and they were equally affected by the chaos they faced. Just before dawn the 91st's veteran commander, Major General Wilhelm Falley, having been suddenly called away to a war game in Rennes, was returning to his headquarters near Picauville when he was ambushed and killed by American paratroops. The 91st was an excellent division, but the sudden apparent disappearance of its

BELOW

Sporting fearsome Mohican haircuts, two men of the 101st Airborne Division – the 'Screaming Eagles' – apply their warpaint to one another.

General Aircraft Hamilcar gliders approaching to land. The British Hamilcar was used with great success in the Normandy landings, and was the first Allied glider capable of transporting a seven-ton light tank. More than 400 Hamilcars were built.

commander meant that it remained inert and largely ineffective throughout D-Day.

While the Americans were landing on the Cotentin, the spearhead of British 6th Airborne approached its landing zone. At 0015 hours on 6 June, six Halifax bombers released six Horsa gliders from their tow ropes at 1500m (5000 feet) over Cabourg, and five minutes later three gliders crashed-landed within 45m (50 yards) of their objective – the bridges at Bénouville over the Caen Canal and Orne River, the eastern boundary of the British beachhead. Led by Major John Howard, an assault party of the Oxford and Bucks Light Infantry charged across the bridges, sending the surprised Germans fleeing in confusion. Other elements of 6th Airborne had been coming down farther east – 68 gliders of the 5th Parachute Brigade landed at Ranville, about a kilometre and a half (1 mile) from the Bénouville bridges. Eighteen gliders were completely destroyed when they ran into the extensive pole-and-wire network ('bird-traps') put up by the Germans. Chester Wilmot, the Australian war correspondent who was going to write the definitive history of the campaign, landed with 5th Brigade and recorded that he 'could see silhouettes of other gliders, twisted and wrecked – making grotesque patterns against

the sky. Some had buried their noses in the soil; others had lost a wheel or a wing; one had crashed into a house, two had crashed into each other.' The divisional commander Major General Richard (Windy) Gale landed at 0300 hours near Wilmot, commandeered a horse in a nearby field, and rode towards Ranville, collecting along the way scattered groups of 6th Airborne. By 0600 hours he had established a divisional headquarters at the Château de Heaume in Ranville, and had the equivalent of several battalions dug in to the east, just in time to prepare for German counter-attacks, which were going to continue throughout the day.

Hand-to-hand fighting

Meanwhile the most important mission given to 6th Airborne that night had run into difficulties. Lieutenant Colonel Terrance Otway's 9th Parachute Battalion was assigned the task of destroying a German battery just back from the coast at Merville, about 6.5km (4 miles) to the north-east of Ranville, which could hit the entire length of Sword Beach. Ten minutes before Otway's men were over the drop zone, 100 RAF Lancasters attempted to drop 1814.4-kg (4000-lb) bombs on the battery, but most landed south at Varaville. A few minutes later as the 9th's Dakotas passed over Varaville, they were hit by heavy flak. The pilots dived and wove, and the flight formations disintegrated. When they jumped the paratroops came down over a wide area, with scores of men drowning when they dropped down straight into the swamps of the Dives River. By 0400 hours, instead of the 600 men with mortars, anti-tank guns and jeeps he had expected, Otway could muster only 155, none of whom had more than light weapons. At 0430 hours two of three Horsa gliders scheduled to crash-land among the battery casements appeared overhead. One overshot the target, and the other, hit by flak from the battery, crashed amongst the trees to the rear of Otway and his men.

Knowing that, if he delayed, the British landings would be brought under heavy fire, Otway led his men into a furious assault. By 0600 hours, after bitter hand-to-hand fighting, the battery was in British hands; 110 dead and wounded Germans lay piled in the bunkers, along with 65 paratroops. Unfortunately, Otway now discovered he had no way of destroying the guns. Grenades down the barrels had no effect, though smashing the sights did put them out of action temporarily. Having done all he could, Otway and his 80 men set off to clear Le Plein, which was their next task, allowing the Germans to reoccupy the battery, and eventually bring it back into action.

With the airborne-forces assault under way, feint attacks were being made against beaches near Boulogne by motor launches pumping huge quantities of smoke from special generators, and towing balloons with reflectors, while squadrons of Bomber Command dropped 'window' (strips of aluminium), which further confused German radar. At about 0300 hours beams of German searchlights were sweeping the Pas de Calais, and shore batteries had opened up on radar blips, while German night-fighters hunted the decoy air force. Meanwhile 160km (100 miles) to the south-west, between 0315 and 0500 hours, 1056 Lancaster, Halifax and Mosquito aircraft of Bomber Command flew in 10 groups, each of about 100 aircraft, to attack the 10 largest German positions on the actual landing beaches. In all, about 5000 tons of bombs were dropped, with around 500 tons falling on each position.

Under cover of this activity, convoys of the invasion force had been sailing towards a rendezvous point designated Area Z, south-east of the Isle of Wight. From here they had moved along a series of 10 mine-swept channels, the Americans steering for the south-west and Utah and Omaha Beaches, while the British and Canadians steamed south-east for Gold, Juno and Sword, their navigation assisted by the blinking lights on the conning towers of two midget submarines, lying just a few hundred metres off shore. Despite heavy weather, by 0500 hours the invasion fleet was in position, covering a sea area 80km (50 miles) west to east, and 32km (20 miles) north to south. In this 2600 square kilometres (1000 square miles) were more ships than had ever been assembled in one place and at one time in history – 5726 transports and landing craft, and 1213 warships and bombardment vessels, crammed with 287,000 men. The warships, ranging in size from battleships to torpedo boats, included three American and four British battleships, and 23 British, American, French and Polish cruisers.

Furious bombardment

As the last aircraft of Bomber Command wheeled north, at 0510 hours the 152mm (6-inch) guns of the cruiser HMS Orion opened up on the battery at Mont Fleury about a kilometre and a half (1 mile) south of Gold Beach. Over the next 20 minutes warships began bombarding another 29 positions along 80km (50 miles) of Normandy coast, the fall of their shot being directed by no fewer than 160 spotter aircraft. Some of the German batteries proved tenacious. Four guns in massive reinforced concrete casements at Longues on Gold Beach kept up fire for more than two hours, and fell silent only after the British cruisers Ajax and Argonaut had fired 179 shells at them, and managed to shoot two through the embrasures of the batteries. Some batteries, like that at Bénerville, fell silent when they received their first 16-inch shells, but sprang back into life later in the day.

The response of the German navy was confined to three torpedo boats based in Le Havre – *Mowe, Jaguar* and *Falke* – which were attempting to attack the British battleships *Warspite* and *Ramillies* under cover of a smoke screen laid by the RAF along the eastern

BELOW
A member of Britain's Glider Pilot Regiment in typical dress. Unlike their American counterparts, British glider pilots were fully trained combat troops who fought on the ground after landing their gliders. The Glider Pilot Regiment would be virtually destroyed at Arnhem, three months after D-Day.

flank of the landing zone. They succeeded instead in hitting the Norwegian destroyer *Svenner*, which sank rapidly. The Luftwaffe were nowhere to be seen. At first light 36 British and 16 American fighter squadrons patrolled above the beaches, four squadrons of P-38 Lightnings circled the Channel, while another 30 fighter squadrons remained in reserve in southern England.

As the landing craft moved towards the shore, the fire of the heavy naval guns was joined by fire from the destroyers, banks of rockets screaming in from specially adapted landing craft, and finally direct fire from 119mm (4.7-inch) and 6-pounder guns mounted on landing craft. In all, the bombarding forces fired 50,000 shells and rockets, about 10,000 for each of the landing beaches. Only a few minutes before troops were to land on their respective beaches, a final wave

of 1600 bombers of the US Eighth and Ninth Air Forces passed overhead, attacking the immediate hinterland.

H-hour for Utah and Omaha, the westernmost beaches, was set at 0630 hours, one hour after low tide. Farther east, along the British beaches, where the tide came in later, H-hour was set for 0730 hours. At first light off Utah troops of the US 4th Division clambered down landing nets into their LCTs for the 11km (7-mile) trip to the beach. At 0600 hours, while it was still about 6.5km (4 miles) from the coast, German gunners got the range of the invasion force and hit and sank Patrol Craft (PC) 1261, the boat guiding the assault forces to the landing beach. The rest of the force pressed on, but at about 4400m (4800 yards) from the coast the landing craft were caught in a strong lateral current running off the beach. The bombardment had

also obscured traces of landing marks vital to navigation. All these factors meant that when American troops waded ashore at 0631 hours, they were about 2000m (2200 yards) south of their intended landing site. The assistant divisional commander of 4th Division, 57-year-old Brigadier General Theodore Roosevelt Jr, son of the famous president, was a veteran of three assault landings in North Africa and the Mediterranean. Coming ashore with the first waves, Roosevelt realised that the accident had been fortuitous, as the section of the beach they had landed on was virtually undefended. Discovering a causeway, by 0930 hours he had moved the leading elements to within 2.5km (1.5 miles) of Ste Mère Eglise. Casualties had been amazingly low – 197, of whom 60 had been lost at sea when their landing craft had foundered.

Just across the Vire estury to the east, a very different situation faced American troops. For 10km (6 miles) from Grandcamp Les Bains to Pointe de la Percée, the coast rose in a series of cliffs and small promontories. About half way along was Pointe du Hoc, whose 90m (100-foot) cliffs made it a formidable position. Here the Germans had been constructing one of the most powerful batteries of the entire Atlantic Wall, six 155mm (6.1-inch) guns in massive bunkers of reinforced concrete and steel. With a maximum range of some 16,500m (18,000 yards), Pointe du Hoc's guns could easily reach the invasion assembly area to the north, the Utah Beach landing to the west and the Omaha Beach landing to the east. Allied airforces had repeatedly bombed the headland and since 0500 hours the 406mm (16-inch) guns of the American battleship Texas had been pounding it. But there could be no guarantee that this means alone would knock out the batteries. That task had been given to three companies of the 2nd Ranger Battalion, commanded by a former Texas high-school football coach, Colonel James E. Rudder. After being transported to the foot of the cliff in amphibious DUKWs, they were to scale it, then knock out what was left of the German's positions.

Rudder's force was scheduled to land at 0630 hours. Rough seas and poor navigation delayed its arrival until 0710 hours. The destroyers USS Satterlee and HMS Tarlybant closed to within 3200m (3500 yards) of the shore and opened up on the top of the cliffs, forcing the Germans to keep their heads down. From their DUKWs pitching in the

swell at the base of the cliffs, the Rangers fired up rockets attached to grappling hooks and rope ladders, which arced up over the cliffs. As the naval gunfire lifted, the Rangers swarmed up the ladders. The Germans came out of the bunkers and showered them with grenades. Some exploded, toppling Rangers from their ladders, but the Rangers fielded many, lobbing them back over the cliff top.

German guns destroyed
The Rangers were strong, agile and lightly equipped, but it still took them 10 minutes to scale the 30m (100 feet). Fighting their way through a moonscape of craters and twisted wreckage, squads of Rangers attacked each of the German bunkers, destroying them with satchel charges. However, none housed the 155mm (6.1-inch) guns. Rudder guessed that the Germans, knowing that Pointe du Hoc would suffer massive bombardment, had repositioned the guns, and that because the guns needed the fire-control mechanism in the command bunker at the very tip of the

An American soldier diverts the minds of his comrades from the misery of seasickness with a little musical entertainment. The Channel crossing proved to be unpleasant – many soldiers suffered from seasickness.

Pointe, they would not be very far away. Just after 0800 hours he sent a fighting patrol inland to search for them. About an hour later, after crossing the coast road about 1.5km (1 mile) south of Pointe du Hoc, the patrol discovered the camouflaged guns, with the gunners huddling against hedgerows in a nearby field. Scaring the gunners away with a few bursts of automatic fire, the Rangers destroyed the breeches of the guns with thermite charges, and set fire to piles of propellant, which lay nearby.

Rangers forced back

So far the operation had been an outstanding success, but now things began to go wrong. A communications breakdown prevented word that the Rangers had taken Pointe du Hoc from reaching the headquarters ship some 16km (10 miles) to the north until late that night. In the absence of any word from Rudder, HQ decided that the mission had failed and therefore diverted the reinforcement battalions to Omaha Beach. The Germans, quickly recovering, put in counterattacks, cut off the party south of the road, and steadily pushed Rudder back to the tip of the Pointe. The Rangers had to hold on for three days before a relief force fought its way through from Omaha, by which time only 90 of Rudder's 225 men were still in action.

American troops landing at Omaha 6.5km (4 miles) to the east had faced a different set of problems. The beach, a magnificent sweep of sand 275m (300 yards) wide at low tide and extending 6400m (7000) yards east from Pointe de la Percée to the rocks and cliffs of the appropriately named Côte du Rage north of Ste Honorine, was such an obvious place to land that it had been heavily defended. The Germans had placed three belts of obstacles down to the low water mark, and had then placed barbed wire along the top of a 2m (6-foot) wood and masonry sea wall, which ran the entire length of the beach. Beyond the sea wall was an esplanade, and then a shelf of water meadow between 90m and 365m (100–400 yards) wide, which rose precipitously to 60m (200 foot) bracken-covered bluffs. The Wehrmacht's engineers had laced the entire length of the esplanade with mines, dug a 2m (6 foot) anti-tank ditch at the inland edge of the esplanade, and dug machine-gun and mortar positions on top of the bluffs. But the most formidable defences had been positioned in four gullies, or draws, which intersected the bluffs, and were named after the hamlets built in them – Vierville, Moulins, St Laurent and Colleville. The Germans knew that the only practicable means of getting off the beach was through the draws, and at each of them they had constructed bunkers with

machine guns, mortars, and 20mm (.78-inch), 75mm (2.95-inch) and 88mm (3.45-inch) guns, all with interlocking arcs of fire. And across the Vierville draw, through which a metalled road ran inland, they had constructed a wall of reinforced concrete, 9m (30 feet) high and 3m (10 feet) thick. In all, the beach was defended by some 100 guns and mortars, and about 200 machine guns, manned by the three battalions of Colonel Ernst Goth's 916th Grenadier Regiment, part of the 352nd Division, most of whom were veterans of the Eastern Front, though they had received some 18-year-old conscripts.

Just before dawn, waves of B-17s flew overhead to bomb the defences in the draws, but pathfinders dropped their marking flares too far inland. As a result all the bombs fell south of the beaches, some up to 3km (2 miles) from the coast. The transports were

ABOVE
A B-17 Flying Fortress over the Normandy beaches. Heavy bombers were diverted from the strategic air offensive to attack targets in Normandy and the surrounding areas.

Republic P-47 Thunderbolt USA

LEFT
A Republic P-47 Thunderbolt of the 353rd Fighter Group, US 8th Air Force, Raydon, Essex, wearing its black-and-white invasion stripes. The Thunderbolt proved to be an efficient fighter-bomber.

American Rangers prepare for the assault on Utah Beach. Some are armed with specialized equipment for their role, such as Bangalore Torpedoes for clearing barbed wire, and grapnels to assist in scaling the faces of sheer cliffs.

20km (12 miles) out to sea, half as far again as they had anchored off Utah. In addition, winds scudding in from the north-west made this stretch of water far rougher than Utah. Heavily laden troops of the 116th Infantry Regiment of the US 29th Division and the 16th Regiment of the US 1st Infantry

Division clambered down scaling nets into the rolling and plunging landing craft. As they pulled away, loaded to the brim, waves broke over them, swamping 10 completely within minutes. Most of the 300 men aboard were drowned. Some craft managed to keep afloat, but only just, men bailing out furiously with their helmets. The larger LCTs with their cargoes of DD tanks, seeing the difficulties the landing craft were in, closed to within 6.5km (4 miles) of the shore before launching their Shermans. Even in good conditions, the DD tanks had a freeboard of less than 1m (3 feet). Some of the waves were over 2m (6.5 feet) high, and 27 out of 29 tanks were soon swamped. As they sank, they turned upside down, carrying their crews to the bottom.

Sitting targets

The Omaha landing had been choreographed like a Busby Berkeley musical, with about 30 different assault waves, all timed to arrive at 5–10 minute intervals. But the same current which had pulled the Americans off-target at Utah, now pulled craft eastward, and the assault waves began to become mixed up. The novelist Ernest Hemingway, now a war correspondent, was aboard one of the leading craft, plunging through the high seas. He recorded troops 'wax-gray with sea sickness, fighting it

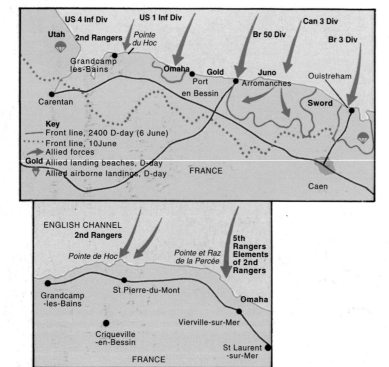

off, trying to hold onto themselves before they had to grab for the steel side of the boat'. Above them heavy naval shells roared landward, 'the concussion and the report... jarring the men's helmets.' Hemingway leaned forward to hear a GI say above the roar of the motor, 'Look what they're doing to those Germans. I guess there won't be a man alive there.'

But smoke and low cloud meant that much of the naval gunfire support failed to find a target. About 900m (1000 yards) from the shore, machine-gun bullets began to splash around the landing craft, while mortar bombs arced overhead. The landing craft of A company of the 116th were the first to ground on the sand, about 275m (300 yards) directly in front of the Vierville draw. As the ramps were lowered, the defenders fired directly into the landing craft, killing most, and forcing the survivors to leap over the sides and hide in the surf. Exactly the same thing was happening to the men of the 1st Division, coming ashore at Les Moulins, 1650m (1800 yards) to the east. As succeeding waves came in, the craft grounded farther

from the shore, until troops, weighed down with heavy equipment, were landing in neck-deep water. All along the beach men were struggling towards the shore in the face of increasingly heavy fire. Some took cover behind concrete obstacles, some lay half-submerged at the water's edge, unable to get across the bullet-swept sand to the relative safety of the sea wall. Life magazine's Frank Capa, who went in with the first wave, lay among the bodies in the shallows, shooting off all the film in his camera. He only shot the one reel: his hands were shaking so violently he could not reload the camera. As the tide began to come in many of the wounded around Capa drowned.

A German officer at Vierville reported by telephone to Kraiss that the invasion at Omaha had been stopped, and that he anticipated an American attempt to withdraw. Watching the disaster from a DUKW about 900m (1000 yards) offshore, the commander of the advanced HQ, Colonel Benjamin B. Talley, the assistant chief of staff to V Corps, had the same idea, and radioed back that the

BELOW

American troops plunge through the shallows at Utah Beach. The assault here was relatively straightforward, unlike that at Omaha, where fierce German resistance and other hardships caused about half the total casualties suffered by the Allies on D-Day.

**M4 Sherman 'Duplex Drive'
USA**

RIGHT
The British-designed amphibious DD tank, fitted with an inflatable skirt and a propeller. Many of those intended to support the landing at Omaha Beach were launched too soon, and sank before reaching the shore.

BELOW
American troops take casualties as they storm ashore. The total number of Allied dead on D-Day did not exceed 2500, a fraction of the expected toll.

landings should be suspended. The message was relayed back to General Omar Bradley on the command ship USS *Augusta*, who at 0900 hours sent an urgent message to SHAEF asking permission to abandon the beachhead. A communications foul-up meant that Eisenhower did not receive it until late in the day, by which time the situation had changed.

The bracken on the bluffs was now on fire, and a smoke haze was beginning to cover parts of the beach. German fire was most intense around the heavily defended draws, and as visibility declined more and more Americans who had had the good fortune to

land between the draws managed to make the relative safety of the sea wall. At 0730 hours the assistant divisional commander of 29 division, Brigadier General Cota, landed with his divisional staff almost halfway between Vierville and Les Moulins draws. Surveying the shambles around him, Cota realised that what was needed was not a general but a platoon commander. Moving from group to group huddled behind the sea wall, Cota found engineers and Rangers, as well as infantrymen from the 29th and 1st Divisions. Quickly organising a company-sized force, Cota got the engineers to clear the barbed wire with bangalore torpedoes and then with the command 'Rangers lead the way', urged his force across the esplanade and up a fold in the bluffs, where they were protected from machine-gun fire. Here Cota set up a radio, which by about 1000 hours had at last established shore-to-ship communications. Having managed to collect together about 600 men, Cota now sent the Rangers west behind the bluffs to attack the Vierville draw from the inland side, while the infantry from the 116th worked their way towards Vierville on the seaward side of the bluffs. By 1100 hours the combined attacks, now supported by properly directed naval gun fire, had driven the Germans from Vierville.

Elsewhere along the beach the tide of battle was slowly swinging the Americans' way. Second Lieutenant John M. Spalding of E Company, 2nd Battalion of the 16th Infantry, part of 1st Division, had landed half way between the Colleville and St Laurent draws. Collecting together 23 men, he led

Utah Beach seen from the air, with troops swarming across the sand. Note the line of amphibious tanks moving up in support of the infantry. Utah was relatively undefended, and the American troops made quick progress inland.

them for 365m (400 yards) through the high reeds of a coastal swamp, and up a fold in the bluffs, to reach the crest where the American cemetery now stands. Spalding then turned west and attacked the east side of the St Laurent exit. At 0815 hours Colonel George A. Taylor, commander of the 16th Infantry, came ashore and rallied small knots of survivors within earshot: 'Two kinds of people are staying on this beach, the dead and those who are going to die. Now let's get the hell out of here!' The better part of two battalions now made their way up the bluffs, some following what was to be called 'Spalding's Trail', and then moved to attack St Laurent and Colleville from the rear. At about 1030 hours two landing craft, LCT 30 and LCI (L) 544 steamed full ahead through the obstacles off the beach opposite Colleville on the eastern side, firing all their weapons at enemy strongpoints. At the same time two destroyers came broadside on to within 1000m (1090 yards) of the beach opposite Les Moulins. With their keels scraping the bottom they pumped

*General Omar Bradley
commanded the American II
Corps in Tunisia and Sicily,
before being appointed to
lead the US 1st Army in the
invasion of Normandy. After
the war, he became Chairman
of the Joint Chiefs of Staff.
He died in 1981.*

BELOW

*The first casualties are
evacuated from 'Bloody
Omaha' as D-Day itself
draws to a close.*

133mm (5.2-inch) shells into enemy positions
to the east, one round passing through the
embrasure of a bunker on the west side of the
Colleville draw. Under cover of this fire engi-

neers drove bulldozers through the dunes at
the St Laurent draw, filled the anti-tank ditch,
and filled the minefield. As Spalding's men
and other elements of the 16th Regiment
were already attacking from the rear, the
German defenders at St Laurent surrendered
a little after 1100 hours.

Beachhead established

Thus by 1130 hours the Americans had captured both the Vierville and St Laurent exits,
and were beginning to move off the beach in
strength. German fire at other strong points
was beginning to slacken noticeably as the
defenders ran short of ammunition. The
352nd Division's commander, Major General
Dietrich Kraiss, was under the impression
until about midday that his forces were holding, and when it became clear that the
Americans had taken Vierville and were
advancing out of the St Laurent draw, he had
no reserves to hand, having despatched them
to the south-west to deal with a dummy parachute drop. Early in the afternoon, Kraiss
moved a battalion-sized force, supported by
12 75mm (2.5-inch) self-propelled guns, into
the Colleville area, but their counter-attack
was soon stopped by naval gunfire. By
evening, the Americans held a shallow beachhead from Vierville to Colleville, and ever
more troops were coming ashore. The price
had been heavy. About 300 of the 566
Rangers had become casualties, along with
hundreds of sailors manning the landing craft

and engineers attempting to clear beach obstacles. But the biggest losses had been incurred by the infantry divisions: the 29th had suffered 2440 casualties and the 1st Division had lost 1744. The price for the 352nd Division had been almost as high, with 2500 prisoners taken, many of whom were wounded, and perhaps as many as 1000 dead.

Armoured attack

The slaughter on Omaha had been going on for more than an hour when landing craft carrying the 1st Battalion Royal Hampshire Regiment grounded several hundred metres east of Le Hamel on Gold Beach, about 10km (6 miles) east of Colleville. The defenders, also of the 352nd Division, put down a withering fire, hitting most of the landing craft. Unlike the Americans, the British had decided that sea conditions were too rough to permit the launch of the DD tanks. Hence the Hampshires found themselves on their own. Soon the commanding officer, his second in command, the artillery support officers and the forward headquarters were either dead or wounded, and all the radios were smashed.

A replay of the American experience at Omaha seemed in the offing, when the corps commander, Lieutenant General Bucknell, ordered the LCTs to brave the obstacles and take the tanks directly onto the beach. The German positions at Le Hamel hit at least 20 of the large craft, but the majority made it to the shore and lowered their ramps. Instead of the expected infantry troops, the waiting German machine-gunners were stunned to see huge armoured vehicles emerging, the 'funnies' of the 79th Armoured Division. Crab tanks flailed paths through the mine-fields up to the beach, oblivious to the metallic scream of the machine-gun bullets spraying all around them. A Crab commanded by Sergeant Lindsay RE, which landed to the east of Le Hamel, smashed through the centre of the strongly defended town, firing and flailing alternately, until it came up alongside the main German emplacement. Edging his tank around to the front, Lindsay (in 79th Division parlance) 'posted a letter': he swung the muzzle of his gun into the embrasure, fired, and blew the 88mm (3.45-inch) and its entire crew out of the back.

BELOW
Second wave Horsa gliders, towed by Dakotas (C-47s) of RAF Transport Command, crossing the Normandy coast on their way to reinforce the 6th Airborne Division. Total Horsa production was 3655, of which 400 were used by the Americans.

In the centre of Gold Beach, another assault battalion, the 1st Dorset, had come ashore to the east of Les Roquettes, this time supported by crabs and other AVREs, and quickly pushed inland. Another battalion, the 2nd Devon, came ashore at Le Hamel, followed closely by five landing craft carrying 47th (Royal Marine) Commando. Since the Hampshires had come ashore the tide had risen considerably, submerging beach obstacles, and three of the landing craft hit mines, killing 43 and forcing the remainder to abandon equipment and swim for the shore. Though drastically reduced in numbers, those Commandos still fully equipped set off inland, bypassing enemy positions, to attack Port en Bessin, on the demarcation line between the British and American beaches, from the rear.

On the extreme eastern boundary of Gold Beach, the 6th Green Howards and the 5th East Yorks came ashore to the west and east of La Rivière respectively. This area was held by the 441st Ost Battalion, part of the 716th Division, who broke and fled when the 5th Yorks and Green Howards overran their main beach defences at about 1000 hours. The commander of the German corps responsible for this sector ordered the 915th Regiment, the reserve of 352nd Division, which had been sent south-west during the night to deal with a phantom paratroop drop, to move post haste to La Rivière, but this was easier said than done. The regiment had to cover nearly 32km (20 miles), partly on foot, partly on bicycles, and partly in French motor vehicles, which kept breaking down. For virtually the rest of the day the road to Bayeux was open, but the British didn't know this, and concentrated on getting their forces ashore and consolidating the beachhead.

BELOW

The debris of a terrible day. The beaches are cleared, and the assault troops have been relieved by others whose task it is to push inland and consolidate before the German counterattacks begin in earnest.

The Canadian 3rd Division, landing farther east on Juno Beach, had a tougher time. As they unloaded in a heavy swell, landing craft smashed into uncleared obstacles, detonating mines. Twenty of the 24 landing craft were lost in one battalion landing alone. All told, 90 of the 306 craft were sunk or disabled during the morning. Only 14 DD tanks of the Canadian 1st Hussars, launched at 3300m (3600 yards) in very rough seas, finally made it to the shore. One of the assaulting units, the Regina Rifles, was supposed to come in to the east of the heavily defended town of Courseulles, but A Company landed too far

to the west, right opposite the town. A mad dash up the beach to the relative safety of the harbour wall ended with 15 dead, blown up in a minefield. The remainder of the Regina Rifles, supported by Centaur tanks of the Royal Marines and AVREs of 79th Division, attacked into Courselles from the east, methodically clearing the town house by house, so that it as not firmly in Canadian hands until mid-afternoon.

About 3km (2 miles) to the east, the North Shore (New Brunswick) Regiment's landing at St Aubin had gone like clockwork. The amphibious tanks of the Fort Garry Horse,

ABOVE

Ashore at last: men of the 13th/18th Hussars, some wounded, moving up Sword Beach. Their DD tanks suffered heavily from the fire of enemy 88mm (3.45-inch) guns emplaced at Ouistreham, greatly reducing their armoured support in the attack.

After the initial shock of the invasion, the Germans were quick to rally and launch counter-attacks. The defence of the beaches was hampered by a lack of ammunition and men in reserve.

launched from only 1700m (1860 yards) out, arrived simultaneously with the infantry, and together they crossed the sea wall and reduced enemy strong points. About 1.5km (less than a mile) to the west at Bernières-sur-Mer things had gone less well. Landing craft carrying the Queen's Own Rifles grounded opposite one of the town's strong points, and when the ramps were lowered German machine guns sliced through the packed craft. Heavy casualties were also suffered by the supporting unit, the Régiment de la Chaudière (known throughout Canada as the 'Chauds'), when four of their five landing craft were hit and the majority of the regiment had to swim or wade ashore. By this time the Queens were street fighting their way through Bernières-sur-Mer, and the Chauds moved in to help, stamping out all but the occasional sniper by 1030 hours.

Throughout the morning the rest of Canadian 3rd Division continued to land, with considerable congestion building up between Bernières and Saint-Aubin. Assault engineers arranged to open up three routes through the shore obstructions and from 1400 hours units of the division were

expanding inland. Pushing 10km (6 miles) to the south-west, elements of Canadian 7th Brigade made contact with British 50th Division at Creully, cutting the Caen–Arromanches road. Meanwhile, the North Nova Scotia Highlanders and 27th Armoured Brigade had pushed south along the Courseulles–Caen road, reaching Villons-les-Buissons only 8km (5 miles) north of its D-Day objective, Carpiquet Airport, 3km (2 miles) to the east of Caen.

German resistance

Sword beach, the destination of the British 3rd Division, lay 5km (3 miles) to the east of Saint-Aubin-sur-Mer and extended some 5km to the mouth of the Canal de Caen and the Orne River. Allied planners, worried about the gap between Juno and Sword which would be left by the main Canadian and British landings, decided to land 48 and 41 Royal Marine Commandos on either side, to speed up the merging of the British and Canadian beaches. As 48 Commando approached the coast opposite St Aubin at around 0900 hours, five landing craft hit mines and one was hit by shellfire. By the

**Churchill Mk VIII Crocodile
Great Britain**

time they reached the beach, 48 Commando was only 200 men strong. Pushing inland, this handful of survivors managed to take the village of Langrune, but further attempts to push eastwards were halted by strong German resistance. Landing about 5km (3 miles) farther east, 41 Commando had an easier time getting ashore, but soon bogged down in the face of heavy German fire.

On the extreme eastern edge of Sword Beach, opposite the town of Ouistreham, Lord Lovat's 1st Commando Brigade landed at the same time as the first DD and crab tanks. The first troops onto the beach were Commandant Jean Kieffer's Free French Commando Battalion. A mortar bomb fell in the midst of one platoon as it charged from its landing craft, killing or maiming most of them. Keiffer led his men east along the coast

road into the streets of Ouistreham, systematically clearing the town, villa by villa. The centre of resistance was in Ouistreham's casino, a strongly constructed building on the esplanade overlooking the sea, with clear fields of fire along the beaches. The Germans had done their best to convert it into a fortress, but the petards of 79th Division's AVREs smashed the walls, and the Commandos stormed the building, capturing the dazed and frightened survivors.

While Kieffer's men fought in the streets of Ouistreham, the bulk of the Commandos under Lord Lovat pushed inland, aiming to link up with the by now hard-pressed paratroops. The route they followed had been carefully selected by Resistance intelligence reports and, as the men moved rapidly to the south-east, they avoided main roads and

ABOVE
The Churchill Mk VIII 'Crocodile' flame-throwing tank. Compressed nitrogen forced fuel from the trailer to the flame-gun, mounted in the normal machine gun position. The weapon had a range of about 110m (120 yards).

LEFT
Debris litters Sword Beach in the aftermath of the invasion. Sword was secured by commandos of the 4th Special Service Brigade, followed by the British 3rd Infantry Division and 27th Armoured Brigade.

major strong points, keeping to hedgerows and farm tracks. Coming from the south they could hear the noise of battle, first distant, then more loudly, the staccato chatter of the airborne's Bren guns intermingled with the tearing scream of the German MG42s. Lord Lovat – perhaps remembering the last time a Campbell had come to the relief of a beleaguered garrison, that of Lucknow during the Indian Mutiny of 1857 – ordered his piper to play 'Blue Bonnets over the Border'. Shortly before 1300 hours the Commandos and the airborne forces joined up.

The Commando assaults on Sword were outstandingly successful, but the bulk of 3rd Division had a very much harder time. The narrow frontage of Sword meant that 3rd Division could only land one brigade at a time, and yet it had the most difficult D-Day objective, the capture of Caen, a medium-sized city with a population of around 100,000. Eighth Brigade, comprising the 1st Battalion South Lancashire Regiment, 2nd Battalion East Yorkshire Regiment, and the armour of the 13/18 Royal Hussars and 79th Division, comprised the initial assault wave. The wind was pushing the sea landward in long rollers, making it difficult to control the direction of the landing craft. The experience of weaving through the iron rails and ramps and pickets with Teller mines on top reminded Major A. D. Rouse of the South Lancashires of 'groping through a grotesque petrified forest'. The BBC's correspondent Howard Marshall, accompanying 8th Brigade, remembered that 'suddenly, as we tried to get between two of these tripart defence systems of the Germans, our craft swung, we touched a mine, there was a loud explosion, a thundering shudder of the whole craft, and water began pouring in.' The DD tanks of the 13/18 Hussars and 79th Division were already ashore, but German 88mm (3.45-inch) guns firing from Ouistreham, and three guns firing from a strong point at La Breche, just to the east of the landing, hit tank after tank, until the whole beach seemed to be a mass of burning armour. The South Lancashire attacked east, but it took nearly three hours to subdue La

Breche, the regiment suffering 107 casualties, including their commander, who was killed.

By the middle of the morning the South Lancashire had taken Hermanville, about a kilometre and a half (1 mile) inland from La Breche, the East Yorkshire were clearing defences south of Ouistreham, and the battalion of the Suffolk Regiment, landing later and passing between the South Lancashire and East Yorkshire, were advancing up the steeply rising slopes of Périers Ridge, about 60m (200 feet) above sea level. Here they ran into two strong points which the British had code named Morris and Hillman. Morris was a relatively small position, four guns and 67 men, who quickly surrendered when the Suffolk attacked, but Hillman was a much tougher nut. It was a fortress about 365m by 550m (400–600 yards), well protected by wire and mines, and it was the headquarters of the German 736th Regiment. The Germans easily repulsed the Suffolk's first attack, and the regiment's commander refused to have his men slaughtered in a renewed frontal assault. A deliberate attack, involving the integration of artillery and air support, with armour and infantry, went in late in the afternoon, but it was not until 2000 hours that the last of Hillman's defenders surrendered.

By nightfall the whole of British 3rd Division was ashore, but had not advanced beyond Périers Ridge, 5km (3 miles) short of Caen. Many weeks were to pass before they would advance any further.

Rommel alerted

For the Germans the events of 6 June had been confusing. The day before, the weather had appeared so bad that Rommel had driven off from his headquarters at La Roche-Guyon to visit his wife at Herrlingen in southern Germany, before seeing Hitler at Obersalzberg. The commander of Seventh Army, General Friedrich Dollmann, was equally sure that there would be no invasion, and on 5 June had sent most of his staff officers to a war game at Rennes in Brittany. The first intimation that something untoward was about to happen came from Fifteenth Army in the Pas de Calais where the army commander, General Hans von Salmuth, alarmed by Allied activity in the Channel, placed his forces on full alert. Von Rundstedt in Paris approved this measure but, given the severity of weather conditions, decided there was little point in alerting forces elsewhere.

At about 0215 hours Speidel was awakened with reports of paratroop landings, but he had no information about their strength or scale. When he finally got through to von Rundstedt by phone, who had no clearer information, both men convinced each other that the landings were merely drops to the French Resistance. By 0430 hours a different picture was beginning to emerge. Radio messages and despatch riders were bringing reports that large numbers of ships had been sighted between the Cotentin Peninsula and the mouth of the Seine. Von Rundstedt still thought that this was a diversionary tactic and that the real landing would come in the Pas de Calais area, but as a precautionary measure he ordered the 12th SS *Hitlerjugend* and the *Panzer Lehr* Divisions to prepare to move to the Normandy coast.

By 0530 hours, when the first shells from the Allied naval bombardment hit the coast, the hidden meaning of all the activity became blindingly clear, but there was considerable delay in transmitting this news to higher

headquarters stationed many kilometres inland. When Speidel finally managed to get a telephone connection with Rommel at 0630 hours, he was still quite oblivious to the bombardment. He only passed on the reports of the paratroop drops, thereby lulling the field marshal into a false sense of security. He soon acquired more definite information, but it

ABOVE
British second-wave troops coming ashore. They were faced with the daunting task of fighting their way forward through extremely difficult terrain.

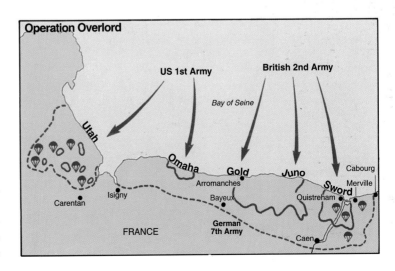

Operation Overlord

RIGHT

On the attack: a Churchill tank rumbles through the narrow streets of a French village. The Normandy countryside, as the Allies were to find out to their cost, was ideal terrain for the German defenders.

took until 1000 hours before he was able to get through to Rommel again to tell him that Allied landings were under way on the Normandy coast. The news galvanised Rommel into action, but it took him most of the day to drive back to his headquarters – Hitler had previously issued an edict forbidding senior German officers to travel by air any longer lest they be shot down.

Down in Le Mans, General Dollmann's headquarters staff remained ignorant of the landings until 0845 hours, when they received news that British troops were coming ashore opposite Caen. They did not hear about the American landings to the west until 1100 hours. Dollmann believed that these latter landings were diversions, and that the earlier British landings were the main

invasion. Von Rundstedt did not share this opinion. Even after he had received definite confirmation of the landings, he continued to believe that they were all feints. The real invasion, he still thought, would soon descend on the Pas de Calais.

Hitler's reaction

This was also Hitler's own view. When the news of the landings reached him at 1000 hours, while he was holding court at Berchtesgaden, he seemed almost relieved. 'They've come at last!' he announced. For the previous two years, increasingly large German forces had been tied down along the Atlantic coast while Allied armies remained poised in southern England. Now that the Allies had committed themselves to decisive action, the German army could crush them. Albert Speer, the armaments minister, was with Hitler on 6 June; his memoirs record Hitler's chain of reasoning that day: 'Do you recall? Among the many reports we've received there was one that exactly predicted the landing site and the day and hour. That only confirms my opinion that this is not the real invasion yet.'

Hitler was at first reluctant to authorise the release of the armoured reserve. Meanwhile, German units were fighting desperately all along the coast, but these were battles fought by battalions and companies who had little or no contact with high headquarters. On the extreme east of the beachhead Major General Edgar Feuchtinger, commanding the 21st Panzer Division (a formation which had

BELOW

Counter-attack: Tiger tanks of the 21st Panzer Division advancing to the Normandy battlefront. The Tiger was rightly feared by the Allies, as it was well-protected and well-armed.

served with Rommel in North Africa), sent his tanks against the paratroops on the Orne bridges before dawn, even though he had not received orders to do so. By 1000 hours the 21st was heavily engaged with the paratroops and was beginning to gain the upper hand when Feuchtinger received his first message from high command, ordering him to break off the engagement and move to defend Caen. It took the 21st the rest of the morning and the early part of the afternoon to carry out the order. They wasted most of the day disengaging and moving. By mid-afternoon many of Feuchtinger's tanks were very low on fuel, but his logistics officers were unable to contact depots in Caen to have more sent forward. Even so, a battle group of 21st Panzer probed around the right flank of British 3rd Division, discovered the still open gap between Sword and Juno, and six tanks and a rifle company succeeded in reaching the coast. At this point transport aircraft and gliders, destined for 6th Airborne's landings east of the Orne, passed overhead. The battle group commander, convinced that he was about to be cut off by another Allied airborne landing, pulled back from the corridor, thus allowing the merging of Sword and Juno to occur a few hours later.

By dusk on 6 June the German response was becoming more coordinated. The panzer reserves, the 12th SS, 2nd SS, *Panzer Lehr* and 17th Panzer Grenadiers, had been ordered to move towards the beachheads. But it was all too late. For the Germans it had been a bad day. They had misinterpreted the true nature of the landings, which was in part the result of Operation Fortitude, and in part the result of a catastrophic communications failure between the various levels of command. The troops had generally fought well, but when reinforcements had failed to arrive and when they ran low on ammunition, they had either surrendered or been overwhelmed. Many Allied leaders had expected a repeat of Gallipoli. Instead 130,000 troops had landed from the sea and another 22,500 had arrived from the air, all for 10,000 casualties, half of them on Omaha. It was true that British 50th Division could have taken Bayeux and did not, and that Canadian 3rd Division had stopped short of Carpiquet and British 3rd Division had not made it to Caen, but for the Allies it had been a good day.

BELOW
The news of D-Day breaks to the world. Railway travellers at a London station eagerly study the evening papers. The reports from Normandy were optimistic, and carefully censored.

CHAPTER THREE

BLOODBATH IN THE BOCAGE

For the Allies, securing a foothold on the coast of France was only the first part of the battle. Now they faced a far harder task: breaking out of the thick Normandy hedgerows.

Allied planners had spent so much time solving the problems of getting troops ashore, that virtually no attention had been paid to the problems which troops might encounter once they were off the beaches. Allied troops had trained in large armoured formations on Salisbury Plain, Dartmoor, Exmoor and the North Yorkshire Moors, preparing for the type of mobile warfare which had characterised operations in North Africa. On the extreme left of the beachhead facing south-east, 6th Airborne had established a small bridgehead across the Orne, overlooking country not unlike that of Salisbury Plain. However, the bridgehead was considered too small to allow armoured divisions to concentrate there in any strength, and certainly not in secret. To the immediate west the situation was even worse. Here British 3rd Division faced the industrial suburbs of Caen, which the Germans were defending. All armies disliked attacking into cities, because it was bloody and took time. To the immediate west of Caen the country was open – but too open. Here Capriquet airfield extended east to west across any advance to the south the Canadian 3rd Division might make, and the Germans were busily defending the southern side of the runway. Farther west, the British on Gold Beach, and the Americans on Omaha and Utah faced very different problems.

From Capriquet, and extending to the swamps and marshes of the Cotentin peninsula, lay the bocage, an intricate patchwork of sunken lanes and small fields bounded by ancient hedgerows; hedgerows more than 2.75m (9 feet) thick at the base and rising to a height of more than 4.5m (15 feet). Large farmhouses or small villages studded the land at intervals of roughly 900m (1000 yards). The farmhouses' thick-walled stone buildings with deep cellars were relics of the time five centuries earlier when Normandy had been a battleground in the closing phase of the Hundred Years War. To make matters worse, about 16km (10 miles) inland the country began to rise to a tangle of hills, the highest of which, 425m (1400-foot) Mont Pincon, lay at the centre of an area the Normans called 'Normandie Suisse', because of its resemblance to the Alpine foothills. The Normandy countryside was an attacker's nightmare and a defender's paradise; an intricate network of natural and man-made obstacles, with thousands of strongly built houses, many of which could withstand all but a direct hit from a heavy bomb or a large calibre shell.

Rommel knew that if the beachhead were to be destroyed, it must be attacked quickly with massive force. He ordered the 21st Panzer and 12th SS Panzer Divisions to concentrate to strike a coordinated blow, but both divisions were already fighting piecemeal with the Allies and could not disengage. By dawn on 7 June elements of 21st Panzer were supporting the attacks of Fifteenth Army's 346th and 711th Divisions against the paratroop and commando bridgehead east of the Orne. Their counter-attacks succeeded in recapturing some ground, but were broken off when the guns of the Royal Navy pulverised advanced units, while the 51st Highland Division moved across the Orne to support the airborne and the commandos. In the centre, the advance guard of the 12th SS Panzer Division was already counter-attacking the Canadians north of Capriquet, a battle group succeeding in cutting off the Regina Rifles in Bretteville. Because speed was now essential, *Panzer Lehr* was trying to advance in broad daylight on the left of the 12th SS against the British 50th Division, but was attacked constantly from the air. Its commander, Major General Fritz Bayerlein, who had served as chief of staff to Rommel in North Africa, described the air attacks as the worst he had experienced. The road out of Vire, he said, was 'a fighter-bomber race course'. The move cost *Panzer Lehr* 80 of its half-track trucks, self-propelled guns and prime-movers. Air attack severely disrupted the movement of several other German formations to Normandy, including a battle group of the St

Nazaire-based 275th Division, which was moving by train to Bayeux on 7 June when it was obliterated near Avranches by waves of medium bombers, followed by Thunderbolts.

The Resistance also played a vital role in preventing the movement of German forces to Normandy. Had one formation, the infamous 2nd SS Panzer Division, *Das Reich*, managed to get to Normandy in the first few days after the invasion, the course of the battle might have been different. *Das Reich* was one of the most formidable formations in western Europe: 20,000 superbly trained, battle-hardened troops with 240 tanks and self-propelled guns, including 100 Tigers and Panthers. However, on D-Day it was still at Montauban to the north of Toulouse, about 650km (400 miles) from the beachhead.

Das Reich delayed

On the evening of 6 June the officer commanding, *Brigadeführer* Heinz Lammerding, received orders to move to Normandy. Under normal conditions the move would have been completed by 9 June, but by that date advance units had only just reached Limoges, still 320km (200) miles south of Normandy. The rest of the division was strung out over 290km (180 miles) of the winding RN 20, all the way back to Montauban. Everything had gone wrong, for although the division had

BELOW

An American patrol advances through vegetation typical of the bocage. Combat took place at very short range, and it was impossible to tell what was going on in the adjacent field, let alone a few miles away.

LEFT
A member of the French resistance poses proudly with his Bren gun, supplied by the Allies just for such an occasion as the invasion. Resistance fighters slowed down the flow of German supplies and reinforcements to the front.

BELOW
Royal Air Force Typhoons launch a rocket attack on a troop train somewhere in northern France. The interdiction of German reinforcements greatly helped the Allied troops fighting in the beachhead.

been in a high state of alert (in the previous three months it had suffered 200 casualties in clashes with the Resistance), on 7 June the Resistance managed to blow up much of its fuel reserves and some of its transport. Panzer grenadiers hastily requisitioned all the fuel and civilian vehicles they could lay their hands on, but the move had been delayed by several hours. During the next 48 hours the situation got much worse as the Resistance ambushed the advance guard on a bridge before Souillic where RN 20 crossed the Dordogne, and hit the long flanks of the stalled column in a dozen other places.

The SS, angered and frustrated by the casualties and delays caused by hidden enemies who quickly melted into the countryside, retaliated with the same brutal tactics which they had used to quell partisan activity on the Eastern Front. On 9 June Lammerding led a panzer grenadier battalion into the town of Tulle, 80km (50 miles) south of Limoges, and caught the citizens in the middle of celebrating their liberation. The SS troops publicly hanged 99 men, women and children from the balconies of houses along the main street and forced their families to watch. The following day, the advance guard surrounded and then occupied the village of Oradour-sur-Glane, 14.5km (9 miles) north-west of Limoges. The SS separated the men from the

ABOVE

The men responsible for the beachhead, from left to right: Hodges, Crerar, Montgomery, Bradley and Dempsey. At this stage of the campaign, Monty was in overall charge. Eisenhower took over on 1 September 1944 – effectively a demotion for Montgomery, although it had been planned even before the landings took place.

women and children, split them into several groups, and machine-gunned them. They herded the women and children into the church, threw in a satchel of high explosives and hand-grenades, and then gunned down the survivors as they sought to escape the flames. In all 642 died – 190 men, 245 women and 207 children.

The advance guard pushed north. When it reached the Loire on 11 June, the Germans discovered that only a single-track bridge had survived sabotage or air attacks. The division following up behind, constantly harassed by Resistance attacks, jammed itself into a bottleneck, a sitting target for the air strikes of the medium bombers called in by Anglo-French SOE teams operating with the Resistance. Meanwhile, on 14 June, advance

elements reached the division's assembly area at Domfront, 80km (50 miles) south of the beachheads. It was now that 'cab ranks' of rocket firing Typhoons, directed in by the SOE, hit *Das Reich*, destroying 16 vehicles in the first attack. The full division finally limped into Normandy on 23 June, far too late to influence the battles for the beachhead.

Montgomery had come ashore on the morning of 8 June, and had found his headquarters caravans parked in the grounds of a château near Cruely. Visited by Churchill, Brooke and Smuts two days later, Montgomery outlined his master plan for the land battle. After initial setbacks, the momentum of the American build-up was increasing, and Montgomery believed it imperative that US forces strike west to take the Cotentin

RIGHT

Wearing its invasion stripes, the black and white bars which signified its allegiance to the Allied cause, Mustangs like this one were responsible for maintaining air superiority over the beachhead and beyond, protecting the bombers that were attacking rear areas.

North American P-51 Mustang
USA

Peninsula and capture the port of Cherbourg. He therefore intended to attract as many of the German forces as he could to the British sector, where intelligence indicated that there was a good chance of a spectacular success. It was clear that the Germans were experiencing major difficulties moving reserves to Normandy and in coordinating their counter-attacks, and that a gap had opened up in the area of Villers-Bocage south-west of Caen, between 12 SS Panzer and *Panzer Lehr*. While 51st Highland Division attacked south along the eastern side of Caen, the newly landed 7th Armoured Division, the famed 'Desert Rats', was to strike directly south through Villers-Bocage and then, moving east, link up with 51st Highland Division and encircle Caen.

'Looney' Hinde

This was a daring plan and required daring men to carry it out. Unfortunately, further down the chain of command were officers who could not think beyond set-piece battles, and other officers who had seen too much action in North Africa, Sicily and Italy and who were very tired. On 12 June Lieutenant General Miles Dempsey, commander of British Second Army, Montgomery's direct subordinate, visited the HQ of Lieutenant General Gerard Bucknell, the commander of XXX Corps, of which 7th Armoured Division was a part, and was horrified to discover that no preparations for the attack had yet been made. When 7th Armoured's tanks

did roll south on 13 June, the divisional commander, Major General George Erskine, regretted that the order had not been received a day earlier, as he was sure that the Germans would now be filling the gap. As speed was of the essence Erskine selected Brigadier Robert Hinde's 22nd Armoured Brigade to spearhead the drive. Hinde, whose often reckless bravery in North Africa had earned him the nickname 'Looney', stormed into Villers-Bocage at 0800 hours on 13 June, and then ordered 4th County of London Yeomanry and a company of the Rifle Brigade about a kilometre and a half (1 mile) north-east along the road to Caen, to a hill marked as Point 213 on Allied maps. The Yeomanry's commander, Lieutenant Colonel Viscount Arthur Cranley, pointed out to Hinde that the road was narrow with deep

ABOVE
Tiger tanks of Michael Wittmann's unit, the schwere SS-Panzer Abteilung 101, move up to the front around 10 June 1944, near the village of Morgny.

LEFT
A British Cromwell tank, seen after a fatal encounter with a Tiger. British, and indeed American, tanks were outclassed by the German Panthers and Tigers that roamed the Normandy battlefield. However, the Allies' overwhelming air power gave them the advantage in the campaign.

RIGHT AND BELOW
*Waves break over the
caissons of one of the
Mulberry Harbours during
the Great Storm, which
destroyed one harbour and
left the other requiring
major repair work. The
storm broke on 19 June and
lasted for three days,
severely disrupting the
timetable of the invasion. It
deprived the armies of
105,000 tons of stores and
20,000 vehicles.*

ditches on either side, and was bordered by thick hedgerows. He wanted to spend some time on reconnaissance but Hinde told him to get on with it. At about 1100 hours the British were on the hill, from where they could see the distant chimneys of Colombelles, the industrial suburb of Caen. And a few hundred metres to the south of Point 213 *Obersturmführer* Michel Wittman, the veteran of many tank battles on the Eastern Front, could see through the vision slit of his heavily camouflaged Tiger tank the turrets of British tanks above the hedgerows, stretching along the road like ducks in a shooting gallery.

Wittmann commanded No 2 Company, 501st Heavy Tank Battalion, which had arrived outside Villers-Bocage during the night, but for the moment he was by himself. Speeding down a farm track which ran parallel to the road, Wittman fired and hit a Bren Gun Carrier, which slewed across the road, belching dense clouds of black smoke. The Tiger roared in towards Villers-Bocage, Wittman pumping another 22 rounds at the British column, each round demolishing a tank or lighter armoured vehicle, while British shells bounced off the German's armour. Entering the town, Wittmann knocked out Viscount Cranley's tank, and then the tanks of the second in command and the regimental sergeant major. Reaching the town square, Wittmann was hit by a storm of British anti-tank fire, and pulled back, destroying yet another British tank in the process. After rearming and refuelling, and joining up with four other Tigers and an up-gunned Mark VI, he returned to Point 213 to complete the massacre of the County of London Yeomanry, and then, reinforced by some tanks from 2nd Panzer Division, again attacked into Villers-Bocage. This time the British were ready, and the Mark IV and three

Tigers, including Wittmann's, were knocked out by a combination of 6- and 17-pounder anti-tank guns, though Wittmann and most of the crews escaped on foot. With 2nd Panzer Division arriving in strength during the evening and throughout the following day, Bucknall ordered 7th Division to abandon Villers-Bocage and withdraw under cover of a heavy American artillery barrage during the night of 14/15 June. In total, for the loss of four tanks, the Germans had destroyed 53 British tanks and other vehicles. The debacle of Villers-Bocage effectively ended Montgomery's first attempt to break out to the west of Caen. It also demoralised 7th Armoured Division, and spread alarm and despondency throughout the Allied armies.

But although Villers-Bocage was a victory for the Germans, it was only of tactical importance, because this action, and all the interdiction operations of the Allied Air Forces and the French Resistance, had bought several vital days in which to establish the beachhead. In the months preceding the landing, literally millions of man-hours had been devoted to working out complex landing procedures for men and materiel. These plans did not survive the first few minutes on the Normandy beaches: all was chaos. Logistics troops on the beaches formed *ad hoc* teams and kept the materiel moving to improvised depots. By the end of the first day 8900 vehicles and 1900 tons of stores had been landed on the British forces' beaches alone. The work was complicated by German batteries at Le Havre, which kept pumping shells onto Sword Beach, but the biggest blow came not from German gunners but from RAF Bomber Command – on 7 June a Lancaster bomb-aimer misjudged his target and dropped a stick of bombs onto the main British ordnance depot just off the beach. The result was spectacular, as 26,000 litres of fuel and 400 tons of ammunition exploded.

The Great Storm

Logistics planners had known that landing men and supplies on open beaches would be a dangerous and uncertain business, and would not produce the military muscle needed to secure the beachhead, let alone allow a break-out. The success of the Normandy landings depended on getting the Mulberry harbours into position as quickly as possible. The first of the 600 caissons and blockships was deposited off Arromanches in the British sector, and off Omaha in the American sector, on 7 June. Eleven days later the American harbour received its first cargo and by 18 June 24,412 tons of supplies and ammunition had rolled ashore from the two Mulberries.

Around midnight on 18/19 June the wind shifted to the north-east, and by dawn had risen to gale force, turning the Bay of the Seine into a seething cauldron. Commanding

BELOW
The American flag flies defiantly over Utah Beach as eagerly awaited support infantry and equipment come ashore.

a convoy of tugs towing 22 caissons in mid-Channel was Lieutenant Commander Taylor. Never before in a long career at sea had he experienced a storm of such unexpected violence: 'It arrived from nowhere, whispering across the water at first and finally rising to a triumphant shout of malignancy calling from the seas an answering mood. It caught the unseaworthy tows unprotected and struck them spitefully until, of the 22 whale tows that sailed from the Solent in fine weather, not one remained afloat.' The full force of the gale hit Omaha beach. Taylor continued: 'Breaches appeared rapidly in the breakwater. Blockships broke their backs and Phoenix caissons disintegrated, and through the breaks the storm struck at the roadways and the piers so that soon they were sinking. Then onto the half-submerged roadways drifting landing craft and equipment piled themselves, till an inextricably jumbled mass of wreckage was torn from the moorings and cast upon the beaches, and along the edge of the sea a long length of whole roadway and wrecked craft trailed brokenly. The destruction was complete.'

Opposite one of the Omaha exits an engineer officer recorded 35 LCMs, 11 LCTs, 9 Rhino ferries, 3 LCIs, and more than 20 other craft chaotically piled up. Mulberry B, at first sight, seemed in no better condition. Taylor recalled that along the beach at Arromanches 'littered wreckage was piled high, casting itself near the high-water mark in a chaotic tangle of steel.' But despite appearances to the contrary, Mulberry B proved salvable, the full impact of the storm having been broken by the Calvados reef lying beyond the harbour. The remnants of the American Mulberry were towed east to repair the British harbour, and by the end of

RIGHT

Strangers in a strange land: an American soldier takes a few moments to study a French phrase book in the shadow of a Browning 12.7mm (.5-inch) anti- aircraft gun.

BELOW

A German grenadier mans a defensive position on the flooded Cotentin Peninsula. He is wearing a camouflage groundsheet, which could be used as a poncho or, with others, built up into a tent. His weapon is the formidable MG42 machine gun.

the month it was receiving 4000 tons of supplies each day. Far more materiel, however, continued to be landed on open beaches. The problem which logisticians faced after the Great Storm, as it became known, was not one of getting supplies ashore, but of finding somewhere to store them in a beachhead.

The Great Storm had not been fatal to the logistic effort, but it did re-emphasise the need to capture a port. This was the task of Collins' VII Corps, which had come ashore on Utah, but first the American beachheads had to be joined up. The terrain behind both beaches was difficult and favoured the defender. Troops trying to move off Omaha came over the bluffs and were confronted by the flooded Aure Valley. It took elements of the US 26th Regiment, part of US 1st Division, until the morning of 8 June to take the small village of Formigny, only about a kilometre and a half (1 mile) behind the Vierville beachhead, and it took the 116th Regiment, reinforced by the Rangers until 9 June to relieve Rudder's men isolated on the tip of Pointe du Hoc. To the south-west, units of the 29th Division, the 175th Infantry and 747th Tank Battalion had advanced slowly behind a barrage of naval gunfire and entered the blazing ruins of Isigny at about the same time.

Slow progress

Across on the Cotentin Peninsula, the 101st Airborne advanced south of its drop zone towards the town of Carentan, on the Cherbourg-Caen railway line, which had to be taken so that the American beachheads could be linked up. On 9 June Colonel Robert Sink, commander of the 506th

Paratroop Battalion of the 101st Airborne, led a patrol through the swamps which lay behind the beaches, until he reached the causeway rising 2-3m (6-9 feet) above the surrounding country, which led south-west to Carentan across the Douve River. Advancing across the causeway, the paratroops quickly came under fire, but Sink's report of the contact was misinterpreted by his divisional HQ, which concluded that the causeway was only lightly defended. The 101st's commander, Brigadier General Maxwell Taylor, ordered the 502nd Parachute Battalion to attack over the causeway, but the soldiers discovered that they could only advance in single file, moving at a crouch, or even crawling, and it took them three hours to advance less than 0.8km (half a mile) across a series of bridges which spanned the Douve and its several branches. The advance was brought to a complete halt by fire from a large stone farmhouse to the west of the causeway, on a hillock which rose sharply from the marshes. After artillery fire had failed to knock out the position, the 502nd's commander, Lieutenant Colonel Robert G. Cole, ordered his battalion to charge the farm. Cole and his second in command, Lieutenant Colonel John P. Stopka, splashed off through the swamp towards the Germans, followed at first by only about 60 of the battalion. Inspired by the example of their officers, or shamed by their own reluctance, more and more men joined the charge until the enemy positions were over-run, and the Germans killed with grenades and bayonets.

As the 502nd and other units closed on the town, Carentan's commander, Major Friedrich von der Heydte was urging the immediate despatch of reinforcements, but Allied airpower and the French Resistance prevented their arrival. The only assistance he got came on the night of 11/12 June when transport aircraft managed to drop 18 tons of infantry ammunition and 88mm (3.45-inch) shells inside the town. German logistic troops had barely begun distributing it when concentrations of naval gunfire, artillery, mortars and tank destroyers smashed into Carentan, setting many buildings ablaze. At 0200 hours on 12 June, the 506th Paratroop Battalion, which had relieved the 502nd, began to attack into the north-east of Carentan. At the same time the 327th Glider Infantry Battalion attacked from the north-west, and at 0730 hours on 12 June elements of the two units met in the centre of the town.

Meanwhile American attacks to the north of the Utah bridgehead had run into heavy opposition and had ground to a halt. More serious was the situation to the immediate west, where a bridgehead established over the Meredet River at Le Motey on 8 June was almost lost when part of the 507th Battalion panicked and fled during a German counter-attack. American VII Corps commander, General Joe Lawton Collins, pushed 90th Division across the Merderet, ordering divisional commander Brigadier General Jay W. MacKelvie to strike for the western coast of the Cotentin Peninsula. Early on 10 June the leading unit, the 2nd Battalion of the 357th Infantry Regiment, attempted to advance behind a creeping artillery barrage, but quickly lost cohesion in the maze of hedges and small fields and went to ground, having gained only a few hundred metres. The 1st Battalion moved up in the afternoon to relieve the 2nd, but it too could make no progress. The 90th Division tried again the following day, and managed a snail's pace. Creeping behind immense barrages, by 13 June it had reached the town of Pont l' Abbé, 3km (2 miles) west of the start line. The town had been levelled – an American officer claimed that only two rabbits had been found alive.

Now alarmed by the lack of progress, on the same day Collins sacked MacKelvie and two of his regimental commanders, and while leaving the 90th in line, decided to reorganise his attack scheme completely. Collins had first

BELOW

The initial Allied advance was slower than anticipated, and the inhabitants of some towns and villages had an agonising wait for their liberators. When they arrived, they were greeted ecstatically – in the majority of cases. Here American GIs celebrate with civilians in Cherbourg.

LEFT
*A paratrooper from the
101st fills jerry cans on a
captured German Sd Kfz2
Kleine Kettenkraftrad in
Carentan. These small and
versatile vehicles were
developed for use by German
airborne forces as supply
and ammunition carriers or
as towing vehicles for light
howitzers and anti-tank guns.*

seen action in January 1943, on the jungle-clad island of Guadalcanal, when he had led the 25th Division against the Japanese. He was now realising that the Cotentin Peninsula had more in common with the islands of the south-west Pacific than with Dartmoor and Exmoor, the areas on which the Americans had trained in England. Fighting through the hedgerows required many more infantry than he had hitherto allowed, so Collins assigned both the 9th Division and the redoubtable 82nd Airborne to 90th Division's axis of advance. The effect was immediate. By 16 June 82nd Airborne had pushed 8km (5 miles) to the west and taken St Sauveur-le-Vicomte; two days later the 9th Division was in Barneville-sur-Mer overlooking the western coast of the Cotentin, its artillery methodically destroying an enemy column caught on the road as it retreated south.

'Air pulverisation'

Regrouping, Collins sent the 4th, 9th and 29th Infantry Divisions north. By 20 June the Americans were fighting their way through the main German defence line, a system of steel and concrete fortifications, which lay in a 10km (6-mile) semicircle to the south of Cherbourg. Collins' troops would probably not have succeeded here had they been facing the Wehrmacht or the SS; however, most of the 25,000-strong garrison consisted of

middle-aged administrative personnel, and over a fifth were units formed from Polish and Russian prisoners. On 21 June Collins requested 'air pulverisation' of some 50 square kilometres (20 square miles) on the outskirts of Cherbourg to demoralise the Germans and force a surrender. At 1240 the following day hundreds of fighter-bombers dived-bombed and strafed from as low as 90m (300 feet). The Luftwaffe was nowhere to be seen, though 24 fighters were brought down by German anti-aircraft guns. No sooner had the fighters wheeled away than wave upon wave of heavy bombers droned overhead, depositing 1100 tons of bombs on Cherbourg's outer defences.

ABOVE
*Sherman tanks advancing
through the difficult and
dangerous terrain of the
bocage. Progress was
painfully slow, for every
hedgerow might hide a
machine gun nest, a
Panzerfaust or an 88mm
(3.45-inch) anti-tank gun.*

Obergruppenführer Paul Hausser, former commander of the formidable 1 SS Panzer Corps on the Eastern Front, replaced Dollmann as commander of Seventh Army.

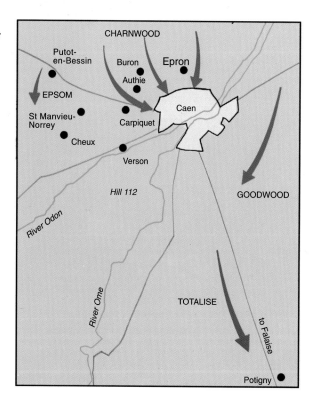

Within 24 hours the three American divisions had penetrated the defence line in many places, and on 25 June the Americans received additional fire support from three battleships, four cruisers, and several destroyers. American fire was so heavy that Cherbourg's commander, *Generalleutnant* Karl-Wilhelm von Schlieben, was driven to shelter in a deep bunker, and lost control of his forces. On the afternoon of 26 June, with Americans fighting in Cherbourg's suburbs, von Schlieben surrendered. German engineers had already reduced the port to a shambles: sunken ships blocked the harbour, toppled cranes lay in a twisted mass of metal, and mines lay everywhere. It took another eight weeks to clear the wreckage, and until November before the port was brought back into full operation. The Germans had been customarily efficient; indeed, so thorough was the devastation that the Americans had to rely on supplies brought across open beaches.

Hitler furious

While the Americans fought to secure Cherbourg, dramatic events had been taking place around Caen. Hitler had flown to France on 17 June for a conference with von Rundstedt and Rommel, during which the Führer had barked angrily 'Don't call it a beachhead, but the last piece of French soil held by the enemy!' Speidel, Rommel's chief of staff, recorded that the hitherto despondent field marshal had begun to feel optimistic and commented on the Führer's 'uncanny magnetism'. But Hitler was offering more than the force of his personality. He ordered two crack divisions transferred to Normandy from the Eastern Front. These forces, combined with those divisions already in Normandy, would give Rommel a significant, if temporary, qualitative superiority by the end of June. On 20 June Hitler ordered a massive six-division strike towards Bayeux for 1 July; this would split the beachhead and enable his forces to defeat the British and Americans in detail.

At exactly the same time as the Führer was concocting his plans, Montgomery was preparing for another attempt to envelop Caen, this time from much closer to the city. Instead of trying to infiltrate an armoured division through the bocage, this time Montgomery intended to launch the three divisions of VIII Corps in 'an all-out blitz attack' on 25 June, Derby Day – hence the code name for the offensive, Operation Epsom. On 22 June Montgomery summoned all the corps and divisional commanders in Second Army to a conference at his tactical headquarters at Creully and outlined his plans. 'We have now reached the "show down" stage,' Montgomery proclaimed. 'The first rush, inland to secure a good lodgement area, is over. The enemy is "firming up" and trying to hem us in... We have thus reached a stage where carefully prepared operations are essential. We must have no set backs. What we take we must hold... the whole army front must flare up and the enemy fought to a standstill. The attack had two phases. At 0415 hours on 25 June the leading battalions of the 49th (West Riding) Division advanced through a thick morning mist towards the villages of Fontenay and Rauray, to secure a start line for the second and main phase of the operation. The mist was so thick that it not only provided cover, but also served to break up the cohesion of the attacking units. By mid-morning the mist had cleared and German fire coming from the bocage to the south-west of Fontenay stopped 49th Division.

At dawn on 26 June a tremendous barrage – more than 700 artillery pieces supplemented by naval guns, the largest concentration yet employed in Normandy – heralded the opening of the second phase. The 15th (Scottish), 43rd (Wessex) and 11th Armoured Divisions – a total of 60,000 men and 600 tanks – advanced on a narrow 3km (2-mile) front east of Fontenay down the main street of the village of Cheux, which descended steeply into a deep gully at the bottom of which was a small stone bridge over the River Odon. Once across, VIII Corps was to swing south-east of Caen and link up with the 51st Highland Division, which would be advancing south-west from the eastern side of Caen. VIII Corps' leading division, the 15th Scottish, attacked into Cheux, and found themselves in a carefully prepared killing zone. Engineers of the *Hitlerjugend* had mined the streets, and loopholed and booby-trapped every house. The Scots had to clear Cheux by close-quarters fighting house-to-house, in which the leading battalion, the 2nd Glasgow Highlanders, lost 12 officers and 200 soldiers. Early in the afternoon the reconnaissance unit of 11th Armoured Division, the Northamptonshire Yeomanry, struggled through the streets of Cheux, and reached the gully of the Odon, where they were attacked from the dense undergrowth by *Hitlerjugend* with *Panzerfäuste* and anti-tank grenades.

BELOW
German SS troops at Cheux, where the 15th Scottish Division walked into a carefully-laid trap and suffered heavy casualties. The village was the scene of savage close-quarter house-to-house fighting.

BELOW

Churchill tanks push towards Caen in the early light of dawn at the start of yet another offensive to capture the city.

BOTTOM

The town of Villers-Bocage was flattened by Allied bombing and artillery fire. Many of France's 300,000 civilian dead in WWII lost their lives during the Allied invasion of Normandy.

About 1500m (1 mile) to the east, the 2nd Battalion of the Argyll and Sutherland Highlanders also fought their way down to the Odon and seized intact the bridge at the hamlet of Tourmauville, over which the tanks of the 23rd Hussars passed in single file. During the next 48 hours the Hussars pushed south up the slopes of a 245m (800-foot) eminence dominating the south-western approach to Caen, which appeared on Allied maps as Hill 112. The Germans had been relying on their dual-purpose 88mm (3.45-inch) guns to hold the British tanks at bay, but constant attacks by Allied fighter-bombers cleared the way for the Hussars. One German

survivor of the first battle of Hill 112 recalled: 'In the early afternoon came the end. About a dozen tanks were rolling towards us, when two formations of twin-engined Lightnings attacked. Where to fire first? At the planes or at the tanks? In the confusion of air attack, the tanks opened fire at us. Gun after gun was knocked out, and the crews with them. Only one thing to do – withdraw!'

Signalling to Brooke on the night of 27 June, Montgomery proclaimed himself well pleased with the development of the battle, and believed that Dempsey would soon have the whole of 11th Armoured Division up on Hill 112. The British were now very close to a significant victory, for possession of Hill 112 would allow them to close off the southern approaches to Caen. The danger posed to the German position was all too apparent to the Seventh Army commander, General Doll-mann, who, having just been informed of the loss of Cherbourg, found the loss of Hill 112 too much to bear, and was dead by the morning of June 29th. It had been a massive heart attack, claimed the German press, though dark rumours circulated that it had been sui-cide, spurred on by his knowledge that he was about to be replaced and recalled to Germany to face a series of unspecified charges relating to his conduct of the battle in Normandy. In fact, the situation was far less serious than

LEFT
Field Marshal Gunther von Kluge (seen here on the Eastern Front), who relieved von Rundstedt as Commander-in-Chief West on Hitler's orders on 3 July 1944. He was implicated in the bomb plot against Hitler just a few weeks later, and committed suicide on 18 August.

Dollmann had imagined. The Hussars on Hill 112 had been reinforced by other elements of 29th Armoured Brigade, one of the components of 11th Armoured Division, but the vast bulk of British forces were still north of the Odon. Too many tanks, trucks and men had been pushed south along too narrow a front. A massive traffic jam had developed in the streets of Cheux, a jam which stretched back to the start line. Because the 49th Division had been unable to advance, the western flank of the jam was open, while small groups of *Hitlerjugend* crawled through the wheat fields by Cheux, sniping at the columns and thereby adding to the confusion.

In the early hours of 29 June Dollmann's successor, *Obergruppenführer* Paul Hausser, who had commanded the formidable 1 SS Panzer Corps on the Eastern Front, was beginning to restore the situation. Hausser ordered the Panzer divisions which had been assembling for the Bayeux offensive to head for Cheux. However, this was hardly a well coordinated or rapid offensive action, for Hausser was forced to feed the divisions in piecemeal as they reached the Odon. By 29 June Montgomery's resident Ultra-reading intelligence officer, Colonel J. Ewart, had received Ultra intercepts which showed VIII Corps in

an increasingly precarious position. The 15th and 43rd Infantry Divisions and the 11th Armoured Division occupied a corridor nearly 10km (6 miles) long and 3km (2 miles) wide, extending north from Hill 112. Ultra revealed that the 2nd, 9th and 10th SS Panzer Divisions and *Panzer Lehr* were advancing from the west, while 1st and 12th SS Panzer Divisions, along with the battered but still capable 21st Panzer Division were advancing from the east.

Allied fears

For Montgomery and Dempsey the situation now seemed very serious. There was already heavy fighting on Hill 112, where 29th Armoured Brigade had been forced to pull back from the southern slopes of the hill. More seriously, a German battle group had broken into Cheux, a move which seemed to presage the cutting off of what was now called the 'Scottish Corridor'. But unknown to the British high command, this was the Germans' high-water mark. British artillery and air power had exacted a fearful toll on the counter-attacks, and Hausser was close to admitting defeat. At that moment, believing that Ultra was providing an accurate picture of both German intentions and capabilities,

A German armoured car in Caen. The devastation caused by heavy bombing seriously hindered Allied attempts to take the town, as the rubble provided excellent cover for the German defenders.

Dempsey ordered 29th Brigade to abandon Hill 112 and pull back north of the Odon. During the next 48 hours German divisions were hit by massed artillery fire and broadsides from battleships and cruisers, while heavy bombers rained down high explosives. The bombers were not particularly discriminating. In an effort to block the advance of the 9th SS Panzer Division up RN 175, Lancasters reduced the town of Villers-Bocage to a heap of smouldering rubble. It was a portent of things to come.

Allied fears

On 30 June Montgomery gathered his army commanders at his new headquarters above the village of Bray near the Cerisy Forest (a highly publicised visit by King George VI had compromised the location of his original HQ), and announced that although the envelopment of Caen had not been carried out, Operation Epsom had nevertheless been successful. Critics, who now included much of the American high command, doubted this assessment of Epsom. It was anything but the 'blitz attack' Montgomery had called for. Instead, it had been a bloody attritional slog in which 15th Scottish Division alone had suffered 2331 casualties, and during which heaps of bodies had created dams in the gorge of the Odon.

But the Germans had suffered more. Epsom had sucked in the divisions Hitler had allocated to the great German counter-offensive. The coordinated seven-division attack scheduled for 1 July was the only hope the Germans had of splitting and then crushing the beachhead. Operation Epsom disrupted and defeated the Germans' only real chance of an outright Normandy victory. But this was not readily apparent to the Anglo-American political leadership, who now began to entertain serious doubts about Montgomery's ability as a general.

The first week of July saw both the British and German high commands in crisis. On 2 July von Rundstedt called Field Marshal Wilhelm Keitel, Chief of OKW, with the news that the counter-offensive was over. When Keitel asked 'What shall we do?' an exasperated von Rundstedt exploded: 'Make peace, you fools!' The stiff-necked old Prussian, now in his 69th year, was not afraid to speak the truth. Three years earlier he had advised Hitler to abandon Operation Barbarossa, and had been dismissed for his outspokenness. On 3 July 1944 the Führer again relieved von Rundstedt of his command, replacing him with Field Marshal Gunther von Kluge, who was given instructions to hold the existing line, no matter what the cost. Von Kluge was a very different character, a pliable 'yes man' who had achieved his present eminence by subservience to the Nazi cause, so much so that on his 60th birthday (30 October 1942), Hitler had sent him a cheque to the value of 250,000 marks, half of which was to be spent on improving his estate. Von Kluge was not in Von Rundstedt's class as a general, but at least he could be relied upon not to present the high command with unpalatable realities.

Churchill under pressure

Within the beachhead, Montgomery's position had become just as insecure as that of his erstwhile German counterpart. He had promised Eisenhower 'to continue the battle on the eastern flank until one of us cracks, and it will not be us'. He had also promised the airmen additional territory for their airfields, and now that this had not been produced, Air Chief Marshal Arthur Tedder, the Deputy Supreme Allied Commander, began urging Eisenhower to dismiss Montgomery. Eisenhower now made his first tentative moves to gain Churchill's support for sacking the field marshal. He knew that Montgomery had been Brooke's choice as Eighth Army commander and that Churchill had been deeply ambivalent. Political pressure was beginning to build up on Churchill. Since 23 June on the Eastern Front the Soviets had been breaking through German defences in Operation Bagration. In addition, since 14 June German V1s had killed 2000 and seriously injured another 7500 in southeast England, and the public knew that the only certain way to remove this menace was for Allied soldiers to overrun the launch sites.

But the headlines in British and American newspapers were proclaiming 'Normandy Front Stalled'. At a staff conference on 6 July in the underground cabinet war room, Brooke recorded that Churchill began by abusing Montgomery because operations were not going faster, and repeated Eisenhower's criticism that he was over-cautious. 'I flared up' Brooke wrote, 'and asked him if he could not trust his generals for five minutes instead of belittling them.... He was furious with me, but I hope it may do some good in the future.' The immediate threat to Montgomery's position had passed, but he was not yet secure, by any means.

Against a background of mounting criticism and pressure, Montgomery launched a third major offensive. Windsor and Charnwood were complimentary operations designed both to expand the beachhead and take the north-western part of Caen. On the evening of 3 July, in Operation Windsor, the British battleship Rodney fired 15 16-inch shells from 24,000m (26,200 yards) onto the village of Carpiquet on the northern side of Carpiquet airfield, just to the west of Caen. At 0500 hours the following morning, the Canadian 8th Infantry Brigade, spearheaded by the Fort Garry Horse, advanced behind a creeping barrage into the village. Units of the *Hitlerjugend* resisted vigorously from concrete emplacements on the western edge of the airfield and, after 24 hours, the Canadian offensive became bogged down.

Forty-eight hours later the main assault, Operation Charnwood, went in against Caen. No army likes house-to-house fighting, and Montgomery was determined not to have his men sucked into a mini-Stalingrad. The trick was to remove the houses. At 2200 hours on 7 July, 467 Lancasters and Halifaxes dropped 2500 tons of high explosives onto the city. Major Bill Renison, second-in-command of the 2nd East Yorks, watching from the north, recalled that 'a cloud of dust rose high into the air and blotted out almost everything, drifting slowly towards us and up the valley of the Orne. By the end of the raid the troops were standing on the end of their slit trenches clapping and cheering; the effect on morale was electric.' Unfortunately, Caen was still packed with French civilians and the result was devastating. Most of the centre and the north of Caen was reduced to rubble, at least 6000 French

BELOW
A soldier of the US 1st Infantry Division in a mottled camouflage suit. This was quickly changed when it became apparent that it conflicted with similar camouflage clothing worn by the Waffen SS.

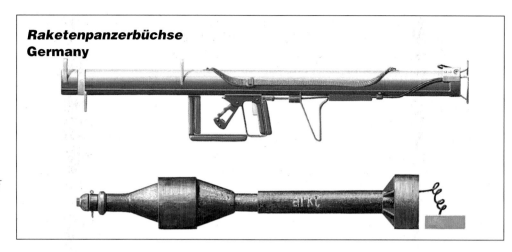

Raketenpanzerbüchse
Germany

RIGHT
The German Raketenpanzerbüchse *was based heavily on the American M1 Bazooka, which had been captured in some numbers in Tunisia in 1943. The confined spaces of the bocage meant that Allied tanks became sitting ducks to well-sited 'Panzerschreks'.*

civilians (mostly women and children) were blown to pieces or died of their injuries, and many thousands were badly maimed. The bombing did disrupt German supply lines, but had very little effect on the German defences, which lay north of the built-up area where the bombs landed. The British and Canadians finally broke through by concentrating overwhelming force, three divisions supported by the gunfire of a battleship, two cruisers and a monitor, along with 250 light bombers, against the German defenders. At Gruchy, to the north-east of Caen, troops of the Canadian 3rd Division charged into the heart of the German positions in 16 Bren carriers of the divisional reconnaissance regiment. The surprised Germans surrendered after a weak attempt at resistance. But in other places the Germans, particularly the *Hitlerjugend*, fought to the death, succumbing only to the liquid fire of the flame-throwers of the Crocodile tanks. The fighting was at close quarters and bitter, and by 9 July the Germans had suffered 6000 casualties. Neither had British and Canadian casualties been light – about 3500 were dead, wounded or missing. However, by the evening of 9 July the British and Canadians held the north-western part of the city. The industrial suburb of Colombelles to the north-east, and the half of Caen which lay south-east of the Orne were still in German hands.

The fighting in Caen had barely died down when Montgomery launched his fourth offensive, Operation Jupiter, an attack by the 43rd (Wessex) Division against German positions on Hill 112 to the west of Caen. It was the start of a vicious attritional struggle, which was to go on unremittingly for weeks. In the first 36 hours, 43rd Division suffered 2000 casualties in an attempt to gain

footholds on the northern slopes. A German counter-attack on 11 July almost pushed the British off, but one battalion, the 4th Somerset Light Infantry, clung on in the face of near-impossible odds. At 0100 hours on 12 July the battalion launched a counter-attack, which immediately ran into heavy resistance. One British survivor, Corporal Douglas Proctor, graphically recalled the horror of that night's attack. 'The leading section commander was attempting to scramble through the barbed wire... a single enemy bullet pierced his belly and as a result exploded the phosphorous grenade he carried in his webbing pouch. Struggling in desperation he became entangled in the barbed wire and hung there, a living, screaming, human beacon. His only release from the fiery hell, as he must have known, was to plead for someone to shoot him as quickly and mercifully as possible.' The attack virtually wiped out 4th Somerset Light Infantry: of the 36 men in Corporal Proctor's platoon who went into action, only nine remained. The battalion was pulled off Hill 112, only for another to take its place. And so it went on, day after day, for another two weeks.

Shermans vulnerable

By the middle of July the fighting in the British and Canadian sectors had become bogged down; the situation in the American sector was no better. After the fall of Cherbourg, Bradley had turned all his forces south. On 3 July VIII Corps, under the command of Major General Troy H. Middleton, struck down the western coast of the Cotentin Peninsula towards Coutances. Simultaneously, Major General Charles H. Corlett's XIX Corps attacked south-east of Carentan, along the Vire River towards St Lo.

In the centre Bradley placed VII Corps under Collins, who had Périers as his objective, a town halfway between Coutances and St Lo. Bradley's intention was to secure the St Lo–Coutances road and use it as a line of departure for an all-out offensive to the south-west, where two good roads ran parallel to the coast down to Avranches, where the bocage gave way to more open country.

The Americans advanced on a very broad front (nearly 48km – 30 miles) through country which was bocage at its worst. In this sort of country it was impossible to maintain contact between units, let alone formations. The dense hedgerows quickly broke up attacking battalions into companies, and then into platoons. The success of the attack therefore depended on the energy and experience of the platoon commander, and often the death or wounding of the officer would bring an advance to a halt. A single German machine gun supported by one or two mortars could hold up an entire attack for hours. The Americans found that when rain was falling and the hedgerows were wet (about one day in three in the summer of 1944) radios could not transmit signals from one field to another. It often happened that a

platoon attack in one field succeeded, while attacks in adjoining fields were defeated, so that coherence soon broke down. In order to maintain the advance, infantry commanders called in tanks, but the high silhouette of the Sherman made them easy targets for German anti-tank guns sited along the farm tracks which ran between the hedges. Tank crews quickly discovered that the Sherman did not have the engine power or the traction to break through the hedges, and tanks which attempted this usually 'bellied-up' over the hedges, exposing their vulnerable undersides to German infantry anti-tank weapons, the *Panzerfaust* and the more formidable *Panzerschreck*. German anti-tank teams stalked tanks in the hedgerows, making them more a liability than an asset.

By 15 July the four divisions which comprised VIII Corps had advanced just 11km (7 miles), at a cost of 10,000 casualties. For VII Corps the situation was even worse. On 4 July one of its divisions, the 83rd, succeeded in advancing just 180m (200 yards), at a cost of 1400 casualties. XIX Corps made no better progress. On 7 July an attempt by 3rd Armoured and 30th Infantry Divisions to exploit a gap in the German defences ended

BELOW
American artillery in action in the bocage. A combination of heavy rainfall and dense hedgerows often made radio communication between adjacent units difficult, if not impossible, resulting in a serious loss of cohesion.

ABOVE

German SS panzer grenadier armed with a Panzerfaust *hollow-charge anti-tank weapon. As they negotiated the high earthen banks that were the hedgerows of the bocage, the American Sherman tanks exposed their vulnerable undersides to these weapons.*

with both divisions mistaking one another for the Germans, and engaging in furious combat. Both divisions called in USAAF fighter-bombers, which strafed both of them without discrimination. Casualties were heavy; by the time the divisions were disentangled, the Germans had plugged the gap.

On 10 July Bradley decided that in order to unhinge the German defences he would have to capture St Lo, which formed the eastern anchor of the German line. The town had been pulverised by successive waves of Allied bombers on 6 June, which had killed more than 800 of the inhabitants and reduced it to a heap of rubble. St Lo itself was important only in a symbolic sense. Of paramount importance were the hills and ridges which ringed St Lo to the north and the west. Here the Germans had dug in some formidable formations – the 3rd Parachute Division, battle groups of the 353rd, 352nd and 266th Divisions, supported by a variety of heavy guns, anti-tank guns and multiple rocket launchers – all commanded by Lieutenant General Eugen Meindl, a tough paratrooper with extensive experience on the Eastern Front. The German defence line consisted of a number of mutually supporting strong points, all of which were difficult for air and

artillery spotters to locate. Directly north of St Lo there loomed a hill, which appeared on Allied maps as Hill 122, which appeared to American observers to be the key to the defence. Two American corps faced this complex of defences, Major General Leonard T. Gerow's V Corps, and Major General Charles (Cowboy Pete) Corlett's XIX Corps, but the commanders of both formations decided a direct attack against Hill 122 would be prohibitively expensive. They decided instead on an alternative strategy, an outflanking move from the east which involved taking the Martinville Ridge and a nearby 45m (150-foot) eminence, code-named Hill 192.

The American attack begins

The Americans were under no illusions as to how difficult attacks on these features would prove to be. US 2nd Infantry Division, tasked to take Hill 192, was allocated elaborate support for its attack after dawn on 11 July, but initially everything went wrong. A morning mist limited visibility to such an extent that an airstrike, planned to proceed the advance, was cancelled. The Americans had unfortunately moved back several hundred metres in order to avoid their own bombs, and when the aerial onslaught failed to materialise, had a much longer way to advance under heavy German fire. Enemy defensive positions, bunkers dug into the base of the hedgerows, were difficult to detect, and the first American assault crumbled with some 200 casualties and the loss of six tanks. Later in the morning 2nd Division resumed the attack, supported by 20,000 rounds fired by the division's own artillery. This time infantry were able to get close to Germans sheltering behind hedgerows, and bombard them with rifle grenades. During the afternoon the defenders began to withdraw, leaving the Americans on Hill 192, looking south to an even higher and more formidable feature, Hill 101. Meanwhile the 29th Division had been supposed to attack along the Martinville Ridge, but a pre-emptive strike by German paratroops during the night with flame-throwers inflicted 150 casualties, thereby delaying the assault. The 29th began to advance late in the morning, but quickly came under fire from Hill 101, which slowed the Americans down. The attack finally petered out on 13 July.

The American commanders now decided that there was no alternative to an assault on Hill 122. Over the next four days fighting swayed to and fro on the hills around St Lo, American firepower eventually wearing the Germans down. On 16 July the 2nd and 3rd Battalions of the 116th Regiment of the 29th Division managed to break into the town, but intense German shellfire cut them off from the rest of the division. The commander of 3rd Battalion, Major Thomas D. Howie, tried to continue the advance, but was killed the moment he broke cover. The rest of the 116th attacked the town on the night of 17 July, linked up with the isolated battalions, and by mid-morning were fighting their way into the centre of the town. That afternoon the regiment took the body of Major Howie, draped in an American flag, to the centre of St Lo, and laid it before the bombed-out shell of a church – a poignant symbol of the death and destruction which the Americans had both endured and inflicted to take this little town. That night, morale in St Lo was very low. It was scarcely higher anywhere else among the Allied armies in Normandy. The campaign was entering its seventh week. Already the Allies had suffered 122,000 casualties, had devastated the once-peaceful province of Normandy, killing and maiming tens of thousands of French civilians, and the break-out seemed as far away as ever.

BELOW
American soldiers during the bitter fighting for St Lo. Bradley decided that capturing this position was vital to kickstart the breakout from Normandy.

LEFT
US troops in action in the bocage. They faced formidable opposition from battle-hardened German units that were only dislodged from their defensive positions with great difficulty. Here the GIs use rifle grenades to help knock out enemy positions in the hedgerows.

BREAKOUT

After weeks of grinding attrition, the Allied breakout attempt turned almost overnight into a racing flood of men and materiel which threatened to sweep all German resistance before it.

On 16 July 1944 Soviet troops crossed the Curzon Line, the pre-war border between Belorussia and Poland, and on the following day marched 57,000 German prisoners through Moscow. Since the beginning of their offensive on 23 June Soviet armies had advanced 480km (300 miles) and had utterly smashed German Army Group Centre. In Normandy, by contrast, the Allies had in some places advanced scarcely 8km (5 miles) since 6 June. Headlines in American and British newspapers contrasted 'Reds Cross Bug River' and 'Reds Roll Towards Lvov', with 'Dempsey's Men Hold All Attacks' and 'British Troops Face Mass Tank Attack'. The Normandy campaign was stalled and Montgomery was running quickly out of ideas, a fact he tried hard later to disguise. His only remaining strategy was to hammer away relentlessly at the Germans, a policy which differed barely from the one advanced by Haig on the Western Front in World War I. The weapons might have changed, but Windsor, Charnwood and Jupiter were reruns of the same grinding attritional battles.

Bradley was not much more optimistic about the American front, and later recalled that 'by July 10 we faced a real danger of a World War 1 type stalemate in Normandy.' At the present rate of advance the Allies would not be at the Rhine until about 1950 – in fact, the war seemed set to last forever. But at this, the nadir of the campaign, Bradley hit on an essentially new approach, though Montgomery would later try to claim that it was he who had the idea. Bradley decided that the advance on a broad front in country like the bocage played to German strengths. Instead, he would concentrate his forces in a rapier-like thrust, technically the same manoeuvre as the British advance at Epsom, but in practice very different. He planned to concentrate the bulk of First Army in the centre of the Cotentin Peninsula north of the St Lo–Périers road, a very straight Roman road, easily recognisable from the air. Just to the south of the road he marked out a 15-square-kilometre (6-square-mile) rectangular area, which the US Eighth Air Force would bomb to oblivion. As soon as the bombing stopped, two armoured divisions and a motorised division would make a dash for Coutances, 26km (16 miles) to the south-west. From here they would advance to Avranches. Once Avranches had fallen, Bradley's divisions would 'turn the corner' and push westwards into Brittany to seize her large Atlantic ports.

The break-out was code-named Operation Cobra. On 10 July Bradley outlined his plan to Montgomery and Dempsey in Montgomery's caravan at Twenty-first Army

RIGHT

Generals Montgomery and Bradley discussing the details of Operation Cobra, which was intended to seize ground west of St Lo from which an Allied breakout could be mounted. The operation turned out to be far more successful than the Allies had envisaged.

BELOW

Much of Operation Cobra's success was due to the dropping of 4000 tons of bombs behind the German front, which destroyed the only German panzer division in position there.

Group Tactical Headquarters. Shortly after the meeting Dempsey wrote down his recollection of the proceedings, and these attributed to Montgomery the major role in devising a new strategy. According to Dempsey, the important moment came when Montgomery said to Bradley, '"if I were you I think I should concentrate my forces a little more" – putting two fingers together on the map in his characteristic way.' In fact this is what Bradley had already decided to do, but to increase his chances of success his attack would need the support of British Second Army. Montgomery and Dempsey readily agreed to support Cobra with massive British and Canadian attacks to the east of Caen, which were to be code-named Goodwood and Atlantic respectively, and which, like Cobra, would be spearheaded by an enormous aerial bombardment. At the meeting on 10 July, Goodwood and Atlantic were scheduled for 17 July, Cobra for 18 July. But within a few hours Dempsey began to change his mind about the nature and extent of the operation, and began to speak about it as if it were the major Allied break-out.

Montgomery did nothing to discourage his subordinate and, meeting with him at 1630 hours on 12 July at Dempsey's headquarters, approved a plan to strike to the south-east with an entire British armoured corps. Later that night Montgomery assured Eisenhower that 'my whole eastern flank will burst into flames on Saturday (19 July). The operation on Monday (21 July) may have far-reaching results.' Eisenhower replied enthusiastically, promising that Bradley would 'keep his troops fighting like the very devil, twenty-four hours a day, to provide the opportunity your Armoured Corps will need, and to make the victory complete.' The following day

Dempsey issued an operational order to VIII Corps, the British armoured corps, which stated that on 18 July it would 'cross R Orne North of Caen, attack southwards and establish an Armd. Div. in each of the following areas: Bretteville sur Laize – Vimont – Argences – Falaise.' The last town mentioned, Falaise, lay 48km (30 miles) beyond the front, and this could mean only one thing – that British Second Army intended Goodwood not merely to support Operation Cobra, but to be a break-out. This, certainly, was what Eisenhower and the rest of the staff at SHAEF believed. This interpretation was reinforced a few days later, when Bradley discovered that some of his divisions were running short of ammunition. Cobra would have to be delayed until supplies were replenished. In the event, bad weather forced a further delay. The two operations thus came to be seen as quite separate, with Goodwood, originally the supporting operation, evolving into the main focal point.

When Dempsey surveyed the front for a start line, he focused attention on the extreme eastern end of the beachhead. On 6 June British paratroops had here secured a small enclave on the south side of the Orne, now held by the 51st Highland Division. For about 10km (6 miles) south of their front the land was flat and relatively open, until it rose almost imperceptibly to the Bourguebus Ridge. It was flanked to the east by the German-controlled industrial suburb of Colombelles, to the west by the Bois de Bavent, a low, wooded ridge. Compared to other areas it seemed almost ideal – a natural corridor for an armoured assault. The only real drawbacks it held as a launching point for an assault were those of size and access. The enclave was a mere 15 square kilometres (6 square miles) in area, reached by only three bridges across the Canel de Caen, and three across the Orne. Chaos would ensue if traffic-control broke down as it had during Operation Epsom.

At dawn on 18 July 1500 heavy bombers deposited 5000 tons of high explosive on Colombelles and the Bois de Bavent. Shortly

BELOW
Sherman tanks advancing through the narrow streets of a French town towards the front. The tanks are Sherman Fireflies, a British conversion armed with a 17-pounder gun, which gave them a much greater punch against the heavily-armoured German panzers.

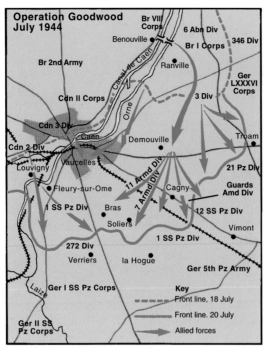

Operation Goodwood
July 1944

Br VII Corps
6 Abn Div
Benouville
Br I Corps
346 Div
Br 2nd Army
Ranville
Ger LXXXVI Corps
Cdn II Corps
3 Div
Cdn 3 Div
Caen
Demouville
Troam
Cdn 2 Div
Louvigny
Vaucelles
Fleury-sur-Ome
11 Armd Div
7 Armd Div
Cagny
21 Pz Div
Guards Amd Div
1 SS Pz Div
Bras
12 SS Pz Div
Soliers
Vimont
1 SS Pz Div
272 Div
Verriers
la Hogue
Ger 5th Pz Army
Laize
Ger I SS Pz Corps
Ger II SS Pz Corps

Key
— — — Front line, 18 July
——— Front line. 20 July
⟶ Allied forces

BELOW

A Sherman tank is hit during the Allied advance and explodes as its ammunition 'cooks off'. Early, petrol-driven Shermans burned easily; the later diesel-engined models were less vulnerable.

afterwards, medium bombers dropped 2500 tons of fragmentation bombs down the corridor as far south as the Bourguebus Ridge. As the bombers departed, 1500 artillery pieces and heavy naval guns began a rolling barrage. Behind this, the Canadian 3rd Division attacked into the rubble of Colombelles,

while the British 3rd Division advanced into the Bois de Bavent. Spearheaded by the Northampton Yeomanry, the advance guard of 11th Armoured division, 29th Armoured Brigade, passed along 17 corridors which had been cleared in the minefields by the engineers of 51st Highland Division. The bombing had been the heaviest in the war so far and had raised morale. Lieutenant Brownlie of the 3rd Battalion Royal Tank Regiment, the leading battalion of 29th Armoured Brigade, remembered that 'the clear blue sky was filled with bombers, which plastered the country ahead. Many of us stood up and cheered.' On a small hill nearby, Chester Wilmot, recording for the BBC, reported that 'I turned and looked out to sea... the Lancasters and Halifaxes were beginning to darken the northern sky... they came over the horizon in a black swarm. For 45 minutes the procession of bombers came on unbroken, and when they'd gone, the thunder of the guns swelled up and filled the air, as the artillery carried on the bombardment.' Advancing behind the barrage, Brownlie recalled that 'to us it was a solid grey wall of shell-bursts. We drove on in formation for about a mile. We had never before driven in formation for more than a couple of hundred

metres, except on exercises. Was it all over bar the shouting?' The only Germans they met were a pathetic handful, stupefied by the bombing, wandering around staring into space.

Rommel responds

Dempsey had intended that 11th Armoured Division should be followed by Guards Armoured Division and 7th Armoured Division, a total of 750 tanks, the largest armoured offensive in British history. Goodwood might have been successful if this momentum could have been sustained. However, huge traffic jams were already building up within the enclave. The assault involved moving not only tanks, but a further 9000 vehicles across the Canel de Caen and the Orne. In addition, tanks began to snag the tapes indicating the lanes which had been cleared through the minefields, so that vehicles lost their way and had their tracks blown off. Instead of an armoured torrent, tanks and trucks emerged in dribs and drabs. By mid-morning, 11th Armoured's tanks were straggling in long columns towards Bourguebus, their accompanying infantry left several kilometres north to deal with small pockets of resistance.

The Germans had picked up a clear picture of British plans some days earlier, thanks to radio interception and direct observation from the single chimney in the Colombelles steel works which was still standing. Rommel could see that the British were planning a major offensive. He responded by ordering additional forces to deploy to a depth of more than 18km (11 miles) from the British front line. North of the high bank of the Caen–Troarn railway, which ran across the British line of advance, Rommel positioned elements of the 16th Luftwaffe and 22nd Infantry Division. They were supported by six groups of self-propelled artillery and anti-tank guns, with four or six pieces per group. Farther south, between the Caen–Troarn railway and the Caen–Vimont railway line, which also ran along a high bank, were two regiments of panzer grenadiers from the 21st Panzer Division, some Panther tanks of 1st SS Panzer Division, and a company of the 503rd Heavy Tank Battalion equipped with Tiger tanks. Farther south again in the villages on the north slope of the Bourguebus Ridge were deployed six battalions of panzer grenadiers from the 1st SS Panzer Division, the formidable *Leibstandarte Adolf Hitler*.

ABOVE
Interception of British radio signals enabled the Germans to build up a clear picture of British plans. Field Marshal Rommel quickly organized Sperrlinie – blocking lines – to stem the British advance.

The gun-line on the crest of the ridge was furnished with 78 88mm (3.45-inch) anti-tank guns, 194 artillery pieces, and 270 multiple rocket launchers. And in woods about 6.5km (4 miles) south of the ridge Rommel positioned the bulk of *Leibstandarte Adolf Hitler* and two battle groups, each of about 40 tanks plus infantry, both from the 12th SS Panzer Division. The German units, totalling about 230 tanks, were experienced and well deployed, with good fields of fire. Rommel had personally inspected these deployments on 17 July, and was pleased with them: he had converted what appeared to be one of the weakest sectors of the German front into one of the strongest. Rommel missed the battle: driving back from his tour of inspection on the evening of 17 July, his staff car was strafed by British fighter-bombers. Rommel, badly injured and unconscious, was invalided back to Germany.

German preparations had been so thorough that Rommel's absence did not really matter. By mid-morning of 18 July, the advance guard of the 11th Armoured Division, the Fife and Forfar Yeomanry, was about 6.5km

(4 miles) south of the start line, passing the heavily bombed and apparently deserted village of Cagny, and approaching the embankment of the Caen–Vimont railway. Trooper John Thorpe, hull gunner in one of the Shermans, recalled the moment when all hell broke loose. They had just climbed the embankment 'when very severe armour-piercing fire comes from a coppice on our left front.... In front, brew-up after brew-up, some tank crews on fire and rolling about on the ground trying to put out the flames in their clothes. Soon, what with burning tanks, burning corn, and mortar smoke, visibility is short. Now all the tanks in front are burning fiercely, and twenty yards [18m] away, I see a tank boy climbing out of a turret spurting flames. He does not make it. After putting one leg up to step out, he falls back inside. Ammunition explodes in the burning tanks. In the still air, huge smoke rings rise out of their turrets.' For all intents and purposes the Fife and Forfar Yeomanry had been wiped out, and this had been achieved in a matter of minutes.

In fact, there had only been four 88mm (3.45-inch) guns in the coppice, which grew in a walled garden in a farm on the north-western edge of Cagny. The gunners had been watching the Fife and Forfar advance for some time, but had decided that as they were a Luftwaffe anti-aircraft unit it was not their business to shoot at armour. Unfortunately for the British, Colonel Hans von Luck, who was commanding Battle Group von Luck, part of 21st Panzer Division, arrived in the village at the same time as the Fife and Forfar were beginning to climb the railway embankment. He was astonished to find the 88mm guns with their barrels pointing skywards and was so enraged when the Luftwaffe commander refused to depress his guns to engage the tanks, that von Luck pulled out his Luger pistol and said, 'Either you will move and shoot the tanks and get a medal or I will shoot you.' The Luftwaffe commander complied with such enthusiasm that he not only engaged the Fife and Forfar's Shermans to his immediate front, but also opened up on some dark shapes about 900m (1000 yards) to the north, and knocked out two of the Tigers of the 503rd Heavy Tank Battalion.

The Panthers strike

At virtually the same time other British tanks to the south-east ran into Panthers of the 1st SS Division, which had been completely untouched by the bombing, having sheltered on the southern slopes of Bourguebus Ridge,

which was well to the south of the bomb line. Without infantry to attack the 88s, and heavily outranged by the Panthers, the 11th Armoured Division took huge casualties. From his tactical headquarters, under a bridge in the railway embankment, 11th Armoured Division's commander, Major General 'Pip' Roberts attempted to call in air support, but as he was about to do so the Marmon Herrington armoured car containing an RAF officer and two radios tuned to RAF fighter-bomber frequencies suffered a direct hit, badly

BELOW

British tanks drive past a wrecked German Tiger. The Tiger was a formidable opponent in a defensive battle.

BOTTOM

A Bren gunner and British infantry in the bocage. The Bren was an excellent light machine gun.

wounding the officer and smashing the equipment. Shortly afterwards, Roberts suffered another disappointment. He suddenly saw Brigadier 'Looney' Hinde, commander of 7th Division's 22nd Brigade, and thought that 7th Division was moving up in support. But Hinde was on a reconnaissance, and when he reached Roberts said to him, 'There are too many bloody tanks here already – I'm not going to bring my tanks down yet.' Roberts had commanded 22nd Brigade at the Battle of Alam Halfa in Egypt on 1 September 1942, when it had stopped Rommel and the Africa Corps in their tracks. Deeply shocked by Hinde's attitude, Roberts later wrote 'I cursed both my old division and my old brigade.'

The Guards Armoured Division, going into action for the first time, showed less reluctance, but moving up in support became hopelessly entangled with the rear elements of the 11th Armoured Division. The confusion was heightened by the sudden appearance of German tank-destroying teams armed with *Panzerschreks*. When the commander of the Guards Armoured Division, Major General Robert Adair, saw a *Panzerschrek* team heading straight for him he had to break off trying to sort out the situation, and order his driver to reverse at high speed. To the east, 3rd Battalion Irish Guards was attacked by the Tigers of the 503rd Heavy Tank Battalion, whose Tigers exacted a fearful toll on the Shermans and Cromwells. The situation was saved when a Sherman commanded by Lieutenant Gorman drove straight at a Tiger and rammed it before it had time to traverse its turret, an exploit which earned Gorman the nickname 'blockhead'.

Seventh Armoured Division was now entering its sixth year of war, and had advanced very cautiously. As the tanks crossed the bridges over the Orne they passed truckloads

BELOW

RAF armourers fitting 27-kg (60-lb) armour-piercing rocket projectiles to the underwing racks of a Hawker Typhoon fighter-bomber. The Typhoons operated in so-called 'cab ranks' over the battlefront, waiting to be called in to attack enemy armour as necessary.

of 3rd Division men who had been wounded in the fighting in the Bois de Bevant, some of whom were screaming in pain. Moving down the cleared paths in the minefields some tank crews lost their way, and had tracks blown off when they detonated mines. Others were not lost, but still drove into the minefield, hoping to lose a track. Literally crawling into the battle, 7th Armoured Division now ran into the back of the Guards, and all cohesion disappeared. Many British tanks fought on, but as individual units. As the Panthers closed for the kill, 'Pip' Roberts managed to use coloured smoke shells to direct a cab-rank of Typhoon fighter-bombers onto the Panthers coming over Bourguebus Ridge and then it was the turn of the Germans to take heavy casualties. British and German tanks continued to slog it out for another two days, until torrential rain on the night of 20 July turned the ground into a quagmire, making further movement impossible.

The operation had not been a total Allied disaster: the Canadians had captured the rest of Caen, and the British, at a cost of 5500 casualties and 430 tanks (more than one-third of the total they had in Normandy) had man-aged to advance nearly 10km (6 miles) and take Bourguebus Ridge.

Eisenhower 'livid'

This, at least, is what Montgomery claimed. But Eisenhower and his staff at SHAEF accused Montgomery of failing to deliver the long-awaited break-out. Montgomery protested that he had made no such claims for Goodwood, but his claims fell on deaf ears. Air Chief Marshal Sir Trafford Leigh-Mallory, usually a supporter of Montgomery, summed up the mood in Eisenhower's headquarters with an incredulous 'Seven miles [11km] for seven thousand tons of bombs!' Eisenhower, described variously as 'furious' and 'livid', picked up Leigh-Mallory's theme and thundered that 'it had taken more than seven thousand tons of bombs to gain seven miles' and that 'the Allies could hardly hope to go through France paying a price of a thousand tons of bombs per mile.' Air Marshal Tedder, deputy supreme Allied commander, long a critic of Montgomery, reminded Eisenhower that Churchill had given him

An M5 Stuart tank, equipped with hedgeclearing gear, demonstrates the importance of this invention for tankers: with spikes fitted, Allied tanks were no longer forced to 'belly up' over hedges in the bocage.

RIGHT

General Lawton Collins, whose VII Corps was chosen by General Omar Bradley to spearhead Operation Cobra, the breakout from Normandy. Much bitter fighting, and many casualties, lay ahead of the Allied armies before this goal was finally achieved.

the power to remove any commander who did not measure up, and now urged him to sack Twenty-first Army Group's commander. Tedder noted in his diary on 21 July 'Eisenhower agreed and is preparing a paper to dispatch to Monty.'

At exactly the same time Montgomery had managed to offend the prime minister, by claiming he was too busy to receive him at his headquarters. Visiting Churchill at 0930 hours on 19 July, Brooke recorded that the prime

minister was raging against Montgomery. 'Haig had always allowed him (Churchill) in the last war as minister of Munitions. He would not stand for it. He would make it a matter of confidence, etc. etc.' Two years earlier Brooke had engineered Montgomery's appointment as commander of Eighth Army, and now Brooke moved rapidly to save Montgomery's career. Flying directly to the airstrip at Twenty-first Army Group's tactical HQ, Brooke left Montgomery in no doubt of the seriousness of the situation. Brooke told him that Eisenhower 'Has been expressing displeasure and accusing Monty of being sticky and of not pushing sufficiently on the Caen front with the British while he made the Americans do the attacking on the right', and that Churchill was taking these complaints very seriously. He now all but ordered Montgomery to invite Churchill to his headquarters.

Monty's masterstroke

Churchill arrived at Montgomery's headquarters on the morning of 21 July 'looking grim-faced and sullen'. Montgomery's aide-de-camp, Captain Henderson, recalled that it was 'common knowledge at Tac that Churchill had come to sack Monty. I mean we all knew it. He came in his blue coat with a blue cap, and in his pocket he had an order, dismissing Monty. There was quite an atmosphere.' Montgomery had been in many tight corners before and was a gifted showman. The briefing began with his intelligence chief, Colonel Bill Williams, giving Churchill details of enemy movements. Montgomery then spoke for another five minutes, summarising how he was going to defeat the Germans. He then played his masterstroke. Williams had just received news via Ultra that a group of German officers had attempted to assassinate Adolf Hitler, and he also knew that Churchill had spent the previous evening aboard the cruiser *Enterprise* in Arromanches harbour, and would not have had time to examine his despatch box. Montgomery now asked Churchill, 'What is going on with this news of a revolution in Germany?' Williams recalled that, 'Winston was completely nonplussed. He sat on the only stool in Monty's map caravan and looked at us in silence for a moment. Then I remember very clearly he produced a long chain with keys on it and unlocked two despatch boxes. They were full of papers all mixed up.' Montgomery and Williams 'scrabbled through these papers.

They were Cabinet papers, Ultra signals and other intelligence reports all muddled up.' The realisation that the war might be about to end left Churchill dumbfounded. He 'began to mumble to himself rhetorical sentences how he would deal with the overthrow of the Nazis and peace proposals, and began to coin phrases for a speech.' Whatever else might have been on his mind quickly paled into insignificance. Churchill left Montgomery in very high spirits, clutching a gift from the general – a bottle of excellent French brandy. Later that day Eisenhower visited Montgomery. The meeting was strained but Eisenhower left satisfied, thanks to the Ultra information that was coming in, that not only was Germany in a political crisis but also that, even if it had not been Montgomery's intention, the Goodwood offensive had ensured that all but two of Germany's panzer divisions were now concentrated on·the British front. If Bradley's divisions could now get to the

BELOW
Crewmen loading belts of 12.7mm (.5-inch) calibre ammunition into the wing bays of a P-47 Thunderbolt. The IXth Tactical Air Force's Thunderbolts performed a tremendous task in support of the Allied forces during and after the hard-fought breakout from Normandy.

open country beyond Coutances, there appeared to be very little the Germans could do to stop them.

Although Eisenhower and Montgomery did not yet know it, the Goodwood Operation had reduced von Kluge, who, since the wounding of Rommel was Germany's principal commander in the west, to near despair. On 23 July von Kluge wrote to Hitler 'I came here with the firm resolve to enforce your command to stand and hold at all cost. The price of that policy is the steady and certain destruction of our own troops.' Von Kluge went on to complain about the 'annihilating power' of the Allied air forces. His forces were short of everything, including ammunition, and desperately needed reinforcements. Von Kluge warned that 'despite all our efforts, the moment is fast approaching when our hard-pressed defences will crack. When the enemy has erupted into open terrain, the inadequate mobility of our forces

will make orderly and effective conduct of the battle hardly possible.' All that stood between the Germans and disaster, then, was a few kilometres of bocage.

Ever since they had first plunged into the labyrinth of hedgerows, American tank crews had been trying to find ways of moving across country without their tanks 'bellying up' over hedges. A tank stuck at an angle of 45 degrees in the air was useless and vulnerable. The crew could not bring its guns to bear, while the lightly armoured bottom was exposed to anti-tank fire. Hundreds of Shermans had been lost in this way. Crews had experimented with a variety of cutting devices to allow a tank to go through, rather than over, a hedge, but all had failed, until a non-commissioned officer in the 102nd Cavalry Reconnaissance Squadron, Sergeant Curtis G. Culin Jr, welded a row of spikes to the front of his tank. It was a brilliant and simple solution. The spikes dug into the bottom of the hedge preventing the tank 'bellying' and, by going forwards and then reversing, the tank behaved like a gigantic garden fork, literally uprooting the hedge. By the last week of July, about three-fifths of all American tanks had been equipped with Culin's spikes. So far, none had been used in combat: Bradley had decided to keep them as a surprise until Cobra was under way.

Napalm introduced

To spearhead Cobra, Bradley chose Collins' VII Corps, which he reinforced to a strength of three armoured and three infantry divisions, totalling about 90,000 men and some 500 tanks. Bradley and Collins were old friends, so that much of the planning took place in informal sessions, and it was soon difficult to tell which general was responsible for a particular idea. The six divisions were to be concentrated on a front of only 6.5km (4 miles) along a stretch of the Périers–St Lo road, facing south-west. Bradley believed that the 'blast effect' from using heavy bombers was essential to success. He wanted an air attack of massive proportions and of short duration. To avoid excessive cratering, which might hamper the advance of ground troops, and to prevent the destruction of villages at critical road junctions, he requested that only relatively light bombs be used. He designated a rectangular target immediately south of the Périers–St Lo road, 6400m (7000 yards) wide and 2300m (2500) yards deep. The air bombardment was to begin 80 minutes before the

BELOW
House-to-house clearance was a task most troops dreaded. It carried a constant threat of sniper fire and booby traps.

LEFT
American soldiers entering a French village with the support of a Sherman tank. While the tanks provided mobile cover and fire support for the infantry, the infantry could suppress any anti-tank threat, such as a German Panzerfaust team.

ground attack with a 20 minute strike by 350 fighter-bombers. Following immediately, 1800 heavy bombers, in an hour-long strike, were to blast the rectangle. Upon conclusion of the heavy bomber attack – the beginning of the ground attack – 350 fighter-bombers were to strafe and bomb the narrow strip again for 20 minutes. Ten minutes after the completion of this strike, 396 medium bombers were to attack the southern half of the rectangle for 45 minutes. While all this was going on another 500 fighters would be patrolling the skies above the bombers, to deal with any German aircraft which might put in an appearance. In all, Cobra was to involve 2500 aircraft delivering 5000 tons of ordnance onto a target area of 15 square kilometres (6 square miles) in just two hours and 25 minutes. In addition to high-explosive and fragmentation bombs, the Americans decided to use napalm, a mixture of jellied petrol and white phosphorus, which had been developed and first used by the Australians against the Japanese eight months earlier in the rugged jungle-clad mountains of New Guinea. Unlike the other weapons, napalm would burn off the hedges and reduce the cover the bocage afforded the Germans. Once the air bombardment was finished the guns would take over. Bradley allocated to VII Corps a substantial proportion of US First Army's artillery assets – nine of its 21 heavy artillery

LEFT
General George S. Patton, seen here, with Omar Bradley, sporting his famous pearl-handled revolvers, led the US 3rd Army in the breakout from Avranches and the race to the Seine in August 1944.

battalions, five of its 19 medium battalions, and all seven of its light battalions – amounting in all to 258 guns, in addition to the artillery already controlled by the divisions of VII Corps. For the estimated duration of the attack – five days – First Army logisticians allocated to VII Corps almost 140,000 rounds of artillery ammunition.

First Army intelligence estimated that, thanks to Operation Goodwood, VII Corps faced no more than 17,000 German troops with fewer than 100 tanks in support. But von Kluge, while withdrawing panzer divisions

from the American front, had been replacing them with infantry divisions, so that actual German strength was closer to 30,000. Cobra was set to commence at 1300 hours on 24 July, but the overcast sky and thick cloud induced Air Marshal Leigh-Mallory, who had flown to Normandy to watch the bombardment, to order a postponement. Unfortunately, 300 heavy bombers which had already taken off failed to receive the message,

and deposited 550 tons of high explosive and 135 tons of fragmentation bombs on both the Germans and the US 30th Division, which lost 25 killed and 131 wounded. Collins had been warned about the postponement, but when he saw the bombs dropped decided that the ground attack must go ahead. Unfortunately, the assault battalions of 30th Division were stunned and demoralised, and more than an hour elapsed before their officers could get the men moving. The two other attacking divisions, the 9th and the 4th, immediately ran into problems, and most of their battalions were unable to advance more than about 90m (100 yards) for several hundred casualties.

The first day of Cobra had degenerated into a fiasco, and Bradley had no choice but to launch Cobra again at 1100 hours on 25 July. The weather had cleared and 1500 B-17s and B-24s came in groups of twelve to drop more than 3300 tons of bombs, to be followed by the 380 medium bombers, which dropped another 650 tons. Then came 550 fighter-bombers, dropping more than 200 tons of bombs and several thousand gallons of napalm. The first waves were on target, but as clouds of dust and smoke obscured terrain features, bombs once again landed on the Americans. An officer in 4th Division remembered that 'they came right on top of us... we put on all the orange smoke we had but I don't think it did any good, they could not have seen it through the dust.... The shock was awful. A lot of the men were sitting around after the bombing in a complete daze.' Farther back, Ernest Hemingway described hearing a sound like 10,000 rattles in the sky, which quickly became a roar like an approaching express train. Hemingway survived, though he was badly shocked. All told, 600 Americans had been killed or wounded. The dead included Lieutenant General Lesley J. McNair, commanding general of US army ground forces, the second-highest-ranking officer in the US army, who had been present as an observer. Once again, units preparing to attack had been badly disrupted; some did not advance at all, and others went forward with great reluctance. The evening of 25 July was one of the worst of the entire war for Eisenhower. It seemed clear that Cobra would not achieve even the modest gains of Goodwood, and he apologised to Bradley for agreeing to the use of heavy bombers against tactical targets. He said 'I gave them a green light this time. But I promise you it's the last.'

Collins' gamble

At VII Corps tactical headquarters that evening Collins was puzzling over reports coming in that German resistance, although still stiff in some places, appeared uncoordinated. This could mean one of two things: that the bombing had indeed broken German resistance, in which case he should commit his armoured divisions to the battle, or that, warned by the bombing of 24 July, the Germans had moved their main line of defence to the south, in which case he could be sending his armoured divisions into a trap. Collins gambled and decided to commit his armoured divisions the following morning. Organised in two columns, each supported by 200 fighter-bombers, Collins' armour set off

LEFT
On a hot summer's day, before a riot of flowers, a Frenchwoman distributes milk to thirsty American soldiers. More than four years of German occupation were now at an end for the population of this village.

on the morning of the 26th for the towns of Marigny and St Gilles. Equipped with their bocage-tearing spikes, Shermans were able to move around positions which would once have held them up for days, and to hit them from the rear or from the flanks. By late afternoon Collins was almost certain that his forces had achieved a clear penetration of the enemy defences. Deeming that the situation demanded speed rather than caution, he ordered his infantry divisions to continue their attacks through the night. On 27 July there was no mistake: despite the difficulties of the terrain, the momentum of the American advance was picking up. On 28 July the Americans knew that they were winning. The country was beginning to open up and drivers could now get their tanks out of low gear. Late that evening the advance guard of VII Corps rolled into Coutances.

Rapid progress

After 52 days of grinding attritional struggle, the Americans had ripped through the extreme western end of the German line. It was now that they reaped the benefits of the British army's slogging matches: the Germans had nothing left to stop them. On 29 July they raced the 26km (16 miles) to Avranches, and on 30 July crossed the Selune River into Brittany. The Germans now suffered another

BELOW

An Allied soldier near Tracy Bocages in early August. He is armed with a captured German MP40 sub-machinegun, a common practice amongst Allied troops, as the German weapon was very highly regarded.

blow. Even at the end of July, the German high command still believed that a substantial American army under General Patton was stationed in eastern England, waiting to descend on the Pas de Calais. Anticipating an attack, they kept substantial forces north-east of the Seine. On 1 August the nightmare became reality, but Patton's army, the newly formed Third, did not oblige the Germans by attacking across the Straits of Dover. Instead it surged through the gap at Avranches on the German's broken left flank.

During the next five days Patton's tank columns tore over north-western France. Third Army's 4th Armoured Division raced across Brittany to Lorient, 6th Armoured Division was outside Brest by 6 August, while 83rd Infantry Division closed on St Malo. Meanwhile, with the German left flank wide

LEFT
*The Canadian offensive was
supported by a heavy artillery
and air bombardment.
Unknown to the Canadians,
the Germans had found
protection in the deep
shafts and tunnels of an iron
mine complex. They were
able to move substantial
forces through the tunnels
as required.*

open, Eisenhower decided to devote the rest of Third Army not to the occupation of Brittany but 'to the task of completing the destruction of the German army... and exploiting... as far as we possibly can.' To this end, on 5 August, Third Army's XV Corps, under Major General Wade H. Haislip, emerged from the Avranches gap and struck south-east. By 9 August XV Corps' advance guard had reached Le Mans, 145km (90 miles) south-east of Avranches. The Seine lay 190km (120 miles) to the west; 95km (60 miles) to the north lay the British and Canadian front at Caen.

While the Americans were making their spectacular breakthrough, the Canadians and British kept up the pressure. On 25 July the Canadian II Corps launched Operation Spring, an assault south of Caen towards the small towns of May-sur-Orne, Verriers and Tilly-la-Compagne, designed to ensure that the Germans could not move any divisions westwards. Unknown to the Canadians, the Germans had ensconced themselves securely within this area deep within a complex of iron mines. Here they had complete protection from air and artillery bombardment, and could move substantial forces through the tunnels to any area of the front which was threatened. This was the strongest German position in Normandy; on 25 July alone the Canadians suffered 1500 casualties, of whom nearly one-third were killed. It was their worst day of the war, with the single exception of Dieppe. Gains were negligible.

As the Canadian attack faltered, Montgomery received an urgent message from Brooke. Eisenhower had again been

complaining to Churchill about the apparent inability of the British to advance, and Brooke warned that the army 'must attack at the earliest possible moment'. This was a tall order. Three-quarters of the German armour was still concentrated against the British. As Montgomery wrote to Dempsey, another Allied attack in the area of Caen 'was unlikely to succeed'. Scanning the map of the front, the British commanders agreed that the only prospect for success lay in moving the whole of XXX and VIII Corps about 32km (20 miles) west of Caen, almost to the British boundary with the Americans, where Ultra intercepts indicated that there were no German armoured formations.

Dempsey launched this operation, code-named Bluecoat, on 30 July. Advancing south along the boundary with the Americans, 11th Armoured Division, the spearhead of VIII Corps, smashed into and defeated a battle group of 21st Panzer Division, and came within 3km (2 miles) of the town of Vire, only 38km (24 miles) east of Avranches. Both Dempsey and Montgomery sensed that a major British victory was in the offing – all VIII Corps now had to do was to drive due west to Avranches, thereby trapping the still-substantial German forces south of St Lo. Unfortunately, all was not well on VIII Corp's eastern flank. XXX Corps should have advanced in tandem with VIII Corps, but the heavily defended Mont Pincon lay directly to the south. It was scarcely surprising that after some minor gains, XXX Corps' attack became bogged down, leaving the whole of VIII Corps' eastern flank exposed to German counter-attack. Alerted by Ultra that two panzer divisions were indeed moving west, Dempsey decided that he could not afford to take a risk and halted VIII Corps' advance. Montgomery felt that XXX Corps' failure to advance had cheated him out of a victory which would have matched that of El Alamein. On 3 August he sacked the commanders of both XXX Corps, and XXX Corps' most famous formation, 7th Armoured Division, along with about 100 of 7th Armoured's subordinate officers, including Brigadier 'Looney' Hinde.

Hitler's blunder

Even though Bluecoat had failed, Allied high command fully expected that the Germans in Normandy, mindful of the rapid American advance eastwards from Avranches, would soon begin to withdraw towards the Seine to form a new defence line. This was exactly what many German commanders planned to do. However, 2100km (1300 miles) to the east, in the Wolf's Lair in East Prussia, Adolf Hitler was convinced that his forces were on the verge of a major victory. Hitler, having survived the 20 July assassination attempt, was now convinced that the numerous disasters which had befallen his forces since 1942 were the work of treacherous anti-Nazi generals. Now that the Gestapo was weeding them out, the scene was set for a return to the spectacular victories of 1940 and 1941. Poring over the map of Normandy, it was obvious to the Führer that Avranches was the key to the American advance – every item of equipment to sustain Patton's divisions had to pass through that town, and the American-controlled corridor around Avranches was only 26km (16 miles) wide.

Having been promised an early-morning fog by meteorologists, on the night of 6/7 August four panzer divisions advanced from Mortain to Avranches, just 32km (20 miles) to the north-west. That first night the panzers penetrated 13km (8 miles) into American lines, and cut off some American battalions. For a short time it seemed that Hitler's gambling instinct might indeed pay off. But as dawn broke there was not a cloud in the sky. By mid-morning the sky over Avranches was filled instead with Allied fighter-bombers, forcing the Germans to go to ground during the hours of daylight. For the next 72 hours the Germans lay hidden by day, and attacked by night.

Eisenhower flew to Bradley's headquarters for a crisis meeting on 7 August; the American commanders decided to keep pushing divisions through the Avranches gap, come what may. If the Germans succeeded in plugging the gap and cutting off the American Third Army, Eisenhower personally guaranteed airdrops of 2000 tons per day to Patton's divisions. To Bradley and Eisenhower the Mortain counter-attack seemed like a gift from the gods of war. The Germans, by ignoring Patton's surge to the east, and pumping more and more men and machines westwards towards Avranches, were helping

to create the very conditions by which a large part of their army in northern France could be encircled. On 8 August, when the eastern spearhead of Patton's Third Army, Haislip's XV Corps, reached Le Mans, Bradley ordered it to turn north and head via Alençon and Argentan for the British sector of the Normandy beachhead. Now all Bradley had to do was to convince the British to strike south towards Argentan, and meet up with the Americans.

Quite independently of Eisenhower, Bradley or, for that matter, Montgomery, Lieutenant General Simmonds, the commander of the Canadian II Corps, had planned to

BELOW
A German StuG III assault gun in action in Normandy. The StuG III was a well-regarded weapon, feared by the Allies, as its low silhouette and powerful gun made it a fearful opponent for Allied armour.

LEFT
American troops advancing on an isolated farmhouse in the Mortain area. The German attack at Mortain gave the Allies momentary pause, but it could not stem the flow of American men and materiel into Brittany and southern Normandy.

attack south from Caen to Falaise on 8 August. This was the 26th anniversary of the great Canadian assault on the German army during the Battle of Amiens in World War I. This assault had contributed greatly to breaking the morale of the imperial German army, and had ushered in the German collapse. Simmonds was hoping that history would repeat itself. The experience of numerous disappointing failures had hardened the Canadians' determination to succeed. After dusk on 8 August, 1000 heavy bombers blasted the flanks of the corridor leading down to Falaise, leaving the corridor itself untouched. With no preliminary bombardment, two columns of tanks rolled forward, and with them went infantry in 'Kangaroos', tanks from which the turrets had been removed. At long last the Allies had an armoured personnel carrier. The surprise was complete. By dawn the Canadian columns, now joined by Major General S. Maczek's recently landed 1st Polish Armoured Division, were pushing towards Falaise.

Canadians annihilated

The Germans counter-attacked at 1130 hours. In one of the most extraordinary battles of the campaign, Michael Wittmann drove his lone Tiger at a squadron of Shermans, only to find that instead of reversing they came straight for him; he had had the misfortune to run into part of the Polish Armoured Division. Wittmann destroyed many of the Polish tanks, but still they kept advancing. Some got around his flanks, and five Shermans, coming up behind him, fired volleys at point-blank range, which blew Wittmann and his Tiger to pieces. The Canadians and Poles beat off the German counter-offensive, and at 1400 prepared to resume the attack. Five hundred B-17s flew overhead to pulverise the Germans, but ended up by repeating the Cobra disaster. Many bombs dropped short, more than 300 Canadians and Poles were killed and wounded, and many tanks were destroyed. The attack got off to a bad start. The following day a Canadian battle group, the 28th Armoured Regiment and the Algonquin Regiment, became hopelessly lost in the advance. It ran into two German panzer groups and was fired on simultaneously by the Polish 1st Armoured Division.

BELOW

Michael Wittmann's Tiger after its destruction by Sherman tanks of the Polish Armoured Division. The Shermans, coming up from the rear, blew the Tiger to pieces with volleys fired at point-blank range.

RIGHT

British troops in support of a Sherman tank, which can be seen in position at a gap in the hedgerow. The Sherman's high hull and turret profile made it readily visible to enemy gunners.

Caught between the Germans and the Poles, the Canadians were annihilated.

Operation Totalise would have petered out but for the extraordinary situation developing to the south, where the Americans were pushing towards Argentan. It was imperative for some of the British forces to get to Falaise. During the next four days a revitalised Totalise, renamed Tractable, was put together. Totalise had relied on innovation and surprise; Tractable was an all-out onslaught. Massed artillery put down a creeping barrage, part high explosive and part smoke, to mask movement. Behind the wall of explosives came 300 tanks and four brigades of infantry, riding with the tanks in Kangaroos. Above, nearly 800 Lancasters and Halifaxes flew towards German positions.

Then everything went wrong. Once again many of the bombers dropped short of their target, killing and wounding more than 400 Canadians and Poles. Ignoring the casualties, the armoured columns pressed forward, but in the dense clouds of smoke they soon lost their cohesion and collided with each other. Now in total disarray, the Shermans and Kangaroos rolled down to a stream, the Laison, which ran across the line of advance but which had been considered too small to

worry about. It may have been small (only 3.5m (4 yards) wide) but its banks were steep – a natural anti-tank ditch. The armoured columns were left milling around in confusion on the north side. Eventually fascine-carrying AVREs managed to bridge the Laison at several points. The tanks continued to advance, but the dash had become a crawl. On 15 August the Canadians finally entered Falaise. It had taken a week to cover 22.5km (14 miles). During this time the Americans had advanced nearly 97km (60 miles) north of Le Mans, and were now at Argentan, less than 32km (20 miles) to the south. On 11 August Patton had told Haislip, 'Pay no attention to Monty's Goddamn boundaries. Be prepared to push even beyond Falaise if necessary. I'll give you the word.' On 16 August Patton radioed to Bradley for permission to move north of Argentan, saying half in jest 'Shall we continue to drive the British into the sea for another Dunkirk?' Bradley said he preferred 'a solid shoulder at Argentan to the possibility of a broken neck at Falaise', and ordered Patton to stay put.

Hitler still believed that armoured counter-strokes would bring Germany victory. He ordered Field Marshal von Kluge to maintain pressure at Avranches, and to strike simultaneously at Falaise and Argentan to prevent the Canadian and American jaws meeting. On 15 August von Kluge made a tour of inspection of forces inside what was clearly now a pocket. Like Rommel, he was strafed by fighter-bombers and barely made it out alive. That evening he informed Berlin: 'No matter how many orders are issued, the troops cannot, are not able to, are not strong enough, to defeat the enemy. It would be a fateful error to succumb to a hope that cannot be fulfilled.' Without waiting for Hitler's reply, von Kluge ordered the troops to begin withdrawing from the pocket. In a rage Hitler dismissed von Kluge, ordered him back to Germany (the hapless von Kluge took cyanide rather than return) and, on 17 August, replaced him with Field Marshal Walther Model, a dedicated Nazi fresh from the Eastern Front. Model had survived many difficult situations in Russia, and he quickly realised that there was nothing to do other than to continue the withdrawal, while striking at Falaise and Argentan with any armour he could lay his hands on in order to keep the jaws open for as long as possible.

By 19 August the German situation was desperate. The Polish 1st Armoured Division had advanced south-east, and a Polish battle group of 1800 men and 80 tanks held the ridge of Mont Ormel in the middle of the corridor. From here they directed artillery fire and airstrikes against the German columns retreating on either side of the ridge.

BELOW

Full speed ahead: the breakout from Normandy achieved, members of the FFI wave to Allied tanks racing on for Paris and the Seine past the wreckage of German vehicles.

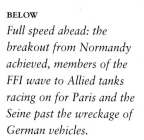

Oberfeldwebel Hans Erich Braun, one of the survivors of the 2nd Panzer Division, was on the receiving end. He remembered the withdrawal as a passage through the circles of hell: 'The never-ending detonations – soldiers waving to us, begging for help – the dead, their faces screwed up still in agony – huddled everywhere in trenches and shelters, the officers and men who had lost their nerve – burning vehicles from which piercing screams could be heard – a soldier stumbling, holding back the intestines which were oozing from his abdomen – soldiers lying in their own blood – arms and legs torn off – others, driven crazy, crying, shouting, swearing, laughing hysterically – and the horses, some still harnessed to the shafts of their ruined wagons, appearing and disappearing in clouds of smoke and dust like ghosts – and the horses, again, screaming terribly, trying to escape the slaughter on the stumps of their hind legs.'

Taking reserves from outside the pocket, Model sent two panzer divisions against Mont Ormel. Even though they were heavily outnumbered, the Poles fought back, their morale sky-high. Their radios were tuned to the BBC, which broadcast regular reports from Warsaw where the Polish home army had risen against the Germans. Apart from on the streets of Warsaw, there was nowhere else

that these Poles would have preferred to be; the Germans were everywhere and the Poles were killing them in large numbers. At that very moment, 32km (20 miles) south, Major General Jacques Philippe Leclerc's recently landed French 2nd Armoured Division was attacking north from Argentan. The French, too, had another battle on their minds. On Saturday 19 August Paris, like Warsaw, had risen in insurrection. Leclerc's men fought at Argentan until, on 21 August, the jaws snapped shut, and the encirclement was complete. Twenty-four hours later, the columns of the French 2nd Armoured division were racing for their capital. The battle for Normandy was over.

A costly victory

During the 11 weeks of fighting very little had gone according to plan, either for the Allies or the Germans. The Allies had expected huge casualties on the first day; instead, with the exception of the Omaha debacle, casualties had been lighter than anticipated. The Germans, expecting a landing in the Pas de Calais, continued to believe until late July that Normandy was a diversion, albeit a very powerful one. They had therefore failed to concentrate sufficient force quickly enough to crush the beachhead when

it was in its infancy. For their part, the Allies had anticipated a quick advance off the beaches, and the development of manoeuvre warfare throughout northern France, in which their massive numerical superiority in armour and aircraft would give them a decided advantage. The Germans were not strong enough to crush the beachhead, and for many weeks the Allies were not strong enough to break out.

Again and again the Allies launched set-piece offensives, supported by massed artillery fire and aerial bombardment, for very modest gains. Again and again the Germans were able to resist from heavily fortified and inge-niously camouflaged positions, redeploying their largely horse-drawn artillery and their largely non-mechanised and non-motorised infantry by night to those areas of the line in which a breakthrough was threatened. The result was static, attritional warfare: the side with the most men and materiel would even-tually win. The casualties reflected the nature of the fighting: between 6 June and 22 August the Allies lost 200,000, the Germans 400,000, and the French (both Resistance and civil-ians) about 100,000 – a total of some 700,000 in 77 days. It had cost great deal to break the German line, but now the campaign in north-west Europe could enter a new phase.

ABOVE

The hell of Falaise, where 50,000 Germans and all the heavy equipment of the German 7th and 5th Panzer Armies were trapped and subjected to relentless attacks by Allied fighter-bombers. The bulk of the personnel had, however, already escaped across the Seine.

CHAPTER FIVE

OPERATION ANVIL/DRAGOON

By August, with the Germans in Normandy in full retreat, the whole of France was ready to rise against its occupiers. Their chance came when the Allies landed in the south.

Throughout June and July 1944, while fighting raged in Normandy, the rest of France had been very far from quiet. The FFI, the French Army of the Interior, had been growing steadily through-out the early summer. By late May the Maquis (the Resistance) had gathered some 10,000 fighters in camps in the Mont Mouchet region of the Massif Central. RAF and USAAF Dakotas supplied them with rifles, bazookas and grenades, although, apart from a few SOE teams, the paratroops they were expecting did not arrive. On 6 June large bodies of Maquisards conducted raids up to 150km (95 miles) away in the Loire Valley. An entire German division, 12,000 strong, was despatched to deal with them. The Germans struck on 10 June, and for the next 10 days a battle was fought that was equal in ferocity to anything that was happening on the distant Normandy beachhead. The Resistance destroyed the initial German attack, inflicting 3100 casualties, but the Germans called up an additional 8000 troops with heavy weapons and air support. In the early hours of 21 June the Resistance, run-ning short of ammunition, broke off the battle and withdrew into the Massif Central.

In the south-east another uprising was under way. The steep, thickly wooded slopes of the plateau of Vercors to the south-west of

Grenoble made the area a natural fortress. During the course of 1943 the Resistance had set up many camps in the forest. By 6 June 1944, some 4000 Maquisards had assembled on the plateau and had hacked out an airstrip for the Allied transport aircraft they were con-vinced would soon arrive. One of their leaders, Eugène Chavant, had gone down to the Mediterranean coast, rendezvoused with an Allied submarine, and had spent a week in Algiers during which he had been told that an invasion of the south of France was immi-nent. Reassured, Chavant had returned to the Vercors on 5 June, and issued the orders for a general uprising. Like the Maquisards of Mont Mouchet, the men of Vercors raided and carried out demolitions. They brought the traffic to a halt over wide areas of south-eastern France.

German intervention

The Germans could not ignore an open insurrection. On 13 June 1500 Germans moved along the road leading up the 910m (3000-foot) escarpment and were beaten back by 300 Maquisards, who lobbed grenades into the struggling columns from the cliff tops. The following day the Germans launched a set-piece attack, a creeping artillery and mortar barrage, behind which 3000 German infantry advanced and overran the outer

OPPOSITE
French tank crewmen advancing through the south of France pause to give a chocolate bar to a young girl. By August, German forces in the south were relatively weak, and by and large the Allied landings went smoothly.

defences of the Maquisards. The steep slopes of the Vercors, however, proved too much, and the attack bogged down. For the next five weeks, the Germans and the Maquis waged attritional warfare. Increasingly desperate appeals to the Allies for assistance elicited a supply drop on 14 July, when 80 American aircraft dropped 1000 containers by parachute, packed with small arms and ammunition, but not the heavy mortars and anti-tank guns the Maquisards needed to combat the Germans effectively.

Luftwaffe in action

The following day more aircraft were over the Vercors, but this time it was Luftwaffe bombers, depositing a rain of incendiaries on the tinder-dry forests. On 19 July, with fires raging on many parts of the plateau, the Germans threw two divisions, totalling more than 20,000 men, around the Vercors. For 48 hours, German battle groups tried to force their way onto the plateau from eight different directions, slowly pulverising Maquis strong points with mortar fire and attacks by JU 87 Stukas, just about the last time these aircraft were used in Western Europe. The Maquis withdrew systematically, making the Germans pay a heavy price for every few hundred metres. At 0930 hours on 21 July,

about 20 gliders drifted noiselessly out of the southern sky, leading the Maquis to believe for a few moments that the long-awaited invasion had begun. But as they swooped in low to land on the still uncompleted airfield, the Maquisards recognised them as German DFS 230 gliders. Opening fire with a single machine gun, the French managed to kill the pilot of one glider, causing it to crash, but the rest were coming in threes and fours, overwhelming the handful of defenders. Soon about 500 paratroops were moving in behind the main Maquis positions, hitting them with accurate mortar fire. During the next 24 hours the Germans ran amok amongst the villages, killing everything that moved. Some of the wounded, who were discovered hiding in caves by the SS on 23 July, were dragged 'out by their hair, their legs. A dozen or so were loaded on a few hand-barrows, were thrown onto German lorries like sacks, and beaten and stabbed to death. The bodies were driven away and thrown into ditches along the road.' Another 50 or so, who had crawled into a thicket, were discovered by the SS, and dragged out and beaten to death, one at a time. In all, some 750 Maquisards died in the battle for the Vercors, with the remainder withdrawing east towards the Alps, pursued by the German 157th Division.

RIGHT
Members of the Resistance fighting openly against their German occupiers in the Mediterranean coastal town of Hyeres. Actions like these throughout France tied down German troops, and hindered the flow of reinforcements and supplies to the front.

Resistance fighters gather in a French town, proudly displaying their arms. For much of the war the British in particular had been supplying the Resistance with arms, and this activity reached new heights in 1944, before and after the Normandy invasion.

Most of the German forces trying to deal with the insurrections in southern and south-central France belonged to Army Group G, which had responsibility for the defence of France south and east of the Loire – in effect about half the country. The commander of Army Group G, General Johannes Blaskowitz, a Prussian officer of the old school who despised the Nazis, and had clashed with Hitler in 1939 over the excesses of German occupation policy in Poland, operated from a headquarters in the small farming village of Rouffiac, about 10km (6 miles) from Toulouse. As news of the battles with the Maquis began to filter in over an increasingly imperfect communication system, Blaskowitz confided to the war diary: 'The situation we have now is intolerable and unacceptable: there is no way for the German troops to distinguish between friend and enemy. Much bloodshed could be avoided, bloodshed of innocent French civilians, if the situation could be remedied by making sure that the Germans know who is friend and who is the enemy, who is peace-loving civilian and who is terrorist.' Believing that the honour of the German army was at stake, Blaskowitz ordered that captured Maquisards were to be treated in accordance with the Geneva Convention as prisoners of war. In fact, Blaskowitz had no control over the forces who were fighting most of the counter-insurgency campaign and who were responsible for most of the atrocities.

Counter insurgency forces

The most feared was the *Sicherheitsdienst*, known as the SD, the security service of the Nazi Party, which operated out of a head-quarters based in Paris, and was part of Himmler's SS empire. It was the SD, frequently and incorrectly confused with the Gestapo (who operated only in Germany) which was responsible for intelligence gathering throughout France, and prisoner interrogation. Blaskowitz attempted to distance the Wehrmacht from SD counter-terror, by forcing the SD to bury their victims in public funerals, though as the summer wore on it was clear he was fighting a losing battle. Less feared, but hated even more, was the Vichy French *Milice*, a 30,000-strong para-military police force, whose members had sworn an oath of allegiance to Pétain on their knees after undertaking a night's vigil. For the *Milice*, the battle with the FFI was literally a life-and-death struggle, for they knew the best they could hope for in a liberated France was a summary execution. The summer of 1944 saw what was, in effect, a civil war throughout large parts of France, with both the Maquis and the *Milice* giving no quarter in a conflict

RIGHT
Liberation was the opportunity for many to take revenge on real or alleged collaborators. Here a woman accused of sleeping with the enemy is marched through the streets in shame.

BELOW
A German soldier does his laundry on a train evacuating him from the south of France. The speed of the Allied advance meant that the Germans were forced to race to avoid being trapped behind Allied lines.

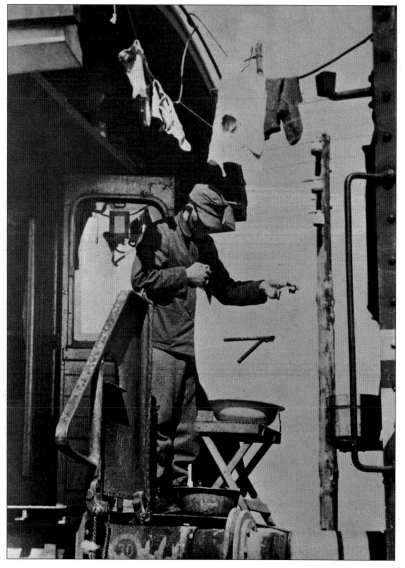

of increasing barbarity. By the 31 July the SD had recorded 7000 individual Maquis attacks throughout southern France, 6000 on French collaborators and 1000 on the Germans. That day Blaskowitz reported to von Rundstedt that Resistance activity had reached a point where 'control over the greater part of the area can no longer be referred to. Only where German troops are in evidence can peace and order be preserved.'

Weakening German forces

As the FFI grew stronger and bolder (it was estimated that by 1 August about 150,000 Frenchmen had declared their allegiance), Blaskowitz became weaker, as his forces were siphoned north to the battle in Normandy. The 2nd SS Panzer Division (*Das Reich*) had been the first to leave on 8 June. Over the next eight weeks it was followed by the 9th Panzer Division, and the 271st, 272nd, 276th, 277th, 338th and 708th Infantry Divisions, and the 341st Assault Gun Brigade. There was even a shortage of anti-tank rockets, as most of these had been sent to Normandy. During the same period Army Group G received only two understrength infantry divisions as replacements, and now had only a single panzer division, the 11th, which had been badly mauled in Russia, and was in process of being rebuilt. All the other formations were static divisions, filled with over-age German soldiers and troops from Eastern Europe. There was even a unit of Indian volunteers, raised from British Indian prisoners of war captured in North Africa. The Germans attempted to mask their weakness by elaborate deception operations, moving troops between locations to make it look as though reinforcements were pouring in. So extensive were these movements that headquarters had to keep colour-coded lists of real and fake units to avoid confusion.

The primary role of the two main components of Army Group G, 1st and 19th Armies, was to defend the south-western and Mediterranean coasts of France respectively, though Blaskowitz no longer believed this possible, and was continuing to advocate a withdrawal from the coast and the establishment of a new position in central-eastern France, where the Germans would be operating on a much shorter logistic line and would have the advantage of interior communications. With his understrength divisions guarding a coast from the Loire to Biarritz on the Bay of Biscay, and from the Spanish to the Italian frontier on the Mediterranean, and supported by only 30 light naval craft and about 200 aircraft, Blaskowitz knew that any Allied assault would quickly break through

the thin defensive crust. OKW continued to brush aside his recommendations, and Blaskowitz had no option other than to position forces along the coasts, and push ahead with defence works. By June, nearly 1000 permanent fortifications had been built along the Mediterranean coast, almost 62,500 mines had been laid, and about 1000 medium and heavy guns were in position.

Landing site predicted

Unlike the situation on the Channel coast, where an Allied landing could come almost anywhere, the topography of the Mediterranean coast made it possible to predict the site of a landing with more accuracy. The Mediterranean coast was divided by the delta of the Rhône, low swampy country in which a landing was virtually impossible. This meant that a landing would have to come either to the west of the Rhône, on the wide sandy beaches between Perpignan and Sète, or to the east of the Rhône, in the small cliff-lined bays of the Côte d'Azur. The western beaches were ideal for an amphibious operation, but the communication network ran north-west through Languedoc to the Garonne and the

BELOW
An alleged collaborator is dragged out of hiding by his hair. Scenes like this one were frequent occurrences in the second half of 1944.

B-17 Flying Fortresses drop supplies and arms, but not the men and heavy weapons they expected, to Resistance forces in the Massif Central in France. At its height, the battle tied down over 20,000 German troops.

Atlantic coast. If the Allies were to land here they would be advancing in exactly the wrong direction. A landing on the Côte d'Azur would be a more difficult operation, but opened the prospect of an advance north across eastern France, which would allow the Allies to cut off German forces fighting in Normandy. Blaskowitz therefore concentrated defensive works to the west of the Rhône delta. The large ports of Toulon and Marseilles were obvious Allied objectives, and both were defended by about 200 guns apiece of medium and heavy calibre. In addition, another 45 batteries were positioned along the coast between the Rhône and Agay, many of them camouflaged with the same ingenuity

the Germans had displayed in Normandy, while between Marseilles and Nice German engineers constructed 600 concrete pillboxes, from which even static divisions could conduct a formidable defence.

The troops in this area came under the command of Lieutenant General Frederick Wiese's Nineteenth Army, with a headquarters at Avignon. Weise, who had worked as a Hamburg policeman until Hitler had come to power, and had only been a colonel at the beginning of the war, was a dedicated Nazi who had won spectacularly rapid promotion in the bloody fighting on the Russian Front. On paper Weise commanded 10 divisions, but one was busy suppressing the Vercors uprising, and several more had been diluted with eastern troops – Poles, Armenians, Georgians, Ukrainians, and Azerbaijanis – soldiers who had already demonstrated their unreliability in Normandy. There were, however, four divisions of high quality, which were being rested and rebuilt after being mauled in Normandy. There was now only one panzer division in southern France, the 11th, with 200 tanks, and thus the most formidable formation in Army Group G. After spending nearly three years in Russia, 11th Panzer had been moved to Bordeaux in April 1944 for rest and rebuilding. It had suffered heavy casualties, but its surviving officers and non-commissioned officers were amongst the most experienced and skilful panzer soldiers in the Wehrmacht. The division's commander, 44-year-old Lieutenant General Wend von Weitersheim, an aristocratic cavalry officer, had so distinguished himself in Russia that he had been awarded the Knight's Cross with Oak Leaves and Swords, Germany's highest decoration.

Blaskowitz's Army Group G comprised about 500,000 men, of whom 250,000 were either on the Mediterranean coast or within easy reach of it. Convinced that the Allies would land on the Riviera, and that the forces deployed there were too weak for anything other than token resistance, on several occasions Blaskowitz had urged OKW to allow 11th Panzer Division to be moved eastwards, but on each occasion the high command had refused. Blaskowitz also recommended that the whole of Army Group B should be withdrawn from south-western and southern France, so that the battle could be fought in the interior with the Allies on extended supply lines and without their naval guns in support. This, too, had been ignored. In short, Blaskowitz believed that southern France was the wrong place to fight the battle.

British reluctance

Blaskowitz was not alone in his reluctance to fight on the Mediterranean coast. The entire British political and military establishment – the prime minister, Winston Churchill; the Chief of the Imperial General Staff, General Alan Brooke; the commander of the Mediterranean theatre, General Sir Henry (Jumbo) Wilson, and the commander in Italy, General Sir Harold Alexander – were very much opposed to any such operation. A landing on the south coast of France, code-named Anvil, had been agreed at a conference at Quebec in

BELOW
Field Marshal von Rundstedt, the man in overall command of the defence of southern France, discusses the coastal defences during an inspection visit in December 1943.

August 1943, where it was envisioned that it would take place simultaneously with the Normandy landings, and draw troops away from the Channel. The British had agreed initially not because they believed that such an operation was really necessary, but because agreement to Anvil meant that a relatively large number of landing craft would have to be kept in the Mediterranean. Although the Anglo-American alliance appeared united, in reality the Allies were often pursuing different and sometimes conflicting objectives. Churchill's reason for keeping landing craft in the Mediterranean was to support the campaign in Italy, but he also planned to move them to the Far East when the situation permitted, so that British forces in India and Ceylon could begin the reconquest of British colonies in South East Asia. Roosevelt and his administration were determined that this was not going to happen, and the transfer of landing craft was subject to innumerable delays.

In early June 1944 Eisenhower recommended that Anvil take place on 15 August.

By this time Churchill had another plan. He attempted to persuade the joint chiefs of staff to use the forces earmarked for Anvil for a landing near Trieste on the Adriatic, from where they would advance north-east through Ljubljana towards Vienna and the Danube. The advantage, Churchill argued, was that this move would cut off German forces in the Balkans, and also secure western Allied control of much of the Danube basin before the Soviets arrived. When the joint chiefs refused, Churchill went over their heads and appealed directly to Roosevelt, denouncing Anvil as 'bleak and sterile'. In a candid reply to Churchill, Roosevelt explained that, 'For purely political reasons over here, I should never survive even a slight setback in Overlord if it were known that fairly large forces had been diverted to the Balkans.' Refusing to give up, Churchill now concentrated on Eisenhower, arguing that the landings should be shifted from the Mediterranean coast to Brest, ostensibly to allow troops to be fed directly into the battle for Normandy, though in reality Churchill knew that a landing on the Atlantic coast would have to be much smaller, thus allowing sufficient forces to be kept in Italy to make the Lubjania option possible. On 5 August Churchill and an entourage arrived at Eisenhower's headquarters at Southwick House near Portsmouth, and in a six-hour debate attempted to browbeat the hapless supreme commander into agreement. Eisenhower refused to budge, and the meeting ended with Churchill literally weeping tears of frustration, and threatening to resign as prime minister. Later that day Eisenhower reported to Marshall, 'So far as I can determine he attaches so much importance to the matter that failure in achieving this objective would represent a practical failure of his whole administration.'

American commitment to Anvil

The American high command, from Roosevelt on down, were totally committed to Anvil. The ostensible reason was that the campaign in north-west Europe could not be sustained without the capture of Marseilles and Toulon, and the additional 35,000 tons of unloading capacity this would afford the Allies. The difficulty with this argument was that both ports were 640km (400 miles) from the battle area, and the problem of transporting supplies such a distance over demolished

BELOW

German troops perform routine maintenance on their anti-tank gun in the south of France. Before the Allied invasions in June and August 1944, the south of France, with its good food and sunny climate, was seen as a 'soft' posting by German units.

LEFT
General de Lattre de Tassigny (second from right) poses with Truscott and other US generals in North Africa. De Lattre was uniquely placed within the complicated French politics of the time to be acceptable to both the ex-Vichy and pro-de Gaulle parties.

BELOW
A Goumier *of the Free French forces. Many of these ex-Vichy troops were now available to the Allies, but de Gaulle was reluctant to use them in France.*

roads and wrecked railway lines almost negated the value of the extra harbour capacity. The British well knew the real reason, but it was so politically contentious that they could not directly challenge American motives, lest they blow the alliance apart. The problem lay in the closeness of the American relationship with the formerly Vichyite French army in North Africa, which was violently hostile to Britain and to the man it saw as Britain's protégé, General Charles de Gaulle. Churchill did not want southern France falling under the control of an anti-British and anti-de Gaulle French colonial army, which would be an unwelcome by-product of the Anvil landing.

However American insistence on the landing was motivated by much stronger considerations than a desire to spite the British. When the Americans had landed in Corsica following the German evacuation in September 1943, they found the island under the control of a Communist-dominated Maquis, which they had some difficulty suppressing. Information coming out of southern France suggested that Communist-inspired uprisings were taking place everywhere, and that in some places, for example, the Vercors, the Communists had managed to set up local administrations. It was therefore imperative that the extreme right-wing French colonial army be landed in France as soon as possible, not so much to annoy the British, but to prevent two-thirds of France falling to the French Communist Party. For their part the British regarded the employment of the French North African army in Metropolitan France for such a purpose with something approaching horror. Secret Foreign Office appreciations argued that the use of Moroccan, Algerian and Senegalese soldiers to suppress French Communist guerrillas would only serve to make the situation worse, and might lead to prolonged domestic strife. It reminded some too much of Franco's employment of Spain's Moroccan troops to suppress the Spanish Republic in the summer of 1936, which had led to three years of bloody civil war. It was little wonder, then, that Churchill had shed tears when he failed to dissuade Eisenhower from Anvil.

Planning begins

At the end of 1943 US Seventh Army had opened a secret headquarters for an Operation Anvil planning group in the white Moorish-style buildings of the *Bouzare'a Ecole Normale* in the hills above Algiers. In December General Jean-Marie de Lattre de Tassigny flew in from London to lead the planning phase, and to take command of French forces in North Africa. De Lattre de Tassigny was about the only French senior officer who could cooperate successfully in this politically volatile environment. In 1940 he had remained loyal to Pétain and Vichy, but in November 1942 he had disobeyed Pétain and ordered his troops to resist the German occupation of Vichy France, an act of defiance which earned him a 10-year prison sentence. After three failed attempts to escape, he was finally successful. He made his way to London and threw in his lot with de Gaulle. He was thus a very rare creature, at least nominally under de Gaulle's command, but acceptable to the Vichyite officers who led France's North African army.

Thorough preparations

De Lattre's task in the early months of 1944 paralleled that of General Frederick Morgan (COSSAC) in London, who was then planning for Overlord. Like Morgan, de Lattre had his staff had to analyse a mass of information coming in from the Resistance. The general later recalled the extraordinary thoroughness of the preparations. 'Every imaginable detail was given in a complete guide to every beach between Mentone and Port Vendres: topography, hydrography, climate, tides and currents, the nature of the soil, information relating to means of communication, industrial resources, electricity and water supplies, hospitals – all was tested, classified and numbered with as much care as the least particular regarding the enemy's dispositions. The smallest concrete block, the most modest machine-gun emplacement, the narrowest

minefield, were scrupulously located and checked on the innumerable photographs taken by reconnaissance planes.' From these researches a plan of campaign gradually emerged. De Lattre's main objective was to capture Toulon and Marseilles, but because of the strength of the defences he knew that there was no prospect of attacking them head on. Eventually he decided to take Cavalaire, just to the east of Toulon, as the western limit of the landing, and to spread the landing eastwards over the 70km (45 miles) of coast separating it from the beach at Agay, which was just to the east of Cannes. He therefore intended to land exactly where Blaskowitz had predicted the Allies would come ashore.

De Lattre worked extremely well with Lieutenant General Alexander Patch, commander Seventh Army, whom he described as a 'resolute commander, of high and clear intellect, and exceptional steadfastness'. Like de Lattre, Patch was a highly experienced soldier. He had formed and commanded the Americal Division in the bitter fighting against the Japanese on Guadalcanal in the Solomons in the winter of 1942-43. He was also a skilled diplomat who made much of his Scottish ancestry when negotiating details with the ever-suspicious Frenchman. In the summer of 1944 Patch chose Major General Lucian K. Truscott to command American

BELOW

B-25 Mitchell bombers from the Fifteenth Air Force on their way to bomb German defences on the Riviera before the Anvil landings. After the aerial bombardment, the defenders were shelled by several Allied warships.

American glider troops prepare before take-off from Voltone Aerodrome in Italy in the early hours of the morning of 15 August. Soon they would be in France, fighting against an enemy that was expecting them.

forces in Anvil. Truscott, who had begun the war as a colonel, was now one of America's most successful fighting generals. He had raised and trained the US Rangers, the American equivalent of the British Commandos, and had accompanied them on the disastrous Dieppe operation in August 1942. He had then commanded a small task force which captured Port Lyautey during the North African landings in November 1942, had commanded Eisenhower's advanced command post in Tunisia in the spring of 1943, and had then commanded US 3rd Division in Sicily, at Salerno and at Anzio.

Diplomatic gaffe

Unfortunately, Truscott was no diplomat. Invited to lunch by de Lattre, he took it upon himself to inspect some French troops without the French general's permission, thereby committing a serious breach of military protocol. Truscott reported that 'conversation lagged during the luncheon. Everyone attended to the business of eating, the sounds of mastication dominating the scene. It finally came to a close and we learned the reason for the cool reception. De Lattre was in a towering rage.' Suddenly the French general burst into an angry tirade, but Truscott cut him short, saying that 'if that was all he had to discuss, we were wasting our time.'

Though the two men later came to regard each other with grudging respect, relations

Not a supply drop, but the real thing: part of the Anglo-American 1st Airborne Task Force being dropped near Le Muy, an important transport and communications hub, on 15 August.

were never close, a tension which was reflected in the plans for the landing, which kept the French and American components well apart. The first phase of the landing was to involve French Commandos and American-Canadian special service forces, which were to seize coastal batteries and create diversions. Simultaneously, a 10,000-strong Anglo-American paratroop and glider force was to land behind the beaches, seizing road junctions and capturing strong points. The main landing would comprise Truscott's VI Corps, composed of the 3rd and 45th Divisions, and somewhat surprisingly, the 36th Division, which had twice been mauled in the Italian campaign, and was led by a new

DUKWs, amphibious trucks, come ashore on 'Alpha Red' beach, near Cavalaire. Unlike the Normandy landings of a month and a half ago, German forces in the area were not very substantial, and their morale was not very high. Marseilles, for example, fell a month earlier than expected, on 28 August.

commander, Major General John E. Dahlquist, who had no combat experience at the head of a division. Twenty-four hours later the advance guard of de Lattre's forces, now named Army B, was to land at St Tropez, from where, after the arrival of reinforcements, it would advance to invest Toulon and Marseilles, which were scheduled to be captured on D+20 and D+40 respectively. In the meantime Truscott's VI Corps was to have surged up the Rhône Valley, linked up with Patton's Third Army advancing from Normandy, and cut off Blaskowitz's Army Group B.

On 10 August, 2000 transports and warships, the largest armada the Mediterranean had ever seen, was assembling in ports as far apart as Algiers, Palermo, Valetta and Naples, where the embarkation of the 94,000 soldiers who would take part in the initial landing was under way. On the afternoon of 13 August senior American officers with the largest of the convoys in Naples harbour were astonished to see Winston Churchill moving amongst the ships in a British motor launch, acknowledging the cheers of the American soldiers with his now famous 'V for Victory' sign. Knowing he would not get his way, Churchill had flown to Italy on 8 August, and had then managed to bully his way into being allowed to accompany the landing force,

something the king had forbidden him to do on 6 June in Normandy. Because he felt that he had been dragooned into accepting the landings, Churchill proposed that the code name be changed from Anvil to Dragoon. Possibly this was intended as a joke, but staff officers took the prime minister literally, so that it became known as Anvil-Dragoon.

Commando landings

Just before midnight 800 French Commandos led by Colonel Georges-Régis Bouvet landed at the base of the steep cliffs at Cap Nègre, from where heavy German guns could hit the landing beaches. Scaling the cliffs in silence, they took the Germans completely by surprise. In what was one of the most successful special operations of the war, the French worked their way systematically from bunker to bunker, killing some 300 Germans and taking another 700 prisoner, all for fewer than 70 casualties. Meanwhile, 40km (25 miles) south-east of Toulon, American and Canadian special service troops were coming ashore in kayaks and on electrically powered surfboards on the islands of Port-Cros and Île du Levant, where aerial reconnaissance had detected heavy batteries. In the event, this imaginative operation proved abortive, because the guns turned out to be skilfully fashioned mock-ups, made from drain-pipes and sheets of corrugated iron. The largest setback the Allies suffered during the night occurred to the west of Cannes, where a force of 67 French Commandos came ashore in the middle of a newly laid minefield, and as they attempted to withdraw were strafed by Allied fighters, which had mistaken them for Germans. The force was annihilated, 27 being killed and 40 captured by the Germans.

The airborne assault was taking place at the same time. Just after midnight, five transport aircraft dropped 300 life-sized dummies, dressed as American paratroops and rigged with explosive charges on La Ciotat, about halfway between Marseilles and Toulon. It had the desired effect, distracting German attention from the actual drop zone at Le Muy, a vitally important intersection where the Route Napoléon ran northwards to Grenoble, and National Highway 7 branched west from the Route Napoléon to Avignon, and then north up the Rhône Valley. Beginning at 0430 hours, 535 transport aircraft and 410 gliders, escorted by a swarm of fighters, deposited 9700 soldiers with 213 guns and mortars and 220 jeeps of the Anglo-American 1st Airborne Task Force in the area around Le Muy. By sheer luck some of the paratroops landed in Draguignan, the headquarters for Nineteenth Army's LXII Corps,

which commanded the divisions on the actual invasion beaches. Isolated and under heavy attack, the headquarters was now reduced to fighting for its own survival, rather than attempting to coordinate the activities of the divisions on the beaches.

Le Muy captured

The seizure of Le Muy was more difficult. Exactly a week earlier, the commander of Nineteenth Army, General Wiese had ordered corps and divisional commanders to a map exercise which had taken place in a large hall in Draguignan. This quickly revealed the critical importance of Le Muy, and Wiese had ordered the garrison reinforced by a battle group, Regiment Bründel, from the 244th Division. The commander of 1st Airborne Task Force, Major General Robert T. Frederick, at 37 the youngest general in the American army, had assigned the capture of Le Muy to the British Airborne Brigade. British airborne forces had already acquired a formidable reputation, but the British commander, Brigadier Pritchett, was under strict instruction from the supreme commander in the Mediterranean, General Sir Henry Maitland Wilson, to conserve his brigade for future deployments in the Balkans, not waste it in attacks on positions which the enemy, thanks to the Normandy breakout, would

American GIs wade ashore during the Anvil landings. Anvil was predominately a French and American operation, reflecting Britain's reluctance to commit scarce resources to yet another front, when they were needed in both Italy and the north of France.

soon have to abandon. Interviewed after the war, Frederick was still furious at what happened at Le Muy. 'They (the British) didn't even try to take it on the first day and when I asked Pritchett about it he said, "Well, we jumped". "But why don't you go in there and take the town?" I asked him. "No," he said, "there are Germans in there." So I thought, the hell with it, and I immediately sent them back to Italy.' Frederick then ordered the American 550th Glider Battalion to attack Le Muy, who advanced slowly behind all the artillery Frederick could muster. At noon the following day a German emissary came out under a white flag and told Frederick that if he would have his artillery cease firing, they would surrender. Frederick told the German that he was going to increase his artillery fire, and that he had better tell his commander to work out a way to surrender as quickly as he could. Without any further attempt at negotiation, the Germans surrendered Le Muy.

Main Anvil landings

Meanwhile the main landings had been taking place almost with clockwork precision. At 0550 hours on 15 August, the first of some 1300 American, British and French bombers arrived from Sardinia and Corsica, and for the next 100 minutes pounded the Riviera, driving the defenders into their bunkers. At 0730 hours, as the last of the bombers peeled off to the south, the guns of Allied warships took over, pumping some 16,000 shells at German batteries and strong points for the next 20 minutes. At 0800 hours the first Americans came ashore, encountering virtually no opposition. The BBC's radio correspondent, Wynford Vaughan Thomas, who landed with the assault troops, reported that the Germans 'did not have their heart in this job. Already many of them are walking down the dusty roads to the prison cages, most of them smiling – glad to be out of it.' The only problem came at 1400 hours as units of the 36th Division were heading in to land at the little port of Fréjus, which commanded the highway to Le Muy and the interior. Preceded by drone boats, remotely piloted craft filled with high explosive which were to be detonated over underwater obstacles, the 36th were still several thousand metres off shore when they noticed the drones behaving erratically, and then putting about and heading back towards the landing craft. Though it has never been fully explained, it is likely that this incident was one of the first examples of successful electronic counter-measures, as it was known that German signallers were trying to jam the drones' remote controls. The landing craft also put about, and landed the Americans further along the coast, from where they advanced and took Fréjus the following day.

Unlike their counterparts in Normandy on 6 June, the Germans on the coast of the Mediterranean had not been surprised. Two

BELOW

American GIs take cover by the side of the road. The speed of Truscott's advance forced General Blaskowitz, the German commander, to retreat in order to save his forces from capture.

days before the landing, OKW had finally given Blaskowitz permission to move 11th Panzer from Bordeaux to the Riviera, but Allied fighter-bombers meant that it could only move at night, and by the morning of 15 August it was still on the west bank of the now bridgeless Rhône near Avignon, waiting for its engineers to construct pontoons across the river. It was to take another three days for part of the armour of 11th Panzer to get across the Rhône, and then it was immobilised by lack of fuel, which was finally brought downriver from Lyons. Meanwhile, at midday on 17 August, Blaskowitz finally received orders from OKW to abandon southern France, with the exception of the fortresses of the Gironde near Bordeaux, and the ports of La Rochelle, Marseilles and Toulon, all of which were to be reinforced and held 'to the end'.

German withdrawal

Blaskowitz now had a few hours to organise one of the most complicated withdrawals ever undertaken by the German army. With Patton advancing east along the north bank of the Loire, Blaskowitz had to delay Truscott's advance north up the Rhône to prevent a junction of the American forces for as long as possible. To this end he ordered Weise to throw 11th Panzer down the east bank of the Rhône in a delaying action, while the with-

drawal crossed the river between Valence and Lyons. To make matters more difficult, the retreating columns would have to avoid the Massif Central, which was now firmly in the hands of the Maquis, so that the columns would have to make wide diversions to the north and the south. Blaskowitz ensured the withdrawal was carefully arranged in 25km (16-mile) phases, but this meant that the rear guards would not be leaving the Atlantic coast for at least a week, and stood a very good chance of being cut off. By 20 August the Germans were in full retreat, using virtually every type of motorised transport they could lay their hands on, including school buses, farm tractors and motor cycles. Thousands of soldiers were also on bicycles, towed by ropes attached to troop carriers, thousands were in horse-drawn wagons, and thousands more were on foot pushing their belongings and supplies in wheelbarrows and perambulators.

Fortunately for Blaskowitz, Truscott's troops did not press inland immediately, but waited for a logistical base to be developed. On 17 August, de Lattre had landed at St Tropez with 16,000 troops, the advance guard of what would become Army B, and began to put into effect his master plan for the capture of Toulon. While Brigadier General Charles Diego Brosset marched his 1st Infantry Division west along the coastal highway, Major General Aimé de Goislard de

FFI troops were important in helping the Allied advance. Here they clear away German wreckage, whilst French Shermans roll forward in the background. The policy of recruiting Resistance members into the regular army meant that the more radical of them could be 'tamed' and controlled by the army's discipline.

GIs march three German prisoners in front of their column during the advance northwards. Many Germans seemed to welcome the opportunity to surrender, as the war now seemed lost to all but the most fanatical.

Monsabert led his Algerian 3rd Infantry Division through the mountain fortifications north of Toulon, then moved south to invest the city from the north and west.

Supported by heavy naval gunfire, de Lattre began the assault on 20 August, his troops systematically reducing the 30 forts on the outskirts, and pressing the defenders into an ever-tighter perimeter. French casualties, 2700 killed and wounded, were not light, and the Germans lost about 8000. On 28 August the German commander disobeyed Hitler's order to fight to the end, and surrendered the surviving 17,000 members of his garrison. Meanwhile a French tank column, supported by the 7th Infantry Regiment of the Algerian 3rd Division, had reached the outskirts of

Marseilles on 21 August, where the Maquis had started an uprising. The task-force commander, Colonel Léon Jean Chappuis, was all for driving straight into the city, but was forbidden to do so by de Lattre, who was reluctant to use North African troops in French urban fighting. They might, he explained, 'be contaminated by the disorder of a city in a state of insurrection'. At 0500 hours the next morning, at the Madeleine crossroads just to the west of the city, with his tanks and soldiers surrounded by cheering citizenry, and the road into Marseilles apparently clear, Chappuis disobeyed orders and took his column into the city. The ensuing battle was ragged and confused street fighting – not the battle de Lattre intended to fight – but it was successful. The Germans surrendered Marseilles on 28 August, a full month earlier than de Lattre had estimated.

Truscott's trap

By this time Truscott had sent an armoured task force under the command of Brigadier Fred W. Butler, closely followed by Dahlquist's 3rd Division due north and then, on 21 August, due west to Montelimar on the Rhône. Just to the north of the town the road ran through the Cruas Gorge, a narrow defile between the Rhône and a ridge, several kilometres long and 300m (1000 feet) high, and it was here that Truscott planned to trap and annihilate the Germans. But this possibility was equally apparent to the highly skilled General Wend von Weitersheim and his vastly experienced 11th Panzer Division. Moving up onto the ridge, on 23 August 11th Panzer counter-attacked, its 88mm fire destroying American armoured vehicles one by one. On 26 August Truscott, furious that the Montelimar choke point had still not been closed, flew to Dahlquist's headquarters and threatened to relieve him. But by now the bulk of the retreating Germans, by bunching up and travelling in daylight, had already cleared Montelimar. American fighter bombers and long-range artillery fire exacted a fearful toll on the packed columns. Passing through the area a few days later, de Lattre saw that 'for tens of kilometres there was nothing but an inextricable tangle of twisted steel frames and charred corpses – the apocalyptic cemetery of all the equipment of the Nineteenth Army, through which only bulldozers would be able to make a way.'

Blaskowitz's Army Group B finally established a new line north of Dijon on 3 September, the same day as Truscott's troops entered Lyons. But on that day British Second Army entered Brussels, Hodges's First Army was at Mons, and Patton was across the Meuse. Truscott finally linked up with Patton on 11 September, about 65km (40 miles) west of Dijon, trapping the last 20,000 of Blaskowitz's rear guard, who decided to surrender. The military results of Anvil-Dragoon hardly justified the operation, and even the 900,000 American soldiers and 4 million tons of supplies which subsequently arrived through the Mediterranean ports could only be moved by diverting logistic assets from Montgomery, Hodges and Patton. Indeed, the American insistence on using these ports may actually have increased Allied logistic difficulties. The real importance of Anvil-Dragoon was political, in that it allowed the French army to bring the more radical elements of the Maquis under control, by inducting them into the new French army, and bringing them under military discipline. As the new units were formed, North and West African units were rapidly repatriated, thus minimizing the racial clashes which the British had feared would play into the hands of the Communists. In the final analysis the landing was necessary not to defeat the Germans, but to ensure the domestic stability of France, and in this it succeeded admirably.

BELOW
FFI armour rolls through the newly-liberated Avignon, 88km (55 miles) north of Marseilles, on 28 August 1944. Members of the Resistance march alongside the tanks.

CHAPTER SIX

PARIS

As the Allies raced through northern France, Eisenhower faced a dilemma: push on for the German border, in an attempt to end the war quickly, or liberate Paris, with all its potent symbolism?

I n the weeks after D-Day, while large areas of Brittany, the Massif Central, and the Vercors saw Resistance uprisings and rapid degeneration into civil war, the mood of the great majority of the population of Paris remained curiously dispassionate. Vichy officials believed that the great bulk of the population was genuinely neutral; indeed, that the population had no love for the 'Anglo' part of the Anglo-American alliance, and that while they might marginally prefer Americans to Germans, they far preferred Germans to the British. They pointed out as evidence of this the reaction of Parisians to a heavy RAF night raid on 21 April, which should have hit the Renault factory, but instead hit Monmartre, killing and injuring hundreds and badly damaging the Sacré Coeur. On Sunday 26 April Marshal Pétain had made his only official state visit to Paris to inspect the damage. For the only time in his life Pétain learned what it was like to be a popular politician. As his motorcade drove to Notre Dame for high mass, it passed through streets lined with tens of thousands of cheering people. So many had turned up at Notre Dame that the cathedral was soon packed to capacity, and the service, conducted by the ultra right wing and violently anti-semitic Cardinal-Archbishop of Paris, Mgr Emmanuel Suhard, had to be relayed on a loudspeaker system to the crowd

outside. And as Pétain left Notre Dame the crowd roared a deafening 'Vive la Maréchal'.

Fickle Parisian support

The German ambassador to Paris, Otto Abetz, was less sanguine about the depth of attachment to Petain. In a report prepared on 10 June he wrote 'According to evidence confirmed daily, the city of Paris seems calm but may hide a certain agitation that could blow up from one moment to the next.' Abetz knew the modern political history of the capital very well and knew that the crowds which had cheered hysterically for Pétain in April could be cheering just as hysterically for de Gaulle before the year was out. A much more likely explanation for the relative calm – indeed apathy – in Paris was that compared to virtually everwhere else in German-occupied Europe, and in Great Britain and the USSR, life in Paris was remarkably easy. By comparison with London and Berlin, Paris had been bombed only lightly, and was now home for a growing band of successful businessmen, entertainers and writers, including the British humourist PG Wodehouse, who sought relative safety from air attack in a congenial environment. It was true that by August 1944 electricity was available only between 22.30 and 24.00, but as France was on double summer time power surged through the grid at exactly the time the sun set. It was also true that apart from military and police vehicles motorised traffic had virtually disappeared from Paris streets, but they had been replaced by hundreds of thousands of bicycles, and thousands of horse-drawn cabs and carts. In addition the Paris Metro, one of the most extensive in the world, continued to function, with trains running every twelve to fifteen minutes, rather better than Berlin or London.

Food shortages

By early August Parisians were complaining loudly about food shortages and reduced rations, but these were a relatively recent occurrence, and could be circumvented by a thriving black market. The wine ration, for example, was reduced to two quarts per person per week (about three bottles), but most Parisians seemed to have little difficulty obtaining additional supplies. Restaurants were allowed to open for only four nights out

of every seven, but there was never a night in Paris when one could not find somewhere to have dinner, and dining by candlelight when the electricity went off was rarely regarded as a hardship. More than 200 cinemas were still operating throughout Paris, their electricity supplied by teams of cyclists operating pedal-powered generators, and the Moulin Rouge, the Moulin de la Galette, Shéhérazade, and a dozen other venues still produced live floor shows for the thousands of Germans on leave or convalescing in the city's hospitals.

German soldiers were everywhere, but they still behaved as tourists, and generally went about unarmed. Routine administration of the law, the direction of traffic and so on was left to the Paris police, whose blue uniforms and kepis gave the streets an aura of normality. Internal security against terrorists was in the hands of the *Sicherheitsdienst*, the SD, widely but incorrectly known as the Gestapo, who, dressed in their plain clothes 'uniform' of black leather overcoat and dark stetson hat, could be seen driving to and from their headquarters in the old *Sûreté Nationale* building at 11, rue des Saussaies in Daimler Benz tourers. It was here that the head of the SD, SS General Karl Oberg, a tubby, short-sighted clone of Henrich Himmler, held court. Coarse and ill-educated, Oberg had joined the Nazi Pary in 1931 when his fruit selling business in Hamburg had collapsed. In January 1944 the SD had been reinforced by the Vichyite *Milice*, whose *délégué général* in northern France, Max Knipping, a former pilot, set up his headquarters in the old Communist Party party HQ at 44, rue Le Peletier while his men, some 500 in all, were quartered in the Auteuil synagogue, which had long since ceased to function.

Every Thursday Oberg held a meeting to exchange intelligence between the SD, the *Milice* and the police, and to co-ordinate their activities. Through a network of informers and through interrogation they had compiled files on about half a million Parisians, and had built up a fairly accurate picture of the Resistance in Paris. They knew that, with the exception of a relatively small Gaullist faction, the Resistance in Paris was dominated by the Communist party, and claimed, at least in paper, a strength of some 25,000. But they also knew that the Communist Resistance in Paris was poorly armed, with probably fewer than 1000 small arms, and that they were capable of little more than the occasional

assassination. Oberg granted the *Milice* the right to arrest suspects, to try them before special tribunals, and then to carry out summary executions. They were also granted a licence to launch pre-emptive strikes, and kill those they believed might be about to commit an outrage. The collaborationist commentator Jean Herold-Paquis waxed lyrical on Radio-Paris about the war these Vichyite gunmen were waging in the streets of the city. 'To bloody arguments they reply with a declaration of war. They are against dishonourable men with dishonourable ambitions.'

Violence escalates

In the weeks after the Normandy landing tit for tat violence between the *Milice* and the Resistance began to spiral. On 16 June the *Milice* took Jean Zay, a Jew, who had been minister of education in the pre-war Popular Front government, from the prison where he had been since 1940, and shot him by the roadside. Twelve days later the Resistance struck back, shooting former Deputy and Vichyite propagandist, the devout Catholic and poisonously anti-semitic Philippe Henriot dead, in his flat at the Ministry of Information in the rue Solferino. The Resistance were alarmed, and Oberg and Knipping relieved, when no fewer than 400,000 people filed past Henriot's bier in just four days. The *Milice* struck back on 8 July, murdering Georges Mandel, a minister in Reynaud's government, while transferring him from the Santé prison. On 14 July, Bastille Day, the political prisoners in the Santé seized and barricaded part of the prison and set fire to their cells, but the following morning the *Milice* stormed and recaptured the Santé, summarily executing 28 prisoners against the prison wall.

Against this background of terror and counter-terror life for the huge majority of Parisians went on as normal. Meeting in the Café Flore, intellectuals of the *avant garde* struggled to explain the sense of apathetic detachment which afflicted the vast majority. On 10 June Jean Paul Sarte's second and most famous play *Huis Clos* had opened at the Théâtre du Vieux-Colombier. Sarte's characters, enmeshed in a web of cowardice and betrayal from which escape is impossible conclude at one level that 'Hell is other people.' The German censors recognised that it was not merely about the human condition, but also said much about the condition of the French people as they entered their fifth year of German occupation, but that the play was far more anti-French than it was anti-German. Two weeks later Albert Camus' first play, *Le Malentendu,* opening at the Théâtre des Malthurins, caused the censors a little more worry. They were perfectly happy to accept the premise that man – particularly Parisian man – was evil at his core and that freedom was illusory. What they were slightly more concerned about was Camus' secondary theme that even though freedom was an illusion, man should still strive for it, because man could not hope for a future unless he knew how to renew the very basis of his existence.

ABOVE

French infantry, supported by armour, pictured passing the corpse of a German soldier along a road to the north of Fontainebleau, en route to Paris. The advance of Leclerc's 2nd Armoured Division towards the capital was slowed down by German roadblocks protected by 88mm (2.95in) anti-tank guns.

Roger Villon, the Communist chief of staff of the Paris Resistance, and Henri Tanguy (alias Colonel Rol), the commander of Communist military forces in Paris, understood exactly the message of Camus' play, and by the end of June had adopted the slogan 'No Liberation Without Insurrection'. The Communist leadership understood about the humiliation imposed by compromise and knew that the only way to excise the humiliation was through the shedding of blood. 'Paris is worth 200,000 dead', was Colonel Rol's chilling assessment. A bloody insurrection would also radicalise the population and make more acceptable a post-war government with major Communist participation.

The worst possible fate, Villon and Rol believed, would be for Paris to wait supine until American and French Gaullist troops arrived to drive the Germans out. But there was one major stumbling block in the plan for a mass insurrection; the entire Resistance in Paris had just 600 pistols and sub-machine guns, just enough to ensure that any attempt at insurrection had a very good chance of ending in a massacre of those involved in the insurrection.

De Gaulle's military representative in Paris, Jacques Chaban-Delmas, and his *délégué général*, Alexandre Parodi, did their best to quell Communist ardour, and they half suspected that some Communists were using the threat of insurrection as a means of forcing the British Special Operations Executive (SOE) to begin supplying arms directly to the capital. In the preceeding few months SOE had parachuted into France 76,290 Sten guns, of which only 114 reached Paris, and 27,961 pistols, of which 18 ended up in the capital. This discrepency was in part a reflection of the difficulty of smuggling firearms into the capital, and in part an indication of the desire of SOE not to arm what was a predominantly Communist movement.

Von Choltitz

This was the situation when a new German commander, Lieutenant General Dietrich von Choltitz, arrived in Paris on 9 August. Parisians were aware of the failed attempt to assassinate Hitler on 20 July, but were surprised when familiar figures amongst the German hierarchy in Paris began to disappear, including the commander of the Paris garrison, General Heinrich von Stulpnagel. The new man came with a formidable reputation. In May 1940, as a lieutenant colonel, he had called in the aircraft which had levelled the dock area of Rotterdam, leaving more than 700 dead. Two years later he had captured Sevastopol in the Crimea, and systematically demolished the city. And in the steady retreat from Russia, which began in the summer of 1943, Choltitz had commanded rear guards which had scorched the earth as they withdrew, ripping up railway lines, demolishing factories and blowing up bridges.

Shortly before taking up his appointment, Choltitz, who had been commanding a corps in Normandy, was summoned back to Hitler's HQ at Rastenburg for detailed personal instructions. Choltitz found the Führer 'in a state of feverish excitement. Saliva was literally running from his mouth. He was trembling all over and the desk on which he was leaning shook with him. He was bathed in perspiration and became more agitated.' Hitler's orders were unambiguous; on the departure of the Wehrmacht, Paris 'must be utterly destroyed…nothing must be left standing, no church, no artistic monument.' The infrastructure, too, was to be demolished, with gas mains torn up, electricity pylons blown up and the water supply system smashed and polluted, so that 'the ruined city may be a prey to epidemics'.

Convinced that Hitler had gone mad, Choltitz returned to Paris to set up his HQ in the Hotel Meurice near the Place de la Concorde, and to wrestle with an appalling dilemma. He was perfectly happy to defend the outskirts of the city and he was willing to fight through the capital, but he had no desire to go into history as the man who had systematically destroyed one of the world's most splendid cities. However he knew that to disobey Hitler would result in his own execution, and very probably the arrest and execution of his wife and children in Germany.

Gunshots near Paris

On Sunday 13 August the crowd at a race meeting at St Cloud to the west of Paris picked up the distant sound of artillery fire coming from the direction of Chartres, nearly thirty miles to the south west. Elements of Patton's 3rd Army had indeed entered the city that day, but their army commander had no intention of going on to Paris, ordering his forces instead to swing to the south east and bypass the capital. At SHAEF HQ, which had recently been set up at Granville on the western coast of the Cotentin Peninsula, Eisenhower had an even greater aversion to a drive on the French capital. In strictly military terms there was little to gain sending Allied forces into Paris, and much to lose. If the Germans chose to defend Paris, an entire army could be sucked into an urban battle in which the advantage, at least initially, would be with the defender. Even if Paris was liberated with very little fighting, the responsibility of feeding the population would fall onto Allied logistics, which even then was having problems sustaining the advance. Either way, the liberation of Paris would divert the Allies from their true objective, which was to drive towards the German frontier as rapidly as possible, bypassing Paris to the north and south. Indeed, the earliest date for the liberation of Paris which Eisenhower could envisage was 15 September.

Police disarmed

To the people of Paris and their occupiers, however, the news that guns could be heard from Chartres heralded the imminent arrival of the Allies. The effect on all elements of the population was dramatic, but the effect was most profound on the Paris police. Throughout the occupation the gendarmes had loyally co-operated with the German administration, and in July 1944 had arrested more than 4500 enemies of the state, including 500 Jews, who were held at the concentration camp at Drancy before being shipped to Auschwitz in one of the last trains to leave Paris on 15 August. Like virtually every other organisation in Paris, the police had been infiltrated by Communist and Gaullist agents, who had set up secret movements, of which the largest was the Communist-inspired *Front National de la Police*, which was particularly strong in the working class industrial suburbs of Saint-Denis and Asnieres on the northern outskirts of Paris. The SD and the *Milice* had become increasingly worried about the reliability of the police in these districts if and when the Allies arrived, and the arrival of the news on the morning of 13 August of fighting around Chartres pushed Oberg into action. Without consulting von Choltitz, he sent the SD to disarm the commissariats of Saint-Denis and Asnières, and intern the personnel. Though von Choltitz countermanded the order in the afternoon and the police were released, the damage had been done. At a meeting of the *Front National de la Police* the chairman, Serge Lefranc declared 'We cannot accept such an humiliation! We must give the order for a general strike of the

Although a member of the 2nd Moroccan Division, this private's uniform is typical of the American-supplied clothing worn by the Free French troops in the last years of the war. His boots are French, however, and his rifle is the trusty British .303in (76.2mm) Lee Enfield.

Parisian Police immediately.' Lefranc quickly won the support of the Socialist-influenced *Police et Patrie* and the Gaullist *Honneur de la Police*, and on Tuesday 15 August virtually all 15,000 police went on strike. They kept their arms, wore plain clothes, and picketed their stations, but for the moment avoided any direct confrontation with the Germans.

In the meantime von Choltitz had been making preparations to evacuate his administrative personnel from the city. Archives were being packed, papers from the military government were being burned, and rosters were drawn up for what would be the last trains east. On 15 August he received news of the Allied landings on the Riviera, and on the 17th of the withdrawal of Army Group G from the south and south west to a line from Orléans to Dijon. Whatever happened, it was evident that Paris would soon be on the front line, and on that day von Choltitz gave the order for the withdrawal of non-essential personnel. All day long on every throughfare from the Sorbonne to the Gare de l'Est and the Gare du Nord, hundreds of trucks, loaded cars, ambulances full of wounded on stretchers, were in file or overtaking and crisscrossing one another, or interspersed with long columns of Wehrmacht cyclists. That day too, in the wired-off council housing estate in the working class suburb of Drancy near le

Bourget airport, the commandant of the detention centre, *Hauptsturmführer* Alois Brunner, ordered the deportation of the remaining 51 Jews to Auschwitz. Amongst them was Marcel Bloch-Dassault, who was to survive the camp to re-establish France's aircraft industry after the war.

On the night of 17 August, cinemas, nightclubs, bars and restaurants all over Paris closed down and put up their shutters, in preparation for the fighting they now expected. By removing his administrative personnel, von Choltitz had minimized the likelihood of isolated units providing targets for Resistance attacks. Including the *Milice*, he had about 16,500 men under his command, some light field guns and anti-aircraft guns, and about 30 tanks, mostly obsolete French Renaults. Von Choltitz had no intention of destroying the city; instead he intended to hold major communication routes running from the west to the east through Paris, so that German forces escaping from Normandy could retreat through the city. He placed garrisons at about a dozen choke points on the road system like the Porte Mallot, Porte D' Orléans and the Place d' Italie, and detachments in bunkers watching 30 or so of the major bridges across the Seine, and then concentrated the remainder in an inner core which extended from the Majestic Hotel overlooking the Arc de

RIGHT
General Philippe Francois Leclerc, commander of the French 2nd Armoured Division, chats to one of his tank crews resting beside their camouflaged Sherman after an engagement. Leclerc was killed in an air crash shortly after the war.

ABOVE
The Parisian Liberation Committee, pictured in August 1944. Its members, from left to right, are Maynial-Obadia, Rigal, Leo Hamon, Colonel Rol [Tanguy], Carrel, Demare, Tollet, Mme Lefaucheux, and Marrane.

Triumph down the Champs Elysées to his HQ in the Hôtel Meurice overlooking the Tuileries. Centres of purely symbolic importance which lay outside this area, like the Hôtel de Ville, the Elysée and the Place de la Bastille, he conceded to the Resistance.

Power vacuum

During 18 August, it became clear to Parisians that a curious power vacuum was being created in many parts of the city, as the Germans concentrated on those areas they intended to defend while the police, all in plain clothes, gathered around their precincts. In the complete absence of the Germans or the police, a group of Communist resistants occupied the town hall in Montreuil, a working class suburb in the east of Paris, while others plastered the walls of the city with posters signed by 'elected Communists, both living and dead', calling for an uprising. Alexandre Parodi, de Gaulle's representative in the city, was now sufficiently alarmed to radio London urging 'General Koenig [commander of the FFI] to hasten the occupation of Paris by reason of the situation created by the strike of the police...' That night Parodi persuaded Yves Bayet, head of the Gaullist *Honneur de la Police* that they, too, must make a gesture, lest the Communists take over large parts of the city. At 0700 on 19 August several hundred police, singing the long-forbidden *Marseillaise*, marched into the Préfecture, the police HQ on the Ile de la Cité opposite Notre-Dame,

and as they raised the equally proscribed *Tricolore*, Bayet proclaimed, 'In the name of the Republic and Charles de Gaulle, I take possession of the Préfecture of Police.'

Annoyed that Gaullists had beaten them to the punch, later that morning a crowd of about 2000 largely Communist Resistance members took over the Hôtel de Ville, Colonel Rol occupying the Prefect's office. Meanwhile other groups set about seizing any weapons they could lay their hands on. Two German trucks broken down at Levallois were found to contain four machine guns, 12 submachine guns, 250 pistols and several dozen boxes of ammunition. At Clichy, two German trucks collided at the intersection of the boulevard Victor-Hugo and the boulevard Jean-Jaurès, and nine machine guns, 15 submachine guns, and eight Mauser rifles were captured. Workers at the Hotchkiss factory handed over 20 newly-manufactured submachine guns, and theft from an ill-guarded German depot secured a truckload of stick bombs. By these methods the Resistance steadily increased its firepower.

Shots in the streets

Since the main roads were clear, and German patrols could still pass freely up and down them, von Choltitz felt no need to intervene. The only exception was the Préfecture, from which the police could take pot shots at convoys passing through the Île de la Cité, if they so chose. Early in the afternoon some of

ABOVE
Although the liberation of Paris was not accompanied by heavy fighting, snipers were a constant menace and had to be hunted down. Here, FFI fighters use trees for cover. The photograph is probably posed, as people in the boulevard seem quite unconcerned.

von Choltitz's ancient Renault tanks rolled up to the Préfecture, and after surrounding it, opened fire. Without anti-tank weapons there was little the defenders, now numbering some 500, could do, except act as targets for the mercifully inaccurate fire of the Renault's main armament. German infantry could almost certainly have stormed the building, but von Choltitz could not see the point. Parodi telephoned the order to evacuate, but this was not thought feasible by those trapped in the building.

That evening with intermittant fire echoing from the Île de la Cité, von Choltitz entered into negotiations with Raoul Nordling, for many years Swedish consul general in Paris, who was acting on behalf of the Gaullist and some elements of the Communist resistance. Nordling propsed a ceasefire so that the dead and wounded could be evacuated from the Préfecture, and in the hope that the seizures of buildings and arms then going on throughout the city might not develop into a bloody insurrection. Von Choltitz was reluctant to let the police off the

hook, but as the negotiations continued, he received a telephone call from Hitler, which ordered him specifically to prepare all 60 bridges over the Seine for demolition. The Führer also reminded von Choltitz that 'Paris must not be allowed to fall into the hands of the enemy except as a field of ruins.'

Compromise

Von Choltitz knew that if a full scale insurrection did develop his ability to influence the situation would rapidly diminish. It was conceivable that the SS might be ordered in, as was happening in Warsaw, and that Paris would indeed be reduced to a pile of rubble. Von Choltitz therefore agreed to accept Resistance occupation of public buildings, as long as the Resistance agreed not to attack German-held strongpoints and to allow German troop movements along several major arteries. The German commander also agreed to treat captured Resistants as prisoners of war, rather than executing them as terrorists. The agreement was not for a cease fire but for a controlled uprising, where each side could emerge with minimum casualties and honour satsified.

Unfortunately the agreement had been drawn up without the consent of Roger Villon or Colonel Rol, who furiously denounced it. When Parodi protested, saying the alternative was the destruction of Paris, Villon shouted back, 'So what if Paris is destroyed? We will be destroyed along with it. Better Paris be destroyed like Warsaw than that she live another 1940.' During Sunday 20 August Communist Resistance members, now reasonably well armed, attacked German patrols, in one brutal action hitting four truckloads of German soldiers with Molotov cocktails and then machine-gunning the burning men, an incident which Resistance cameramen captured on film and later supplied to Allied newsreel companies. On Monday 21 August, three new Communist Resistance newspapers appeared – *Le Parisien Libre, Défense de la France* and *Libération* – each carrying the huge banner headline 'Aux Barricades!' And barricades were already being built all over the city. Men, women and children tore up paving stones, cut down trees, tore down railings, turned over buses and carts, then piled the debris in streets and alleyways, though not in the broad boulevards which the Germans had said they would fight to keep clear. Even so, the number of clashes increased, so that by Monday evening bursts of gunfire throughout the city merged, so that they were more or less continuous.

During the next three days Resistance gangs attacked isolated German patrols, sniped at strongpoints, and were themselves fired at, usually with heavier armament. In his memoirs, published six years after the event von Choltitz made light of the fighting. 'From time to time inflammable liquid was thrown from house-tops on to my supporting tanks as they escorted my patrols. It was tiresome, but it did not lose us a single tank...None of my strong-points was ever attacked.' By January 1945, the Ministry of the Interior had received 123,000 letters from people demanding to be incorporated as bona fide members of the Resistance, and there may well have been that number who manned one of the more than 400 barricades, but modern scholarship suggests that only about 3000 civilian Resistance members, assisted from time to time by about 3000 police, actually engaged in gun battles with the Germans. The entire episode quickly became the subject of myth. Hundreds of Parisians, for example, swore that the Germans had employed 150 Tiger tanks in the battle, whereas in reality von Cholititz had but one modern tank – a Panther – which had broken down in the Luxembourg Gardens while withdrawing, had been abandoned, and which was much filmed when it was hit again and again by Molotov cocktails.

Battle casualties

The mood of most Parisians during the days of skirmishing was one of pleasurable excitement, with young men and women re-enacting the heroic struggles of 1871, 1848, 1830 and even 1789. But people did die. During the week of fighting the Resistance – Communist, Gaullist and police – lost 901 killed and 1455 wounded, and they claimed to have killed 2788 Germans and

LEFT
A dejected and apprehensive group of German officers pictured after their capture by French troops during the liberation of Paris. The photograph was taken in the Hôtel Majestic, the former Paris HQ of the Wehrmacht.

wounded another 4911, though the great majority of these had actually been injured in the fighting in Normandy, and had been evacuated to hospitals in Paris. The actual number of Germans killed and wounded in the fighting was probably fewer than 1500. When they compiled their statistics in 1945, the Resistance also claimed that 582 French civilians had been killed in the fighting, but most of these had been collaborators, summarily executed by the Resistance. Some, like captured *Miliciens*, were lucky to escape with a quick execution, while many others were condemned to death on the basis of the flimsiest evidence. In many cases old scores were being settled. Girls who had made themselves unpopular by sleeping with Germans could expect, at the very least, the public humiliation of having their heads shaved. One Resistance member remembered a weeping mother saying, 'My little Josiane, it's too horrible. Her hair has been cut off, monsieur. Poor little Josiane! If she went to bed with Germans, it was because she's seventeen, monsieur, you follow me? But why ever cut off her hair for it? It's a crying shame, monsieur. She's just as willing to go to bed with Americans!'

The slightly Opéra Bouffe style in which the Paris insurrection developed did not mean it did not have the potential to turn into something much worse. By 21 August two delegations had slipped out of Paris and travelled westward along back roads, hoping to make contact with the Americans. One was led by Rolf Nordling, younger brother of Raul, who travelled under German protection, and carried a personal plea from von Choltitz to Eisenhower urging the Supreme Allied commander to begin the occupation of the city as soon as possible. Nordling was to explain that Von Choltitz had deliberately frustrated Hitler's orders to destroy the city, but that if he were to delay much longer the Fuhrer would replace him with someone who would see the orders carried out. The other delegation was led by Major Roger Gallois, Colonel Rol's chief of staff, who carried a demand that the Americans supply arms and ammunition for the Resistance and send troops. As luck would have it, Gallois made contact with the Americans first, and was ushered into the presence of the profoundly anti-Communist General George Patton at his advance headquarters on the morning of 21 August. When told of the Frenchman's mission, Patton was less than sympathetic. 'They started their goddamned insurrection. Now let them finish it!' was his retort to the interpreter.

Patton sent Gallois and his delegation to the headquarters of General Bradley,

commander of 12th Army Group, where they arrived on the morning of 22 August. Here they were met by Brigadier General Edwin L Sibert, Bradley's intelligence officer, who could see much more clearly than Patton the political costs which might be incurred if the Communists succeeded in taking Paris as the result of a bloodbath which American intervention might have mitigated. Meeting with Eisenhower later that day, he found that the supreme commander was already under pressure from de Gaulle and the British. De Gaulle had flown from Algiers to Cherbourg on 21 August, and accompanied by General Koenig, had driven to Granville to persuade Eisenhower to order an Allied advance on Paris. The meeting had been stormy. De Gaulle had impressed upon Eisenhower the danger of a Communist takeover in the city, but the supreme commander had refused to be moved by considerations he felt were purely political. De Gaulle had then threatened to withdraw Leclerc's French 2nd Armoured Division from Eisenhower's command, and order it Paris at his own volition, a threat which Eisenhower had met with the tart observation that, because Leclerc's division was dependent on American logistics 'it couldn't move a mile if I didn't want it to.'

Forces north of Paris

The French 2nd Armoured Division had landed in Normandy on 29 July, since when it had advanced with Patton's Third Army, assisting in the capture of Le Mans and Alençon. With 16,000 men and 2000 vehicles, it was the only substantial Fighting French formation in northern France. Its commander, Lieutenant General Philippe Leclerc, was in fact the Viscount Philippe de Hauteclocque, who had thrown his lot in with de Gaulle in 1940. Like de Gaulle, Leclerc was an ardent French patriot, who hated the Vichyites and the Communists in about equal measure, and had no desire to enter Paris at the behest of a revolutionary committee. Leclerc was also aware that the Americans did not intend an early occupation of Paris, and so he had been taking steps to circumvent them. His men had been hoarding supplies; they had deliberately failed to report vehicle losses, so that the gasoline ration would not be cut. In addition, his men had 'borrowed' extra supplies in nighttime visits to American depots. Acting on his own volition, Leclerc had already sent a strong reconnaissance patrol towards the capital,

intending to feed reinforcements to it when it encountered the Germans, but it had been stopped and turned back by Bradley as it passed through Chartres.

In the meantime, pressure continued to grow on Eisenhower to reverse his policy. On 22 August de Gaulle sent him a letter delivered personally by General Alphonse Juin, now chief of staff of French national defence, who had caused Eisenhower considerable difficulties in North Africa. De Gaulle warned that he was about to withdraw Leclerc's armoured division from American command and order it to Paris, and that if Eisenhower tried to block its progress the supreme commander would have to accept full responsibility if Paris were to be destroyed. This letter had considerable force. Three weeks earlier, as Soviet armies reached the eastern bank of the Vistula opposite Warsaw, the anti-Communist Polish Home Army had risen up and seized the city, only to discover that the Soviets had no intention of coming to help them. By 22 August much of Warsaw was in ruins, as SS divisions supported by siege artillery systematically destroyed the city, district by district. The parallel between the Soviet attitude to Warsaw and his own attitude to Paris was obvious, and Eisenhower scribbled in the margin of de Gaulle's letter, 'It looks now as if we'd be compelled to go to Paris.' Still he did not give the order, and he only cracked when the following morning the BBC, acting on information received from the British Special Intelligence Service operating in Paris, broadcast the news that large parts of the French capital had been liberated by the Resistance which was now

ABOVE
General de Gaulle returns to Paris in triumph. In 1940, during the latter stages of the Battle of France, de Gaulle had commanded the French 4th Armoured Division, which fought with great gallantry against hopeless odds. His arrival in the city shortly after its liberation enabled him to consolidate his position in French politics.

ABOVE

*De Gaulle on his march
towards the Place de la
Concorde, before driving to
mass in Notre Dame. His
calmness whilst shots were
fired impressed observers.
Although Vichy supporters
and German troops were
still at large in the city, it is
now thought that the
Communists were trying to
embarrass de Gaulle.*

under heavy German counter-attack. Indeed, BBC executives later claimed they had 'shamed' Eisenhower into taking action.

Arrival in Paris

On 23 August Leclerc's 2nd Armoured division, closely followed by US 4th Division, raced for Paris, the urgency of its mission now underlined by the belated arrival of Rolf Nordling's mission at Bradley's HQ with the news that all that stood between Paris and systematic destruction was von Choltitz. By late afternoon the division was rolling into Rambouillet only 20 miles south west of Versailles. Meeting that night in the magnificent Chateau de Rambouillet, which de Gaulle had commandeered as his advance HQ, the leader of the Free French and Leclerc pondered the alarming intelligence that a German battlegroup of some 60 tanks lay directly to the north east. Without informing the Americans, de Gaulle and Leclerc decided to send 2nd Armoured 17 miles to the east, and then strike due north, approaching Paris from the south west in three mutually supporting columns.

It was a wet, miserable day. German roadblocks covered by 88mm anti-tank guns slowed down the advance, but equally serious were the cheering crowds, who swarmed

around 2nd. Armoured as it passed through each village and town. At 17.30 Leclerc was still 10 miles from Paris, and he knew that he could not be in the city for at least another twelve hours. He therefore ordered a detachment of three Shermans and six half-tracks commanded by Captain Raymond Dronne, who knew the area well, to take back roads around the German defences and get to the Île de la Cité with the news that help was only a few hours away.

It took Dronne only two hours to drive into central Paris and reach the Préfecture, where an excited Parodi broadcast on a newly-established radio station 'I have beside me a French captain who has just entered Paris, the first. He has a red face, is dirty and unshaven, and yet one wants to embrace him.' At exactly the same time in the Hôtel Meurice, von Choltitz heard a peal of bells from Notre Dame. He immediately phoned Army Group HQ and, holding the telephone to the window, let General Speidel listen to the bells, informing him that they heralded the arrival of a Franco-American Army. Von Choltitz concluded by saying '...my dear Speidel, there is nothing left for me to do but to say good-bye to you. Look after and protect my wife at Baden-Baden, and my children too.'

Shortly after 0800 Leclerc's advance guard reached the Porte d'Italie. An American radio correspondent described the scene: 'From where I am speaking to you I can hear the explosions of shells and the spatter of machine-guns: Boche machine-guns, machine-guns of the regular army, and the machine-guns of the FFI.' A British correspondent reported that 'shooting continues in the streets of Paris, while Allied troops arriving in greater numbers fight side by side with the FFI and the people of Paris. French and Allied flags are appearing at all windows and everyone is singing the *Marseillaise*.' Later in the day, as fire began to diminish, the BBC's Howard Marshall described how 'all along the French advance route soldiers and people are embracing one another, women and children wave French and Allied flags, shouting 'Vive la France! Vive de Gaulle!' The Australian correspondent Chester Wilmot, who was later to write the definitive history of the campaign, summarised the 2nd Division's progress for British listeners. 'From the Porte d'Italie to the Île de la Cité, Leclerc's units have had a delirious welcome. Men, women and children literally rushed the tanks shouting with joy –

joy which for four years and two months had been supressed.' For the Frenchmen of Leclerc's division, and for the Americans who were following them, this was to be the finest day of their lives.

Official surrender

At 1500, as Leclerc sat down for a belated lunch at the Préfecture, 20 uniformed gendarmes arrived from the Hôtel Meurice with von Choltitz, who had just surrendered to them. After an exchange of military courtesies, a document for the capitulation of German forces in Paris was negotiated, but there were then some difficulties over the signing, not between Leclerc and von Choltitz, but between Leclerc and Colonel Rol, who insisted he should also sign the document as head of the Paris Resistance. Leclerc initially refused, but under pressure from the entire Resistance committee, relented, and even allowed Rol's name to appear above his own. When he arrived in Paris an hour later, and learned that a Communist's name had appeared on the surrender document, de Gaulle flew into a rage, demanded Rol's name be expunged, and confided to Leclerc that the

LEFT
General de Gaulle and General Leclerc in the Préfecture. Leclerc had been determined to enter Paris as quickly as possible; an ardent patriot, the idea of being invited in by a communist-dominated revolutionary committee was abhorrent to him.

pressure he had been subjected to 'proceeds from an unacceptable tendency'.

Amidst all the scenes of rejoicing, de Gaulle was walking a political tightrope. Vichyite factions had still not given up hope, and a few minutes before the general was due at the Hôtel de Ville, Leclerc's military police discovered two *Milicien* waiting to assassinate de Gaulle. As they were led away for execution, one of them, who had already murdered Georges Mandel, spat defiance. 'We'll get you all the same: in a fortnight the *Milice* will be back and then you'll be for it.' De Gaulle planned to walk through the city the following day, Saturday 26 August, to attend a mass at Notre Dame, but once more Vichy reared its ugly head. De Gaulle refused to allow Suhard, the archbishop, or Beaussart, his assistant, to officiate at the mass. In his memoirs de Gaulle enumerated the crimes of the Catholic establishment in Paris, from receiving Pétain to open collaboration with the worst excesses of the Nazis, including the deportation of French Jews to death camps, but added, with an irony that fairly withered, that the Catholic establishment was so unworldy that perhaps it had all escaped their attention. In a passage icy with contempt, de

Gaulle concluded that 'the Cardinal's [Suhard] piety and charity are so eminent that they leave but little place in his mind for the appreciation of the temporal.' Excessive piety having disqualified the likes of Suhard and Beaussart from officiating at Notre Dame, de Gaulle gave the job to Father Huchet, the much decorated chaplain of Leclerc's division.

De Gaulle's moment of triumph

Having signalled to Vichyite churchmen that they would have no role in the new France if he could help it, de Gaulle still faced the problem of the Communists. On the afternoon of 26 August the entire length of the Champs Elysées was crammed with crowds estimated at more than two million. At 1500 de Gaulle arrived at the Arc de Triomphe, placed a floral Cross of Lorraine on the grave, and then preceded by four tanks, Leclerc's soldiers and the police, who linked arms from one side of the avenue to the other, walked down the Champs Elysées to the Place de la Concorde, where he entered a car for the short journey to Notre Dame. A few shots rang out, people hid behind tanks or flung themselves to the ground, but as de Gaulle drove off, the firing died down and after a few

BELOW
French troops and FFI, with the support of an armoured car, advancing on the Chamber of Deputies in the final stages of the liberation of Paris. Some 500 Germans had barricaded themselves inside the Chamber, and had to be forced to surrender.

LEFT
General de Gaulle pins the Cross of Liberation to the standard of the 2e RCP. This unit was a special forces' parachute regimental combat team, and was roughly the equivalent of the British Special Air Service.

minutes the excitement was over. At 16.15 de Gaulle arrived at Notre Dame, where the transcript of CBS's Robert Reid's live broadcast still conveys the emotions of the moment with breathless excitement:

'And now here comes General de Gaulle. The general's now turned to face the square, and this huge crowd of Parisians [machine gun fire]. He's being presented to people [machine-gun fire]. He's being received [shouts of crowd – shots] even while the general is marching [sudden sharp outburst of continued fire] – even while the general is marching into the cathedral...[Break on record]...Well, that was one of the most dramatic scenes I've ever seen. Just as General de Gaulle was about to enter the cathedral of Notre Dame, firing started all over the place.'

With firing now breaking out inside the cathedral, de Gaulle continued to walk calmly and unhurriedly up the nave to where a chair had been set for him in the north transept. The firing continued but did not prevent the congregation singing the Magnificat, but it was thought best to omit the Te Deum. Reid then described de Gaulle's departure. 'I saw him marching down the aisle, this very tall upright figure, with his chin well in the air, his shoulders flung right back. There were battles – there were bangs, flashes all around him, and yet he seemed to have an absolutely charmed life as he walked down the aisle towards the door, because nothing touched him, and he never hesitated for one moment.'

The official line was that the *Milice* and German 'stay-behind' units had been responsible, but de Gaulle was certain that it had been the Communists. They had hoped not to kill de Gaulle, but to humiliate him by forcing him to take cover in public. They failed spectacularly and instead handed de Gaulle a political victory. He moved quickly to capitalise on their discomfiture. Bypassing the American chain of command, De Gaulle asked Eisenhower to back him with a show of force. American high command still had difficulties reconciling political and military objectives, but agreed that, as the US 28th Division was then moving around Paris, it might just as well march directly through the city. Thus, on 29 August, Americans marched down the Champs-Elysées in serried ranks, cheered by thousands of Parisians. Girls threw flowers, rushed into the lines to embrace and kiss the men, and thrust bottles of champagne into their packs. 'It was the day the war should have ended', one recalled some years later. But that evening they were back in action to the east of Paris, and ahead of them lay another eight months of hard campaigning.

CHAPTER SEVEN

ARNHEM

After the rapid advances of August and early September, the Allies looked for a surprise stroke to enable them to move rapidly into the heart of Germany itself: Operation Market Garden.

For the Allies, August 1944 was an extraordinary month. It had begun with the front in Normandy more or less where it had been since mid-June, and it ended with the British, Canadian and American armies well beyond the Seine, with de Gaulle in Paris, and with a Franco-American army advancing up the Rhône. Elements of Patton's Third Army had reached the Seine at Mantes-Gassicourt, south-east of Paris, on 18 August and had launched an attack from bridgeheads on the east bank of the river two days later. Farther south and east, the advance guard of Patton's 4th Armoured Division reached the outskirts of the still heavily defended town of Troyes on the left bank of the Seine on 25 August. The advance-guard commander, Colonel Bruce C. Clarke, brought his armour up north of Troyes, where a gully gave them cover, at about 2750m (3000 yards) from the town. Clarke lined up one medium tank company, backed it with two mechanised infantry companies, and charged with all guns blazing. He took the town without losing a man or a vehicle. On 28 August Clarke sped 80km (50 miles) from Troyes to Vitry-le-François without difficulty, crossed the Marne and then swung north along the east bank to take Châlons-sur-Marne at midday on 29 August. The 4th Armoured then turned south-east from Châlons and by the morning of 31 August in heavy rain was driving towards the Meuse.

The Meuse crossed

A light company in advance of the main body surprised enemy outposts at Commercy, neutralised artillery emplacements by shooting the gun crews before they could break open their ammunition, and seized the bridge across the Meuse intact. It then took possession of the high ground immediately to the east in the vicinity of St Mihiel, where Patton had fought and been severely wounded in World War I. Meanwhile, the divisions of Patton's XX Corps drove east from Châlons-sur-Marne towards Verdun, 112km (70 miles) away. The difficult terrain of the Argonne Forest slowed the advance, but German attempts to blow the Meuse River bridge at Verdun were foiled by the French Resistance. By noon on 31 August, tanks of the American advance guard were in town and across the river, and on 1 September, XX Corps was across the Meuse in strength. Patton's forward units were now exactly half-way between the Seine and the Rhine, but the country was becoming more difficult – before them lay the ridges of Lorraine, running north–south like the glacis of a fortress, crowned by the strong defences of Metz, and beyond these lay the fortifications of the Siegfried Line.

OPPOSITE
British troops entering Brussels on 3 September 1944. They received a tumultuous welcome. It was in Brussels, five days later, that Generals Montgomery and Eisenhower planned the airborne drops on the Rhine crossings.

Meanwhile the British, the Canadians and the US First Army had been advancing north-east to the lower reaches of the Seine between Paris and Rouen – the wide estuary and rapid tidal race made the river unbridgeable much above Rouen. A regiment of the US 79th Division reached Mantes-Gassicourt on 19 August and, finding the Germans gone, crossed the Seine that night in single file using an undamaged weir in torrential rain. Farther downstream, the spearhead of British Second Army, the 43rd (Wessex) Division, reached the forest of Breteuil near Vernon on the night of 24 August. The following evening, the artillery of British XXX Corps opened up on enemy positions on the east bank, with 15 minutes of high explosive rounds followed by smoke shells. Simultaneously, British troops began to cross the river in storm boats, but they ran into heavy fire, and seven were soon lost. The British tried again after dark and before dawn had managed to get a battalion and a half across. They fought off a number of enemy counter-attacks while engineers lashed together a pontoon bridge and rafted across armoured cars, anti-tank guns and some tanks. By 28 August, 11th Armoured Division was across, followed by the Guards Armoured Division on the 29th. The Canadian 4th Division crossed farther downstream at Elbeuf

between 27 and 28 August. They suffered 600 casualties against stiff opposition, but, supported by some 500 light and medium bombers, were able to exploit north-east on 29 August.

Troops sweep ahead

With the Seine crossed, Twenty-First Army Group now advanced rapidly, with First Canadian Army fanning out to capture le Havre and Dieppe and to clear the coastal belt north to Bruges. British troops, spearheaded by 11th Armoured Division, tore through the wide, hedgeless fields which lay between the Seine and the Somme, reaching Gisors, some 32km (20 miles) north-east of the Seine, by the evening of 29 August. The following day was an epic in the history of British armour. Advancing rapidly against crumbling opposition, 11th Armoured reached Beauvais by 1700 hours and then drove through the night in pouring rain to reach the centre of Amiens at 0600 hours, driving alongside columns of retreating Germans who did not realise who they were. Shortly after 0800 hours the British captured the tactical headquarters of German Seventh Army, along with a surprised and very annoyed General Heinrich Hans Eberbach, who still thought the British somewhere near the Seine, and a German field bakery which

RIGHT
Exercising his flair for self-publicity to the full, General George S. Patton, commanding the US Third Army, becomes the first US commander to cross the Seine on 22 August 1944. The next day, the American forces resumed their headlong advance towards the German border.

provided 11th Armoured's spearheads with breakfast. At noon the next day, 1 September, the Guards Armoured Division passed over Vimy Ridge north of Arras, and, on 2 September, British tanks crossed into Belgium. A signals officer, finding the Belgian telephone network largely intact, phoned the Brussels exchange and was told that the Germans were pulling out. Spearheaded by the armoured cars of the Household Cavalry, the Guards Division raced through southern Belgium on the glorious late-summer day of 3 September, the fifth anniversary of Britain's declaration of war in 1939, and entered Brussels in the early evening. Chester Wilmot, who had been in Paris, reported that the welcome in Brussels '...was the wildest of all. There had been Germans in the streets only an hour before, and not a flag had been in sight; but by the time we arrived every building was plastered with flags and streamers. The streets were decked with banners – "Welcome to our liberators", "Welcome to our Allies", "Through Brussels to Berlin", they said, "through Belgium to victory". Thousands of women and children had made themselves special dresses in the Belgian colours – such as red skirts, yellow blouses, and black scarves or bandannas.'

In the last two weeks of August 1944, the British and American armies covered dis-

tances which outstripped even those of the spectacular German blitzkrieg of May–June 1940. Some units had covered about 800km (500 miles) and had taken thousands of prisoners. They had been fêted by deliriously happy civilians in Paris or Brussels. German losses had been catastrophic – about 450,000 in the fighting in France, which, when added to the 900,000 who had been lost in Belorussia in June and July, came to an astonishing 1.35 million. It was clear, too, that the Third Reich was in the midst of a political crisis, with Nazi loyalists conducting a major purge of the Wehrmacht's officer corps.

'Victory disease'

Back in the summer of 1940, following its own spectacular victory over France and the British Expeditionary Force, the Wehrmacht had suffered what was now known in Berlin as the 'victory disease', a heady, semi–intoxicated feeling that the war was as good as over, and that all things were possible. Now it was the Allies who succumbed to the victory disease. On 23 August SHAEF intelligence announced that 'two-and-a-half months of bitter fighting, culminating for the Germans in a bloodbath big enough even for their extravagant tastes, have brought the end of the war within sight, almost within reach.' The US army chief of staff, General George

ABOVE
German vehicles burning on the road to Brussels. The Allied advance was constantly hampered by a shortage of fuel and supplies as the speed of movement by the front line forces caused their lines of communication to become overstretched.

*A Coldstream Guardsman,
armed with a Bren light
machine gun, covers a street
in Arras. In May 1940,
Arras was the scene of a
famous British counter-
attack that came close to
disrupting the drive towards
the French coast by
Rommel's panzers. Now the
Bristish tanks were driving
the retreating Germans back
at an even faster rate.*

Marshall, informed senior Allied commanders that the cessations of hostilities with Germany could occur at any time, but would 'most probably extend over a period between September 1 and November 1 1944'. Eisenhower informed the combined chiefs that he might have to face the occupation of Germany much sooner than he had expected, and on 2 September his chief of staff, Major General Bedell Smith, announced to a press conference that, 'militarily the war in Europe is won'. Even the normally level-headed chief of the imperial general staff, General Alan Brooke, succumbed to the victory disease, writing to General 'Jumbo' Wilson, the enormously fat Allied supreme commander in the Mediterranean, 'It has become evident that the Boche is beat on all fronts.'

In-fighting for glory

In this heady atmosphere, the Anglo-American alliance began to fall to pieces, as generals who had thus far cooperated (sometimes with an ill grace) against a common enemy, began to vie with each other for the laurels of victory. In the United States it was an election year, and it was becoming increasingly important politically for Roosevelt's establishment to ensure that credit for the impending victory was seen to go to an American. On 14 August Eisenhower brought US Third and First Armies into a new army group, to be known as Twelfth Army Group, which he placed under the command of General Omar Bradley. The British press interpreted this new arrangement as a demotion for Montgomery, an impression reinforced by the US serviceman's paper, *Stars and Stripes*, which announced the news on 16 August with the headline 'Bradley Heads Army Group. Status Equal to Monty'. With the British and American press attacking each others' generals, Marshall wrote to Eisenhower on 17 August that '...Stimson [US Secretary for War] and I and apparently all Americans are strongly of the opinion that the time has come for you to assume direct command of the American contingent because reaction to British criticism has been so strong by USA journalists that it could become an important factor in the coming Congressional Elections. The astonishing success has produced emphatic expressions of confidence in you and Bradley, but this has cast a damper on the public enthusiasm.'

Stung by the widespread assumption in both the American and British press that he had been little more than Montgomery's figurehead, Eisenhower replied on 19 August that though Montgomery coordinated the land battle, he always operated 'under plans of campaign approved by me. There has been no major move made of which I have not been cognizant or which has been contrary to the general purposes I have outlined.' Eisenhower urged Marshall to issue a press release making clear to the American public that 'no major effort takes place in this theater by ground, sea or air except with my approval and that no one in this Allied command presumes to question my supreme authority and responsibility for the whole campaign.'

Unfortunately, this was not the way Montgomery saw the relationship. On 17 August Montgomery flew to see Bradley and, after lengthy discussion, was convinced that the American agreed with his conception of future operations – that, after crossing the Seine, Twenty-First and Twelfth Army Groups should be kept together under Montgomery's

overall command and advance in a single thrust north of the Ardennes towards the Ruhr. At 0830 hours the following morning, Montgomery sent a telegram to General Alan Brooke which clearly usurped the function of the supreme commander: 'Have been thinking ahead about future plans but have NOT yet discussed subject with IKE. My views as follows. After crossing SEINE 12 and 21 Army Groups should keep together as a solid mass of some 40 divisions which would be so strong that it need fear nothing. The force should move northwards. 21 Army Group should be on the western flank and should clear the Channel coast and the PAS DE CALAIS and WEST FLANDERS and secure ANTWERP. The American armies should move with the right flank on the ARDENNES directed on BRUSSELS, AACHEN and COLOGNE.... BRADLEY

Cheering crowds surround British tanks as the Allies enter Brussels. British vehicles bore a white 'American' star for identification purposes, but any doubts as to the nationality of the liberating troops were soon dispelled.

agrees entirely with the above conception. Would be glad to know if you agree generally. When I have got reply will discuss matter with IKE.' Brooke, who was about to leave for Italy, sent a brief acknowledgement, 'I entirely agree with your plan contained in [telegram] of 18 August.'

While Montgomery was devising a grand strategy which would combine the two Allied army groups effectively under his own command, meaning that he would be seen to have played the dominant role in the impending defeat of Nazi Germany, Bradley had been visiting Patton. Unsurprisingly, the two Americans were devising a different strategy. It was one in which three American corps would drive east towards the Rhine near Karlsruhe, Mannheim and Wiesbaden. Bradley and Patton had both studied the works of the German military philosopher Carl von Clausewitz, and both understood that victory could be achieved not merely through the physical destruction of the enemy, but also through the destruction of the enemy's will.

Both men now believed that the 'violation of the German border' would have a 'tremendous psychological effect' on the German people and the Nazi apparatus, an effect which might produce a collapse in Germany like that of November 1918. Bradley had discussed this informally with Eisenhower before he had met with Montgomery, and thought he had the supreme commander's support.

On 19 August Eisenhower sent a memorandum to both Montgomery and Bradley, announcing that he would shortly take over personal control of the land battle. He outlined a plan of campaign which would send Twenty-First Army Group northeast, towards Antwerp and the Ruhr, while Twelfth Army Group would head straight east from Paris to Metz. This, in essence, was the 'Broad Front' strategy. By allowing the two army groups to advance on divergent axes, it violated the basic military principle of concentration of force, but as it was widely believed that the Germans were already beaten, this did not matter terribly much. Of much more immediate importance was the fact that a broad front would ensure that American commanders as well as British would be seen as having been instrumental in the defeat of Germany.

Political naïveté

Unfortunately, Montgomery lacked both the education and imagination to empathise with his American allies' obsession with their political process. The last general election in Britain had taken place in 1935, and it was anybody's guess as to when the next one might be. Believing he had the support not just of the British political establishment, but also of Bradley, on 20 August he sent his chief of staff, Major General Freddie de Guingand, to Eisenhower with a counterblast. Montgomery asserted that the force must operate as one whole. In addition, 'single control and direction of land operations is vital for success. This is a whole-time job for one man. The great victory in NW France has been won by personal command. Only in this way will future victories be won.... To change the system of command now, after having won a great victory, would be to prolong the war.' When de Guingand reported back that Eisenhower was refusing to budge, Montgomery flew to see Bradley at dawn on 23 August, to find out if he still had the American's support. To his consternation, he discovered that he had taken too much for

After liberating Brussels, the British Second Army pushed on as fast as possible to take Antwerp, the speed of the advance taking the German garrison by surprise. Here, German prisoners are being marched off to a transit camp.

British armour crossing the Albert Canal near Beeringen by means of a prefabricated Bailey bridge on 7 September 1944. Belgian refugees are also making use of the bridge to escape from the area of the front line.

granted. Bradley disagreed with both Eisenhower's broad front, and Montgomery's narrow thrust to the north-east. Instead, after talking with Patton, he now favoured making the major Allied drive south of the Ardennes. He had already promised Patton two extra divisions for a push to the Siegfried Line, and he now told Montgomery that US First and Third Armies ought to advance through the middle of France to the River Saar, and once over it, to the Rhine near Frankfurt.

Now faced with the prospect of Twenty-First Army Group being relegated to minor mopping-up operations, Montgomery invited Eisenhower to lunch at his tactical headquarters at Condé on the following day, 23 August. Accompanied by Bedell Smith, Eisenhower drove over from Granville, but found Montgomery far from a compliant supplicant. Cold with fury, Montgomery refused to admit Bedell Smith to his caravan, though his own chief of staff, de Guingand, was present throughout the discussions. Standing before his map, his feet spread, hands behind his back, Montgomery addressed Eisenhower, as though he were a Sandhurst or West Point cadet, on the importance of the separation of the strategic and operational levels of command, but found that Eisenhower would not – indeed could not – give ground. The supreme commander explained that the American public were clamouring for the land battle to be com-

manded by an American general, and that he had been ordered by General Marshall to take control as of 1 September. Having refused to give way on command, Eisenhower proved more compliant on the subject of the broad versus narrow front. After about an hour of discussion he agreed to give Montgomery control of the Allied strategic reserve, the newly-formed Allied Airborne Army, authority to effect operational coordination between the right flank of Twenty-First Army Group and Bradley's left flank, in effect US First Army, and to give Twenty-First Army Group priority in supplies.

Eisenhower in the middle

Having given way to Montgomery, Eisenhower was immediately assailed by an irate Bradley and a furious Patton. Meeting to coordinate their strategy, Patton argued that the southern advance was much more suitable for armour than the waterlogged country to the north, and suggested to Bradley that they both threaten to resign, as 'in such a show-down we would win, as Ike would not dare to relieve us.' Bradley would not go so far, but lobbied intensively for several days, and was rewarded on 29 August with yet another shift in policy. Eisenhower decreed that instead of operational control of US First Army, Montgomery was only authorised to effect through Bradley any necessary coordination between his own forces and First Army. Three

ABOVE
*Field Marshal Bernard
Montgomery and
Lieutenant General Brian
Horrocks, commander of
the British XXX Corps.
XXX Corps was the land-
bound spearhead of Market
Garden, intended to reach
the paratroopers and other
airborne forces before the
Germans could recapture
the bridges.*

days later, when Eisenhower assumed land command, Montgomery was promoted to Field Marshal, meaning he technically out-ranked the supreme commander. Patton's comment, in a letter to his wife, was suitably pithy: 'The Field Marshal thing made us sick, that is Bradley and me.'

Eisenhower now had the worst of all possible worlds. In his attempts to accommodate Montgomery and Twenty-First Army Group, and Bradley, Patton and Twelfth Army Group, he had attempted to remain neutral by adopt-ing a broad-front strategy, but under pressure had veered first one way, then another and then back again. Eisenhower knew that the only way to placate all interests was to opt for the broad front, but by late August it was clear that Allied logistics were in a state of crisis, which could only get worse. One of the abid-ing images of the Anglo-American landings was of immense quantities of stores being landed, either through the surviving Mulberry harbour or across the wide, sandy Norman beaches, and it is true that depots of

immense size had been constructed, which by the end of July had covered about half of the all the territory the Allies had then captured. Spectacular though the effort had been, by the beginning of September only about half of the 175 ships or so which had arrived off Normandy during the month of August had been unloaded, and 80 ships were at anchor off the coast being used as floating ware-houses. But the problem was not so much lack of supplies but the inability to push the supplies forward as Twelfth and Twenty-First Army Groups advanced. With the rail system throughout northern France effectively destroyed, the only means of moving bulk supplies was by road. The Allies' chief logisti-cian, General J. C. H. Lee, devised a one-way loop highway between St Lo and Chartres, with every available truck using it around the clock. The convoys, named the Red Ball Express after railroad slang for fast freight, began running on 25 August, and on 29 August 5958 trucks delivered 12,242 tons of supplies. That proved to be exceptional. Soon breakdowns (by the end of September more than 8000 American trucks had been written off) reduced the daily lift to an average of 7000 tons per day. The British inaugurated the less well-known Red Lion Express at the same time, but this too was plagued by breakdowns, particularly when 1400 British 3-ton trucks had to be removed from service because of a piston design defect. Above all else, the Allied armies needed fuel, but by the beginning of September one half of the 22 million jerrycans shipped to France had disappeared, severely limiting the capacity of both Red Ball and Red Lion to move petrol, oil and lubricants. In addition, the Red Ball Express alone consumed 1.4 million litres (300,000 gallons) of fuel every day, nearly as much as a field army.

Corruption rampant

The Allied media machine at the time made heroes of the logisticians, but the reality was very different. Lee was incompetent and corrupt, but protected from dismissal by highly placed friends in Washington. On 26 August, for example, he diverted transport resources from supplying Patton's and Hodges's advanc-

ing tanks to moving his hugely overstaffed headquarters of 8000 officers and 21,000 men to newly liberated Paris, where his organisation took over 296 hotels. At the same time, he gave priority to moving thousands of tons of prefabricated housing forward for the construction of depots, and then demanded 13 infantry battalions to protect them from black marketeers. In fact, the entire logistic apparatus from Lee on down was engaged in an enormous web of corruption. Lee set the tone by regularly despatching a bomber to North Africa to fly in oranges for his breakfast. Paris acted as an immense black hole into which a sizeable proportion of American supplies and logistic manpower (it was estimated that about 10 per cent of his command deserted and set up in business in the city) disappeared. It was good news for Parisians in general, who had cigarettes, petrol and food in quantities they had not enjoyed since 1939, and for Parisian women in particular, who suddenly enjoyed an abundance of silk and nylon, unfortunately at the expense of American airborne-forces reserve parachutes.

All front-line units began to resent logisticians, but none more so than the soldiers of

BELOW
Lieutenant General Lewis H. Brereton, commanding the 1st Allied Airborne Army, presents the American DFC to an officer of one of his troop carrier wings. Waco Hadrian gliders are lined up in the background.

Patton's Third Army, who waged a virtual war on their own lines of communication. Patton's logistics officer, Colonel Walter J. 'Maud' Muller, conducted reconnaissance flights to locate Lee's dumps, and would then raid them at night. Patton not only condoned this activity but may well have abetted it – a story made the rounds that he had stood at an intersection and ordered Red Ball trucks scheduled for First Army diverted to Third Army. Third Army logisticians certainly passed themselves off as belonging to First Army when drawing supplies, while Muller's men did a roaring business exchanging captured German helmets, rifles, bayonets and knives for petrol in the rear areas. Muller also forgot to report captured German stocks, which he used to augment Third Army's stocks, even though the synthetic Wehrmacht fuel fouled American engines. On two occasion 455,000 litres (100,000 gallons) of petrol were captured, which enabled Third Army to drive as far as the Marne and later to the Meuse.

Logistic muddle

After the war, the antics of American logisticians inspired the creation of a host of comic characters in written fiction and television, like Milo Mindebender and Ernie Bilko, but at the time the result was chaos. For very good political reasons, Eisenhower favoured a broad front, but by early September it was becoming increasingly clear that until the logistic mess was cleared up there would scarcely be enough to support a single thrust. On 2 September Eisenhower went to Versailles to see Bradley, Hodges and Patton, and 'to give Patton hell because he is stretching his line too far and therefore making supply difficulties'. Patton recorded in his diary that, 'Ike was very pontifical and quoted Clausewitz to us, who have commanded larger forces than C ever heard of.' The meeting went on for several hours and Patton managed to convince Eisenhower that he had patrols as far east as Metz, and if he were allowed to retain his regular allotment of fuel 'we could push on to the German frontier and rupture that Goddamn Siegfried Line.' By the time the meeting ended Eisenhower had given Patton permission to attack towards Mannheim and Frankfurt, and had agreed to Bradley's demand that First Army stay on Patton's left, south of the Ardennes. In an office memorandum dated 5 September Eisenhower summarised the Chartres meeting, concluding. 'The defeat of the German armies is now complete and the only thing

BELOW

Paratroops of the US 82nd Airborne Division wait for the take-off signal on board a C-47 transport aircraft at Cottesmore on 17 September 1944. Cottesmore was the base of the USAAF's 316th Troop Carrier Group.

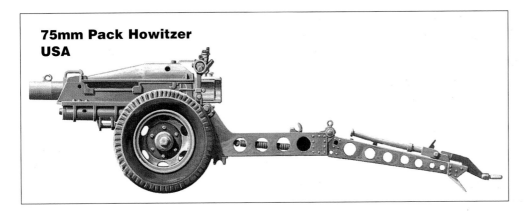

75mm Pack Howitzer USA

LEFT
The 75mm (2.95in) Pack Howitzer M1A1 was an extremely successful US design used throughout World War II in all theatres. Examples were used by the airborne forces involved in Operation Market Garden.

needed to realise the conception is speed.... I deem it important to get Patton moving once again so that we may be fully prepared to carry out the original conception for the final stages of this campaign.'

Montgomery's plan

At exactly the same time Montgomery was planning to advance on Wesel and Arnhem, using airborne forces to seize the Rhine bridges for his armour. His chief planner, Brigadier Charles Richardson, was already thinking in terms of a rapid advance to Osnabruck, which would serve as a convenient site for Twenty-First Army's tactical headquarters, although he fully expected Germany to have surrendered before then. Montgomery had already confided to the commander of the Imperial General Staff that he expected to be in Berlin in two to three weeks. The news that Eisenhower had once again changed his mind at Chartres incensed the British general, who on 7 September rushed off a memorandum urging that all available logistic support be diverted to him, so that he could get a thrust to Berlin. Montgomery added, 'it is very difficult to explain things in a message like this. Would it be possible for you to come and see me?' Eisenhower, who had twisted his leg severely as a result of a forced landing while flying back from the Chartres conference on 2 September, flew to Brussels on 10 September in his personal transport aircraft, a B-25 bomber. Unable to climb out of the aircraft and in considerable pain, Eisenhower asked Montgomery to climb aboard. In the cramped confines of the crew compartment the exchange soon became angry, Montgomery implying that it was Patton and not Eisenhower who was really running the war. Eisenhower at last stood up to Montgomery. Leaning forward, he placed his

ABOVE
Waco Hadrian gliders landing near Zon. The task of the US 101st Airborne Division in this area was to capture vital bridges over the Wilhelmina Canal, the Dommel river and the Aa river. The paras were then to advance on Eindhoven.

hand on Montgomery's knee, and said, 'Steady, Monty! You can't speak to me like that. I'm your boss.'

The discussions went on for another hour, the emotions of both men gradually subsiding. Slowly, Eisenhower became mesmerised by the sheer daring of the plan Montgomery was unfolding, and of the glittering prizes which seemed in prospect. Using much the same reasoning as Patton and Bradley, the normally cautious Montgomery argued that a single, rapier-like thrust towards Berlin could precipitate a collapse of German will like that which had occurred in 1918. This could be achieved by using First Allied Airborne Army to seize a 100km (60-mile) corridor from the Belgian frontier to the lower Rhine at Arnhem, down which would rush Twenty-First Army Group, spearheaded by XXX Corps. Even if Germany did not collapse, the

RIGHT
German troops captured during the Allied advance into Holland, September 1944. This photograph was taken on 19 September, while the British paratroops fighting desperately at Arnhem were still waiting to be relieved by XXX Corps.

Allies would have outflanked the Siegfried Line and secured a bridgehead across the Rhine. An additional reason had been received that very morning by top-secret telegram from the commander of the imperial general staff. Forty-eight hours earlier the long-expected V2 attack on London had begun. The Germans were firing the rockets from mobile launchers in the suburbs of the Hague, and, apart from employing Bomber Command to obliterate the Dutch city, the only hope of preventing further attacks was for Twenty-First Army Group to cut Holland off from Germany. This objective could be accomplished, even if the operation did not win the war by itself. Eisenhower recalled that he had become enthralled with the sheer audacity of the plan – he could not have been more surprised if the ascetic, teetotal Montgomery had turned up roaring drunk. The operation had been code-named Market Garden, with 'Market' denoting the airborne component and 'Garden' the ground-force element, and the two commanders now agreed it would take place on Sunday 17 September.

News that the operation had been approved was received with deep scepticism at Allied First Airborne Army headquarters at Ascot. Since D-Day, airborne forces had been placed on full alert 17 times, and on each occasion the operation had been cancelled. As recently as 2 September a drop by three divisions near Lille and Courtrai, for which British Second Army halted its own advance, had been called off with paratroops actually sitting in the transports while they taxied for take-off, because Bradley diverted First US Army to liberate the area instead. The general feeling amongst the airborne troops was that this, too, would be called off, and in most units the atmosphere was one of casual slackness, in marked contrast to the knife-edged sharpness which had characterised the paratroops before D-Day.

British command snub

First Airborne Army was not a happy organisation. The officer who had recruited and trained the first British paratroops back in 1940, and who since January 1944 had commanded British I Airborne Corps, Lieutenant General Sir Frederick Browning, had expected to be given command of Allied First Airborne Army. Browning also had many additional credentials for high command in the British forces. Educated at Eton and Sandhurst and commissioned into the Grenadier Guards, he had distinguished himself as a company commander on the Western Front in 1916 while still only 20, and had been nicknamed 'Boy', a name which stuck.

'Boy' Browning was on first-name terms with most of Britain's military and political elite, but this counted for nothing in the new subordinate status Britain was beginning to enjoy with the USA. The command of First Airborne Army had gone to General Lewis Brereton, a hard-drinking US Army Airforce officer, who had survived having the aircraft he commanded caught on the ground and wiped out on no less than three occasions, in the Philippines, Northern Australia and in Burma. Brereton got the job in part because he was an American and in part because he knew about transport aircraft, though most pilots regarded his presence as a portent of disaster. Browning had to be content with acting as Brereton's deputy, but this suited neither man. In the three weeks before Arnhem the staff of First Airborne Army's headquarters expanded from 323 officers and men to 1385, meaning that most of them were inexperienced. Brereton and Browning barely spoke to each other, used their own staff officers, and on 4 September discovered that they had planned entirely different operations scheduled to take place 48 hours later. Browning threatened to resign to stop Brereton's plan, leaving relations between the two men at rock bottom.

The command chain and the planning process for Market Garden were problematic, to say the least. So too, were communication systems. Browning's signals section had only been created on 2 September, and there had not been time for exercises to determine whether the sets would work in operational conditions. Nor had direct liaison been established between any of First Airborne Army's headquarters, or any other airforce. In addition, the 1300 C-47 Dakota aircraft, and 250 Albemarles, Halifaxes and Stirlings of the RAF, together with about 2000 gliders, while they were the largest collection of transport aircraft ever assembled, were still only capable of delivering about one-third of the army in one lift.

Airborne troops

Difficulties abounded, but the men commanded by Brereton and Browning were amongst the fittest and best trained of all the Allied forces, and though jaded by the constant raising and then dashing of expectations, were probably also the most highly motivated of any Allied soldiers. US XVIII Airborne Corps under Lieutenant General Matthew Ridgeway was composed of the 82nd and 101st Airborne Divisions, numbering some

24,000 parachute and gliderborne troops, of whom about 10,000 were replacements for the casualties suffered in Normandy. British 1st Airborne Division, under Major General R. E. 'Roy' Urquhart, and Polish 1st Parachute Brigade, under Major General Stanislav Sosabowski, both contained battalions which had considerable combat experience, but these had never before served together as a formation. Waiting in reserve was 52nd (Lowland) Division, a British infantry division organised to be airportable in C-47 Dakotas once the paratroops and glider forces had captured airfields. In all, some 35,000 men were earmarked for the airborne component of Market Garden.

When it was completed on 15 September, the airborne plan involved the capture of bridges over the major rivers and canals at three towns, Eindhoven, about 21km (13 miles) from the start line, Nijmegen, 85km (53 miles) away, and Arnhem 103 (64 miles) away. Major General Maxwell Taylor's 101st Airborne Division was to drop north of Eindhoven, to capture the bridges over the River Aa and the larger Willems Canal at Veghel, over the River Dommel at St Oedenrode, and over the Wilhelmina Canal at Son, and then go on to capture Eindhoven by nightfall. Meanwhile, Brigadier-General James Gavin's 82nd Airborne Division was to

capture the Groesbeek Heights, an area of wooded hills to the east of Nijmegen, followed by bridges over the River Maas at Grave and over the Maas–Waal Canal, and finally the road bridge over the Waal in the centre of Nijmegen. Farther north, Major General Urquhart's 1st Airborne Division would be coming down on heathland west of Arnhem, and then making for the road bridge over the Lower Rhine in the town centre. When he looked at this aspect of the plan, Browning confided to Montgomery, 'I think we might be going a bridge too far', but it was now too late to modify the scheme.

Swift advance

In contrast to the complexity of the air plan, the movement of Lieutenant General Sir Brian Horrock's XXX Corps was simplicity itself. Spearheaded by Guards Armoured Division, the corps was to advance as rapidly as it could up the single, tree-lined double-track road, which ran though country which was almost entirely flat and waterlogged. But the administrative cost of this apparently straightforward movement was enormous. British VIII Corps and three American divisions had been grounded, as were the Allied heavy, medium and anti-aircraft artillery and many engineering units. Half their first-line transport, all their second-line transport, and

BELOW

Dakota transports dropping men of the British 1st Airborne Division at Arnhem. As there are gliders on the ground, this is probably the second lift. There were not enough aircraft available to drop or land the entire division in one operation.

the whole of Twenty-First Army Group's third-line transport were to be used to sustain the advance.

The success of the operation depended on the Germans being on the point of defeat, and it was true that all the evidence up to the beginning of September suggested that this was the case. But the Germans had now had two weeks to recover, and had been effecting a remarkable transformation. The remnants of *Generalleutnant* Kurt Chill's 85th Division had reached Turnhout in northern Belgium on 4 September, and had been ordered to the Rhineland for rest and reinforcement when news of the fall of Brussels caused Chill to ignore his orders and dig in on the northern bank of the Albert Canal. He set up reception centres for stragglers and within 72 hours had formed dozens of broken units into the more or less cohesive *Kampfgruppe* Chill. Meanwhile, scattered paratroop units, amounting in all to about 20,000 men, were formed into what was intended to be the nucleus of First Parachute Army, and on 5 September veteran airborne commander

General Kurt Student flew in to take command. Simultaneously, the largely intact Fifteenth Army, which had occupied the Pas de Calais, was retreating up the coast, and by mid-September had brought into Holland nine divisions amounting to 65,000 men, 750 trucks and 225 guns. By 17 September, paratroop battalions had formed a coherent defensive zone in the area between Eindhoven and Nijmegen, with dual-purpose 88mm guns covering the entire length of the Eindhoven–Nijmegen Road. To the west was *Kampfgruppe* Chill, and behind them was the still effective Fifteenth Army. Around Arnhem the area was beginning to resemble an armed camp. In the woods to the west of the town a Dutch SS Battalion was in training, while to the east elements of 9th, 10th and 11th SS Panzer Divisions were resting and refitting. By 10 September Allied air reconnaissance, reports from the Dutch resistance, and Ultra signals intelligence were beginning to piece together a reasonably accurate picture of German strength, at least in terms of numbers. But the Allied high command had by

ABOVE
Troops of Lieutenant Colonel John Frost's 2nd Parachute Battalion set out on the long approach march to the Arnhem bridge. As they pressed on deeper into the town, progress was slowed by cheering crowds. Little did they know of the ordeal that lay ahead.

German troops manning one of the hastily-arranged – but highly effective – Sperrlinie (blocking lines) that did so much to prevent the 1st and 3rd Parachute Battalions from linking up with the 2nd Battalion at Arnhem bridge.

now convinced themselves that the German will to fight had gone, and that Operation Market Garden would see a resumption of the extraordinary progress which Allied armies had been making since they crossed the Seine.

Market Garden began an hour before midnight on Saturday 16 September as 200 Lancasters and 23 Mosquitos of RAF Bomber Command dropped 890 tons of bombs on four German fighter fields in northern Holland. The bombing continued the next day with nearly 1000 B-17s and P-51 Mustang fighters attacking more than 100 German anti-aircraft positions between the start line and Arnhem. Meanwhile, from 22 airfields in southern and eastern England, the peace of a beautiful late summer Sunday was shattered as the largest aerial armada ever seen in daylight climbed into the sky and flew east. Over the southern part of the North Sea the seemingly endless stream of aircraft and gliders separated into two streams, with 101st Airborne Division taking a southerly route into Holland, while 82nd Airborne and British 1st Airborne Division took the northerly route. Browning, accompanied by his tactical headquarters and his personal chef and wine cellar, took off in

gliders which joined the 82nd Airborne's stream, which was now nearly 160km (100 miles) long and 5km (3 miles) wide. Brereton, who was to oversee reinforcement flights, and would therefore remain at Ascot, nevertheless flew along in a B-17 to watch the drop of the 101st over Eindhoven.

At about 1300 hours the southerly stream ran into heavy flak over Eindhoven, from batteries which aerial reconnaissance had failed to detect. Brereton's aircraft was hit, but as usual the general survived, though several Dakotas and gliders flying nearby were shot out of the sky. In all, the 101st lost 33 Dakotas and about 40 gliders. The stream pushed on through the flak to the drop zone, where Major General Maxwell Taylor jumped with nearly 7000 men of the 101st. At the same time, Brigadier-General Gavin jumped south of Nijmegen, closely followed by the 6500 men of the first wave of the 82nd Airborne. At about 1330 hours Browning's I Airborne Corps headquarters landed near Groesbeek village to the west of Nijmegen, from where Browning would attempt to control the battle.

Meanwhile, the gliders of 1st Airborne Division's 1st Airlanding Brigade had skidded into fields west of Arnhem, followed by

Urquhart's artillery and divisional troop, and about half an hour later by the paratroops of 1st Parachute Brigade. By 1400 hours some 20,000 troops, 511 vehicles, 330 guns and 590 tons of equipment had been safely landed along the 100km (60-mile) corridor.

Hitler alerted

Unfortunately for the Allies, Field Marshal Walther Model was sitting down to lunch in his headquarters at the Taffelberg Hotel at Oosterbeek only 3km (2 miles) east of 1st Airborne's landing zone, and within minutes of sighting the air armada Model had radioed news of the landings to Hitler, and then driven to the headquarters of Lieutenant General Willi Bittrich, the commander of II SS Panzer Corps, who controlled both 9th and 10th SS Panzer Divisions. Shortly after 1430 hours, the 9th SS was on its way to Arnhem and the 10th to Nijmegen. A hundred kilometres (60 miles) south, at Vaught, a small village only 11km (7 miles) west of one of the 101st's drop zones, General Kurt

Student was sitting at his desk in his headquarters when he heard the unmistakable drone of transport aircraft. Student rushed out onto his balcony where he saw an 'endless stream of enemy transport and cargo planes as far as the eye could see'. The founder of German airborne forces turned to the officers who had joined him on the balcony and said with a heartfelt sigh, 'Oh, what I might have accomplished if only I had such a force at my disposal!'

The troops Student was watching, the 506th Regiment of the 101st Airborne, were under orders to seize the main road bridge and two smaller bridges over the Wilhelmina Canal at Zon, but it was blown up by the Germans literally at the last moment. Nor did the 101st make it into Eindhoven, as had been initially intended. Farther to the north the 504th Regiment of the 82nd Airborne Division came down either side of the enormous nine-span bridge over the Maas at Grave, and quickly captured it. Early on the morning of 18 September while preparations

LEFT
British armour and infantry crossing a Bailey bridge on the Bois le Duc canal on the Belgian-Dutch border. Canal bridges, rarely captured intact by the Allies, were prime objectives, as the canals were usually very deep and difficult to cross.

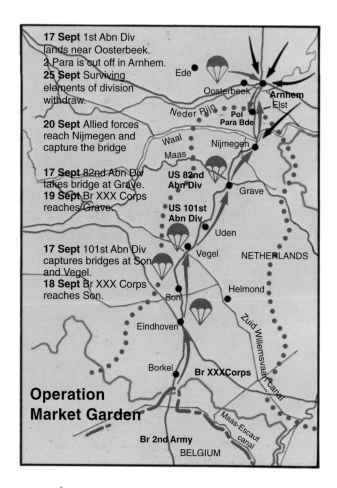

17 Sept 1st Abn Div lands near Oosterbeek. 2 Para is cut off in Arnhem.
25 Sept Surviving elements of division withdraw.

20 Sept Allied forces reach Nijmegen and capture the bridge

17 Sept 82nd Abn Div takes bridge at Grave.
19 Sept Br XXX Corps reaches Grave.

17 Sept 101st Abn Div captures bridges at Son and Vegel.
18 Sept Br XXX Corps reaches Son.

Operation Market Garden

for the reception of glider reinforcements were being made, the 101st advanced south, capturing four bridges on the road to Eindhoven, where they expected to see British XXX Corps, but were greeted instead by delighted Dutch civilians.

At that time, the advance guard of XXX Corps, the Guards Armoured Division, was still 8km (5 miles) to the south. The division's spearhead, the Irish Guards, had set off at 1400 hours behind a narrow rolling barrage up the single road, while Typhoon fighter bombers circled overhead, waiting for forward air controllers to identify targets. For the first 5km (3 miles) to the Dutch frontier the advance went well, but then German 88mms opened up, knocking out nine tanks in a row. The advance resumed after a combination of fighter-bomber attack followed by artillery silenced the 88s. At 1730 hours the Irish Guards reached the bridge south of Valkenswaard and, finding it intact, crossed into the town in the face of determined German resistance. The town was 'a complete shambles with three or four really big fires burning. Germans still firing; other Germans milling about trying to find their way back to

Germany.' In a report broadcast on 19 September, the BBC's Wynford Vaughan Thomas, who was accompanying XXX Corps, prepared the British public for disappointment: 'It is pretty obvious that the enemy is now on the ground in strength. The colonel looked at the map and stroked his chin thoughtfully, then turned to me and said: "Well, it certainly looks as if the picnic is over." The picnic, that wild fantastic chase half-way up France after a beaten army, is obviously over. We're still advancing, of course; at the moment we're getting ready to put in an attack on that strongpoint, but now that attack has to be in some strength if we're to push the enemy out.'

Road clogged

The advance of XXX Corps now slowed to a crawl, with strengthening German opposition exacerbating the traffic jam which 20,000 British support vehicles were already creating on the single road available. It was not until the afternoon of 19 September that British tanks reached the 82nd Airborne's position south of the Nijmegen Bridge, which, because of a command dispute between Model and Bittrich, the Germans had failed to destroy. At 1430 hours on 20 September, after a seemingly interminable wait for assault boats to be transported through XXX Corps traffic jams, the 3rd Battalion of the 504th Parachute Infantry, led by their Lieutenant Colonel, Reuben Tucker, paddled frantically across the river, while Allied fighter-bombers strafed the far shore. The astonishing boldness of the action paid off – German fire was light and poorly coordinated, and Tucker's men were soon closing on the northern approach of the Nijmegen Bridge. At the same time, 30 Shermans of the Grenadier Guards closed on the southern approach, and then began to roll across the bridge. When the British tanks were half-way across the bridge, German engineers attempted to detonate the explosives attached to the central span, but nothing happened. With the Waal crossed, the advance guard of XXX Corps was now only 16km (10 miles) south of Arnhem, but later that afternoon the advance ground to a halt in the face of determined opposition.

By this time (20 September), British 1st Airborne Division had been fighting in and around Arnhem for three days, and its situation was becoming desperate. Things had gone wrong right from the start of the operation. The reconnaissance squadron of 1st

Airborne Division should have driven off immediately to capture Arnhem Bridge in a surprise attack, but unfortunately the gliders carrying the armoured jeeps had failed to arrive. At 1500 hours three battalions of 1st Parachute Brigade had set off following different routes into Arnhem. The 1st and 3rd Battalions ran into German infantry and armoured vehicles, but the 2nd Battalion under Lieutenant Colonel John Frost slipped between German units and at dusk reached the northern end of the road bridge at Arnhem, thus sealing off the shortest route to Nijmegen for German reinforcements. It should now have been a relatively simple matter for Frost to hold on until reinforcements arrived, but unfortunately all was not well at divisional headquarters.

Urquhart missing

On the evening of 17 September, 1st Airborne Division suffered its single worst stroke of bad luck, when Major General Roy Urquhart became detached from his headquarters and for the next 36 hours had to hide from German patrols, several times nar-

rowly avoiding capture. In his absence, his subordinate commanders had a blazing row, which resulted in 1st Airborne launching a number of attacks to secure high ground outside Arnhem, when they should have been concentrating on getting reinforcements to Frost. In addition, fog over airfields in England had delayed the flying in of reinforcements, so that when they did arrive, at 1600 hours on 18 September, the now very alert Germans shot many out of the sky.

Completely isolated and unable to call in air support because of communication difficulties, Frost and the men of the 2nd Battalion had been attacked by Panzer forces rushed north by Bittrich. Incredibly, 2nd Battalion had smashed up a column of 22 SS armoured fighting vehicles which tried to rush their positions. Determined to recapture the bridge, Bittrich ordered up two 100mm guns, which began the process of literally blasting the paratroops out of Arnhem, while more heavy ordnance was being rushed to the area from all over the Reich, including the *Sturmgeschutz* IIIs of the 208th Assault Brigade. By the evening of 19 September

BELOW
The bridge at Arnhem. During the battle, Mosquitoes of the USAAF 654th Heavy Reconnaissance Squadron, based at Watton in Norfolk, made hourly flights over the bridge in an attempt to gather intelligence on what was happening to the British paratroops there. The destroyed SS armoured column can be seen on the approach road to the bridge.

only 250 of Frost's men remained unwounded, in a perimeter which had shrunk from 18 to 10 houses, but every time the Germans attacked they were beaten back. Summoned to discuss surrender, Frost told the Germans that he did not have the facilities to accept their capitulation, a deliberate misunderstanding which was to become the stuff of legend. The bombardment continued into 20 September, the Germans blasting down buildings still held by the British and using flamethrowers to clear the paratroops from the rubble. About midday Frost himself was badly wounded by a mortar blast, and his second in command, Major Gough, took over command of the remaining troops. A little after 1800 hours, Tiger tanks crashed their way across the bridge from north to south, but the Germans found the paratroops' fire still too intense for less heavily armoured vehicles. The fighting went on through the night, but by mid-morning on 21 September British fire began to slacken, and one by one the surviving outposts were overrun, as the paratroops either ran out of ammunition or passed out from sheer exhaustion. They had been fighting for 88 hours without relief, the last 12 of them without food or water; at 1200 hours an SS battle group at last crossed Arnhem bridge.

While Frost and his men were making their epic stand, attempts had been continu-ing to fly in reinforcements to 1st Airborne Division, but because of a combination of deteriorating weather, poor communications and problems in the command chain, all had failed. Under increasingly heavy attack, 1st Airborne had been pushed into an ever-tighter perimeter around Oosterbeek to the west of Arnhem, its only reinforcements some 200 Polish paratroops, who had dropped with the Polish Parachute Brigade at Driel on the southern bank of the Lower Rhine on 21 September, and then swum the river.

Monty's courage

On 23 September, elements of Twenty-First Army Group at last arrived in force on the south side of the river, but after the failure of an attempt by the 4th Battalion of the Dorsetshire Regiment to cross the river on the night of 24 September, Montgomery decided to evacuate the remnants of 1st Airborne Division. As Wynford Vaughan-Thomas had already broadcast on 19 September, it was clear the picnic was over. Market Garden had been designed to exploit the apparent collapse of German will, and when it became clear that the Germans were still full of fight, Montgomery decided there was no point in increasing British casualties by reinforcing failure. Only 2163 men of the 10,005 who had flown into Arnhem made it to the south side of the river during the night

RIGHT

Two *British paratroops in action at Oosterbeek school during the battle for Arnhem. It was at Oosterbeek that remnants of the British 1st Airborne Division made their last stand; the Germans called it the* Hexenkessel *(witches' cauldron).*

of 25/26 September – heavy casualties to be sure, but they would have been much worse if Montgomery had lacked the moral courage to close down the battle.

Allied propaganda tried to portray the operation as 90 per cent successful, because British Second Army was now stuck in a 100km (60-mile) salient in southern Holland, but the public, while making heroes of the airborne soldiers, came to look on it as the loss of an opportunity to win the war in 1944. It was, in fact, no such thing. Market Garden would only have succeeded in ending the war if the Germans had indeed been on the point of collapse, but they were not. As things were, it was providential that Twenty-First Army Group had not been able to cross the Lower Rhine, because if it had done so it would have found itself operating on an inadequate logistic system, in the face of an increasingly formidable enemy. In short, a 'successful' operation may well have resulted in the loss of much of the British army.

ABOVE

Unshaven, dirty and exhausted, but still managing to smile, a mixed group of airborne prisoners marches into captivity after the nine days of battle at Arnhem-Oosterbeek. Even if the airborne operation had succeeded, a subsequent drive into Germany might have proved disastrous.

LEFT

Lt Col John Frost, who led the 2nd Parachute Battalion in the famous stand at Arnhem bridge in September 1944. In the nine-day battle the 1st Airborne Division lost 7212 all ranks killed, wounded and captured. The death toll was 1130.

CHAPTER EIGHT

THE LONG HARD SLOG

After the failure of Market Garden, the Allies realised that the Germans were far from beaten, and that they would in fact face a long hard struggle before victory could be theirs.

The failure of Market Garden came as a rude shock to the Allied high command, and they would never again underestimate the Germans; indeed, in the months to come the problem would often be the reverse, with the Allies basing their planning on wildly pessimistic calculations of German capability. They had assumed that August 1944 would develop like August 1918 – a German collapse – but now they began to suspect that the correct parallel had been with August 1916. The war in Europe could go on for at least another two years, and in his darker moments Eisenhower even thought there would be guerrilla resistance in Germany going on into the 1950s.

The German recovery

The Germans had indeed staged a remarkable recovery. In part it was psychological. The bomb plot of 20 July 1944 gave Hitler, the Nazi hierarchy and millions of ordinary Germans an explanation for the disasters which had been afflicting German arms since the autumn of 1942. After 20 July 1944 it seemed clear that the Reich's war effort was being sabotaged by an internal enemy, the Prussian *Junker* aristocracy who had never been reconciled to the rule of a vulgar, populist dictator. Now that the enemies were being rooted out of the military machine, it

seemed logical to assume that soon the Wehrmacht would again prosper.

It was also the result of an immense increase in military production, the product of Albert Speer's reorganisation 18 months earlier, which was now coming on stream. By the autumn, German factories were well on the way to turning out 40,000 military aircraft for the 12 months of 1944 – as many as had been produced in the USSR. The Western Allies were turning out three times as many, but the latest German machines, particularly the Me 262 jet fighter and the Arado Ar 234B jet bomber, both of which had entered service in the summer, were superior to anything possessed by the British or the Americans, and hinted that Anglo-American air superiority might not last. Since the beginning of the year, German factories had also built 48,000 tanks and self-propelled guns, more than three times the production of 1941, and the Panther and King Tiger tanks were better than anything possessed by the Western Allies. In addition, Krupp, Skoda and other firms had delivered close on 70,000 guns to the Wehrmacht, six times the number cast in 1941.

Although the losses in June, July and August had amounted to a staggering 1.35 million, Hitler's establishment of the *Volkssturm* on 25 September was the beginning of a process which over the next six months would see an additional six million men born between 1884 and 1928 put in uniform and given basic military training. Though the *Volkssturm* was not intended for front-line service, its existence allowed new divisions to be formed from lines of communication troops, and from men in the Luftwaffe and the navy who had lost their aircraft and their ships. From these sources, the remarkably efficient *Wehrkreis* administrative system raised more then 30 new formations, named *Volksgrenadier* divisions, which in a purely numerical sense were twice as strong as the combined British and Canadian armies.

As the Germans retreated to their own frontiers, they had found the business of defence against the Allied tank armies becom-ing ever-easier. Whereas at the beginning of June they had had to defend the entire Channel, Atlantic and Mediterranean coast-line of France, by the end of September they were on a line of only some 725km (450 miles), which snaked from the North Sea to the Swiss frontier, through country which was ideal for defence. The flooded polders and broad estuaries of Holland in the north gave way to broken, hilly and heavily forested country which ran from the Reichswald all the way to the Swiss frontier. For a thousand years this region had marked a linguistic and cultural border between the Romance and Germanic peoples. In terms of topography there were only two relatively easy passages through it, one north of the Ardennes run-ning from Liège in Belgium to Aachen, the

RIGHT

Field Marshal Walther Model, commanding the German Army Group B, visiting the forward command post of a Volksgrenadier *division on the Western Front on 18 October 1944. His nickname was the 'Führer's Fireman', as he was always ordered to take command in troublespots.*

capital of Charlemagne's empire in the 9th century, just across the German border, and the other south of the Ardennes and running from Metz in Lorraine to Saarbrucken. These areas were the natural invasion corridors between France and Germany; both had featured prominently in European military history down the centuries, and because of this, both areas were the most heavily fortified on the European continent. Like their forefathers, the Germans of the Third Reich had enhanced the defensive properties of the frontier region with a system of fortifications, the

Siegfried Line, or West Wall, which ran from the Dutch frontier to Karlsruhe. Between June 1940 and August 1944 it had been neglected, but was now the scene of frenetic activity as a million workers, under the direction of Martin Bormann, Hitler's deputy, threw up tank obstacles and bunkers.

Von Rundstedt recalled

On 5 September Hitler had recalled Gerd von Rundstedt to command the western defences of the Reich, who, using the still-intact staff system, quickly organised three army groups:

ABOVE

A British Bren light machine gun section in action west of the river Maas. From the logistics point of view, with their lines of communication extending only 240km (150 miles) to the Ruhr, the Germans were much better placed for an attritional battle than the Allies.

**Messerschmitt Me 262
Germany**

LEFT

Germany's jet programme was far more advanced than that of Britain or the United States. Aircraft like the Me 262 threatened to turn the tide of the war in the air against the Allies.

Army Group H, under Kurt Student, with responsibility for the area between the North Sea to below Rörmond; Army Group B, commanded by Field Marshal Walther Model, which reached south to the line of the Moselle; and Army Group G, under General Hermann Balck, whose area of responsibility ran from the Moselle to Karlsruhe. An SS group, under Heinrich Himmler himself, held the remainder of the line to Switzerland. By the middle of September, a coherent and increasingly well-manned front line was beginning to emerge, but there was still a doubt as to whether Germany's new armies had regained the will to resist the Western Allies. At the end of August morale everywhere was reported at an all-time low, with even crack units infected with a debilitating cynicism and defeatism. By the end of September, morale, defined as the willingness of soldiers not just to go through the motions of doing their duty, but to exert themselves to the utmost of their capacity, even when not under the supervision of NCOs and officers, was reported as extremely high, even amongst the newly formed *Volksgrenadier* divisions. The defeat of the British attack at Arnhem – with newsreel pictures of columns of Britain's elite paratroops being marched back to prisoner-of-war camps – was in part responsible, but the astonishing recovery of will owed much more to news which was then emanating from Washington.

Postwar plans

On 12 September, Roosevelt, Churchill and their respective staffs met at Quebec for a conference code-named Octagon. Amongst Roosevelt's delegation was the US Secretary of the Treasury, Henry Morgenthau, who had brought with him a plan for the postwar 'pastoralisation' of Germany. Morgenthau's scheme envisaged Germany being divided into two states, northern and southern, after being stripped of the territory it had acquired. No financial reparations were to be demanded, as this would have meant keeping part of Germany's industrial strength operational to pay for them. Instead, all industrial machinery was to be dismantled and transported to to Allied nations, mostly to the USSR. In effect, Germany was to be de-industrialised, with the standard of living being pushed back to that enjoyed by German peasant families 100 years earlier. The German people were to become, in Morgenthau's chilling words, 'the hewers of wood and drawers of water for Europe'. In time, carefully controlled deportation and emigration to North and South America, Southern Africa and Australasia would be used to reduce the German population to some 20 million, about one-quarter of its present size, so that Germany would never again be in a position to threaten the peace of Europe.

The Morgenthau Plan, quickly leaked, was widely discussed in the American press in mid- and late September, and was a propaganda gift to Goebbels, who made sure it had the widest possible dissemination throughout Germany. Not since Rome had defeated Carthage, more than 2000 years earlier, Goebbels claimed, were the consequences of defeat quite so dreadful. Now that they had nothing to hope for, the resolve of the German people stiffened. 'Enjoy the war,' they

BELOW
The Canadian General Henry Crerar, who commanded the 1st Canadian Army in north-west Europe. This formation, which also included units of European origin, was initially responsible for clearing the Scheldt estuary.

LEFT
Canadian troops advancing through Holland. Thanks mainly to the defeat of the British 1st Airborne Division at Arnhem, German morale had risen to a new high, and much bitter fighting lay ahead for the Allied forces.

enjoined one another, for they all knew that a peace would be more terrible.

The failure of Market Garden to precipitate a German collapse meant that the war would now become an attritional slogging match. Unfortunately for the Allies, the Germans were now in a much better position to win this slogging match, because their lines of communication ran back only 80–240km (50–150 miles) from the Ruhr, which, although heavily bombed, now had a productive capacity five or six times that of 1941. By contrast, Allied logistics were still in a shambles, and the Anglo-Americans would have little hope of winning an attritional battle with the Germans until the port of Antwerp, the largest in north-west Europe, with a daily unloading capacity of 40,000 tons, could be brought into the production. The British had captured Antwerp with its harbour facilities intact on 4 September, but Zangen's Fifteenth Army, a component of Student's Army Group H, controlled the banks of the 65km (40-

mile) estuary of the Scheldt. The clearance of the Scheldt was the responsibility of Montgomery's Twenty-First Army Group, but, preoccupied with Market Garden, Montgomery had given the job to General Harry Crearar's First Canadian Army. On 8 October Admiral Ramsay, in charge of naval operations in north-west Europe, sent Eisenhower a report that the Canadians would be unable to accomplish the clearance of the Scheldt until 1 November because they had run into strong opposition and were short of ammunition. A thoroughly alarmed Eisenhower now sent Montgomery orders in terms which were unequivocal: 'Unless we have Antwerp producing by the middle of November our entire operations will come to a standstill. I must emphasize that, of all our operations on our entire front from Switzerland to the Channel, I consider Antwerp of first importance, and I believe that operations designed to clear up the entrance require your personal attention.'

ABOVE

Commandos heading for the beach at Walcheren. Having secured a beachhead, they pushed north and south along the shore, knocking out German installations that included the heavy guns threatening Allied shipping in the Scheldt.

Over the next week relations between Montgomery and Eisenhower deteriorated to breaking point. In a telephone call to Eisenhower's chief of staff, Bedell Smith, Montgomery's denial of Ramsay's charge produced from the acerbic Bedell Smith an explosion of anger. 'Purple with rage', Smith told Montgomery that unless Antwerp was opened soon his supplies would be cut off. Montgomery hit back, blaming the failure of Arnhem on SHAEF's unsatisfactory plan of campaign, and suggesting that the obsession with clearing the Scheldt was really an attempt to divert him into a backwater. Eisenhower now called Montgomery's bluff. He wrote that if Montgomery really found SHAEF's plan 'unsatisfactory, then indeed we have an issue that must be settled soon in the interests of future efficiency... and if you, as the senior Commander in this Theatre of one of the great Allies, feel that my conceptions and directives are such as to endanger the success of operations, it is our duty to to refer the matter to higher authority for any action they may choose to take, however drastic.'

Montgomery backed down, and on 16 October decreed that the clearing of the Scheldt was now Twenty-First Army Group's top priority.

Formidable defences

By this time the Polish Armoured Division and the Canadians had cleared about 32km (20 miles) of the southern shore of the Scheldt to the west of Antwerp, but still had another 40km (25 miles) to go. On 3 October Colonel General Alfred Jodl had reminded von Rundstedt that the opening of the Scheldt was vital to the Allies, and that the mouth of the estuary must be held at all costs. Here German defences were formidable. On the southern shore of the estuary the commander of Fifteenth Army had placed Major General Eberding's 64th Infantry Division, formed from experienced soldiers on leave from the Russian front, around the town of Breskens on what was now an island, about 19km (12 miles) long and 8km (5 miles) deep, created by flooding the country along the Canal de la Lys and the Leopold Canal. It ran from Zeebrugge on the North Sea to the 6.5km (4-mile) Braakman Inlet on the Scheldt. Including elements from the navy and Luftwaffe, the 64th Division mustered about 11,000 officers and men, over 500 machine guns and mortars, some 200 anti-tank and anti-aircraft guns (including 23 of 88mm (3.45in)) and about 70 artillery pieces of 75mm (2.95in) and upwards. There were also five batteries of long-range naval guns in concrete positions near the coast between Breskens and Knocke-sur-Mer. Known to the Allies as the Breskens Pocket, and to the Germans as Scheldt Fortress South, it was here that the Polish-Canadian advance had come to a stop.

Island defences

The northern shore of the Scheldt was formed by the 32km (20-mile) peninsula of South Beveland, which was connected by an 1100m (1200-yard) causeway to Walcheren Island, which was only 36m (40 yards) wide. The 70th Division, a 'stomach' division formed from men who all suffered from gastric ulcers, and who were consequently ill-tempered, had dug in on South Beveland. It was a particularly formidable position

because at Rilland, where the peninsula projected from the mainland, it was only 2.5km (1.5 miles) wide. The most formidable defences of all were on Walcheren Island. Here about 12,000 Germans manned about 50 heavy guns, placed in strongly constructed concrete pillboxes. In addition, the town of Flushing had been turned into a fortress, with several batteries around its perimeter, and numerous houses and warehouses had been converted into strong points, each capable of giving mutual support.

By the time Canadian and British full-scale assaults were under way, the weather had changed. The first rain came in the middle of Market Garden, and then became heavier and heavier. The autumn of 1944 in north-west Europe was one of the wettest on record, with some areas recording up to three times their normal rainfall. This not only made movement difficult, but also severely reduced the effectiveness of air power. Between 10 and 14 October, for example, Bomber Command sorties managed to drop 1150 tons of bombs on the Breskens Pocket, about one-fifth the tonnage Allied bombers deposited on the Germans on a single morning before Operation Goodwood on 18 July. The

BELOW
Assault on the island of Walcheren in the Scheldt estuary. British Commandos and Canadian troops encountered fierce resistance here. Much of the island lay under water, the dikes having been breached by Allied bombers. It was not until 4 November that the last strongpoint was overrun.

Canadian 3rd Division attacked down the Scheldt in scores of Buffaloes, amphibious armoured fighting vehicles each carrying 24 men, and with the support of Canadian 4th Armoured Division, managed to capture Breskens on 24 October. The Canadians now worked their way along the coast, capturing the last strongpoint, near Knocke-sur-Mer, on 2 November. In all the Canadians had taken 12,700 prisoners, but had themselves suffered more than 2000 casualties.

Meanwhile, on 24 October, the Canadian 2nd Division had attacked along the South Beveland Peninsula in mist and drizzle. Sherman tanks, trying to move along dikes, slithered off and made easy targets for anti-tank guns. Infantry moved on through the night without armoured support and near dawn captured Rilland, about 5km (3 miles) from the Canadians' startline. Meanwhile, elements of the British 52nd Division had crossed the Scheldt in Buffaloes, and landing about 24km (15 miles) west of the neck of the peninsula, moved east to crush the Germans against the Canadians. By 31 October, the British and Canadians had pushed the Germans westwards across the causeway onto Walcheren Island.

The British had begun softening up Walcheren on 2 October, when bombers dropped leaflets warning Dutch civilians that their homes were shortly to be subjected to intense and prolonged bombardment. In fact, British plans for Walcheren were going to go much further than mere bombardment. Because about 70 per cent of Walcheren lay below sea level, British planners decided that the easiest way to neutralise the island was to breach the Westkapelle, one of the largest and oldest dikes in Holland, which ran for about 5km (3 miles) around the western coast of the island. The next day, 259 Lancasters and Mosquitos made the first attempt to breach the Westkapelle dike, with 1270 tons of explosives. The bombers came back on the 7th, 11th and 17th of October, depositing a total of 2672 tons of high explosive, by which time all the island was underwater except for the coastal dunes, Flushing, Middleberg and a segment of country on the east.

Hard-won advance

After two more days of aerial bombardment and with the support of the 15-inch (381mm) guns of the battleship *Warspite* and the monitors *Roberts* and *Erebus*, British Commandos landed at Westkapelle and Flushing at dawn on 1 November. The Canadians attacked across the causeway from South Beveland at 1100 hours, but were quickly beaten back by

BELOW
An LCT discharging a flail tank at Walcheren. These and other special armoured fighting vehicles of the 79th Armoured Division proved invaluable in the Allied seaborne assaults that sealed the fate of the German occupation of northwest Europe.

British Cromwell tanks pictured on a Dutch road some 2km (1.25 miles) from the great bridges spanning the Hollandschdiep, the key to Dordrecht and Rotterdam. The advance through Holland was difficult and laborious; by December 1944 the Allies had made little progress.

a German counter-attack. The fighting swayed to and fro for the next two days, the Canadians unable to make much progress over the 1100m (1200-yard) causeway, which a Canadian veteran described 'as straight as a gun barrel'. The Commandos had an easier time, the rising water having created a series of small islands which the British were able to take one at a time. The heaviest fighting was in Flushing, where the Germans fired from the tops of cranes in the dock area, and from ships at anchor in the harbour. The Commandos overran the last strongpoint on 4 November, and later that day persuaded Major General Daser and his 2000 surviving German troops in Middelberg to surrender.

The same day, a flotilla of Royal Navy minesweepers sailed up the Scheldt, sweeping 50 mines, and in the evening a squadron of six of the small ships entered Antwerp. The estuary was riddled with mines, and over the next three weeks 10 flotillas of minesweepers, working from both ends of the Scheldt, removed a total of 276 mines. On 28 November the first convoy of 19 Liberty ships, most over 7000 tons, arrived safely. By early December, with the port under British management, 17,000 dockers were handling more than 20,000 tons of cargo on a daily basis, revolutionising the Allies' logistic situation. Almost overnight the Allies went from one-third too little port capacity to one-third excess, which would make it possible to sustain the attritional battles to come.

While Twenty-First Army Group had been clearing the Scheldt, Hodges's First Army had

Troops emerging from a 15cwt armoured personnel carrier near Nijmegen, Holland, in December 1944. Montgomery blamed Eisenhower's policies for the stalemate on the Allied front, and was determined to force the Germans into mobile warfare.

begun an offensive against Aachen on 12 September. First Army's XIX Corps, attacking from the north, soon bogged down, while Collins'VII Corps, advancing from the south, soon ran into heavy resistance in the Hürtgen Forest. Bitter fighting raged north and south of Aachen, where XIX and VII Corps finally closed the ring on 16 October, after beating off heavy counter-attacks. Hitler ordered the city, the capital of Charlemagne, founder of the First Reich, to be defended to the last, something which the commander Colonel Gerhard Wilck and the troops of the 246th *Volksgrenadier* Division intended to do. In six days of fierce street fighting, during which the Germans attacked the Americans from the sewer system, soldiers of the 26th Infantry Division fought their way across the ruined city. By 22 October the German perimeter had been reduced to the area of Rutscher-strasse on the north-west of the city, where Wilck was holding out in a huge, four-storey reinforced concrete air-raid shelter. The Americans brought up 155mm howitzers and battered the building at point-blank range; Wilck and his staff surrendered after a day.

Bloody as Aachen proved to be, it paled to insignificance when compared with what was

then happening in the Hürtgen Forest. A rugged, hilly area covered in dense pine forest, the Hürtgen ran 40km (25 miles) from the south-west to the north-east, was about 20km (12 miles wide), and was intersected by the West Wall, running north-south. It was packed with mines, barbed wire and pillboxes, with skilfully positioned Tiger tanks covering the best approach routes. Between September and November five American divisions were sent into the forest, about 120,000 men in all, of whom 33,000 became casualties. It was the worst battle experienced by the American army in north-west Europe, and was described by Ernest Hemingway, who wit-nessed part of it, as 'Passchendaele with tree bursts'. A major objective was the town of Schmidt, which controlled the road to the Schwammenauel Dam at the head of the Rör River. Unless the dam could be taken, an eventual crossing of the Rhine would be dif-ficult, as the Germans would be certain to release a flood of water down the Rör and into the Rhine as soon as Allied landing craft hit the water. The 28th Division, the men who had marched through Paris on 29 August, moved to attack Schmidt on 2 November behind an intense artillery barrage, but made slow headway against an enemy fighting from log-covered bunkers. The 28th Division's 112th Regiment eventually got into Schmidt, but on 4 November was counter-attacked by panzergrenadiers, and fled in panic. The 28th's debacle at Schmidt cost it 6184 casualties, one of the bloodiest actions by an American division in war.

Heavy bombing

On 16 November five divisions, spearheaded by the US 1st Infantry Division, 'the Big Red One', tried again. In the largest air attack in support of a ground operation during the war, virtually the entire US Eighth Air Force dropped more than 10,000 tons of bombs on various German positions. Several towns in the Hürtgen were obliterated before the Americans reached the banks of the Rör on 8 December.

In the meantime, Patton and Third Army had not been idle. Angry and frustrated by the logistic priority then being given to Montgomery's Twenty-First Army Group, Patton had confided to his diary on 3 September: 'We will get crossings at Nancy and Metz by the "rock soup" method, and I gave the orders today.... Once a tramp went to a house and asked for boiling water to make rock soup. The lady was interested and gave him the water, in which he placed two polished rocks he had in his hand. He then asked for some potatoes and carrots to put in the soup to flavour the water a little, and finally ended up by securing some meat. In other words, in order to attack, we have first to pretend to reconnoiter and then reinforce the reconnaissance and then finally attack. It is a very sad method of making war.'

Instead of defending on the Meuse as expected, Patton had made an additional 48km (30 miles) and then seized bridgeheads on the Moselle River south of Metz. Receiving a bare minimum of petrol, using captured stores and fuel, and constantly juggling petrol and artillery tonnages to eke out further advances, Patton began simultaneous encircling moves towards Nancy and north and south of Metz, while still moving forces to link with Patch's Seventh Army west of Dijon.

Brushing aside ineffectual German counter-attacks, Patton sent his 5th Division

BELOW
American infantry and armour moving along a French road towards Aachen, on the Franco-German border. The offensive led by General Hodges' US 1st Army against Aachen, begun on 12 September 1944, soon became bogged down.

against Metz, only to see it driven back with 5000 casualties. The Germans were now fighting in Lorraine, terrain they knew well, where the advantage lay with the defence. The Moselle and Saar Rivers ran south to north across Third Army's line of march, and the large forests and stone villages of the region provided rallying points for delay and counter-attack. There was also the weather. The average November rainfall in Lorraine was 63mm (2.5 inches), but November 1944 brought 178mm (7 inches). By the middle of the month it was increasingly difficult for Patton's armour to manoeuvre off the roads. Of even more importance was the effect on air operations. In August XIX Tactical Air Command had conducted 12,292 sorties, but in November the number had fallen to 3509.

On 8 November, in heavy rain, Patton sent his XII Corps towards Metz behind a barrage of 42 battalions of guns, firing 20,000 shells. The next day, Third Army's XX Corps silently crossed the Moselle River north of Metz. Rising floodwaters destroyed pontoon bridges, but finally armour was across, and soon three divisions were systematically reducing the defences of Metz in a concentric attack. Encircled by 19 November, the garrison surrendered two days later. By early December, Third Army finally reached the West Wall along the Saar. It had suffered 55,182 battle casualties, including 6657 dead. Non-battle casualties produced by exposure and disease ran almost as high.

Lack of progress

By mid-December, Allied armies were making little progress on any part of the front. Montgomery was again vocal in his criticism of Eisenhower. The supreme commander was

RIGHT
Soldiers of the First French Army in action with a 75mm (2.95-inch) anti-tank gun against Germans entrenched in the Chateau de Belfort. The ancient city of Belfort was the key to the mountain gateway into southern Germany.

FAR RIGHT
A French mechanic working on a captured Panther tank. Designed in 1941, the Panther first saw action during the Battle of Kursk in the summer of 1943. It weighed 43.6 tonnes (43 tons) and had a top speed of 45km/h (28mph). Unreliable at first, it had become a formidable opponent by mid-1944.

a coordinator, not a commander, Montgomery said, and his policy of 'have a go, Joe', instead of bringing victory all across the line, had brought stalemate everywhere. General Alan Brooke agreed with his protégé, writing in his diary on 24 November that he was very upset about 'the very unsatisfactory state of affairs, with no one running the land battle. Eisenhower, though supposed to be doing so, is on the golf links at Rheims – entirely detached and taking practically no part in the running of the war.'

On 28 November, Eisenhower and Montgomery had a stormy meeting at Twenty-First Army Group headquarters, after which Montgomery reported to Brooke that Eisenhower had agreed that the SHAEF plan had failed and 'we had suffered a strategic reverse.' On 5 December, Eisenhower again met with Montgomery, this time in Maastricht, where Montgomery asserted that the only solution to the stalemate and attrition was to find some means of forcing the Germans into mobile warfare. Just 11 days later, the Germans were going to grant Montgomery his wish, and remove any lingering Allied complacency.

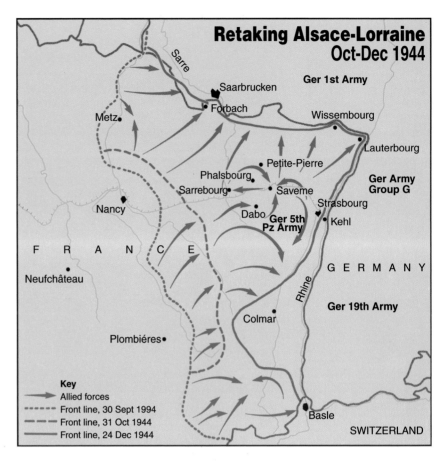

CHAPTER NINE

THE ARDENNES OFFENSIVE

The failure of Market Garden had caused the Allies some disquiet, but at the end of 1944 they were to get a greater shock: a German offensive that seemed set to repeat the success of 1940.

As the Allies had battered against the western defences of the Reich, their armies had moved slowly along divergent axes north and south of the Ardennes, a hilly, heavily wooded area in which the borders of Belgium, Luxembourg and Germany came together. In the far north, Twenty-First Army Group, with the Canadians on the left and the British on the right, was stuck on the River Maas, with a small salient jutting up to just south of Arnhem. Since the clearing of the Scheldt, it had attacked east towards Venlo and Roermond but had achieved only minor success. Supporting Twenty-First Army Group on its right was the newly-activated US Ninth Army under Lieutenant General William H Simpson, a part of Bradley's enlarged Twelfth Army Group, which was pressing towards the River Roer against tough opposition. To its right was Hodges First Army, whose VII and V Corps was still heavily engaged in the Huertgen Forest. The Huertgen battle had pulled Hodges forces to the north, so that the front which ran south for 112km (70 miles) through the Ardennes was held only by the four divisions of Major General Troy Middleton's VIII Corps. On Middleton's right, Patton's Third Army had now penetrated deep into Lorraine, and was everywhere up against the West Wall. Patch's Sixth Army Group after its advance up the

Rhone had by now actually reached the Rhine at Strasbourg, though to its right a dangerous salient, the Colmar Pocket, containing the German Nineteenth Army, remained in the Vosges Mountains. To the south of the pocket French First Army, with its right flank protected by the Swiss frontier, had pushed through the Belfort Gap to reach the Rhine below Basel.

Idea for a counteroffensive

Even as the German front began to consolidate at the beginning of September, General Alfred Jodl, Chief of the Wehrmacht's Operations Staff, had begun to study the feasibility of a counteroffensive. In a briefing to Hitler given at OKW HQ at Rastenburg in East Prussia on 6 September, Jodl argued that the major problem the Wehrmacht would have to overcome before launching a counterstroke would be Allied superiority in the air, which would make the concentration of forces necessary to achieve an offensive difficult. This difficulty could be overcome, Jodl argued, by delaying the offensive until the autumn, when cloud and mist would reduce the effectiveness of Allied aerial reconnaissance and fighter-bombers. It would also be necessary to restrict information, at least in the early stages, to a small number of planners. There remained the problem of where to

OPPOSITE
Private First Class Thomas W. Gilgore of the 121st Infantry Regiment, 8th Infantry Division, US First Army, takes advantage of a lull in the fighting near Huertgen in Germany on 5 December 1944.

launch the attack. By 20 September it was clear from intelligence reports that the Allies, convinced that the Wehrmacht was no longer capable of an offensive, were ignoring the Ardennes. That day, at a packed Führer conference at Rastenberg, Hitler harangued the assembled officers with a speech which suggested that Germany had its back to the wall. 'There can be no large-scale operations on our part. All we can do is to hold our position or die.' No sooner had the conference ended than Hitler invited Keitel, Jodl, Guderian and General Kreipe, a representative of the Luftwaffe, to an inner chamber. Standing over an unrolled map of North West Europe, Hitler exclaimed 'I have made a momentous decision. I am taking the offensive. Here – out of the Ardennes! Across the Meuse and on to Antwerp!'

Sichelschnitt in action

Back in the spring of 1940, it had largely been pressure from Hitler which had caused conventional variants of the old World War I Schleiffen Plan to be set aside, and the radical *Sichelschnitt* to be employed in their place. On that occasion the bulk of Germany's panzer divisions had passed through the Ardennes in just two days, crossed the Meuse, and then, swinging north west, had reached the Channel coast at Abbeville just ten days after crossing the start line, trapping First French Army Group and the British Expeditionary Force in

ABOVE

A German soldier in a well-camouflaged forward observation post checks American movements prior to the German counter-offensive on 16 December 1944. The Germans took full advantage of the adverse weather conditions.

RIGHT

German troops huddle together in dugouts along the Rhine, hiding from Allied aircraft. After long months of retreat, the preparations for a counter-offensive helped raise German morale.

PzKpfw VI Tiger II
Germany

a pocket in north east France and Flanders. In the autumn of 1944 the front was configured in almost exactly the same way. Hitler intended to break through in the Ardennes, take Antwerp, and pin US Twelfth Army Group and British Twenty-First Army Group up against the Maas and the northern part of the West Wall. There was already sufficient evidence in the British and American press to suggest that Anglo-American co-operation was little more than a veneer, meaning that the Allied reaction to a German attack would be slow and disjointed. The attack would not bring total victory, but it could trigger a political crisis in London and Washington, which might see the removal of Churchill and a negotiated peace with the Western Allies, which would leave Germany free to deal with the USSR.

Hitler went on to discuss in some depth how this was to be achieved. He estimated an offensive would require a minimum of 30

ABOVE

The Tiger II tank was a formidable opponent for Allied tank crews.

BELOW

German paratroops riding into battle on a Tiger II. Hundreds of precious tanks and self-propelled guns were used for the operation.

German troops advancing through an American position that has already been overrun. The total surprise achieved by the Germans was made possible by fog and snow, which made Allied air reconnaissance impossible.

divisions, of which ten would have to be armoured. These would have to be organised into four armies. Those to the north and south of the assault area would be composed almost entirely of infantry, with the task of pressing forward to protect the flanks of the main assault from attack. For the main assault he intended to employ two panzer armies, containing a mixture of tank and infantry formations. The aim at all times was to be Antwerp, with no deviation whatsoever. The tanks were to force the Meuse on the second

day, swing northeastward around Brussels and reach Antwerp on the seventh day, before the Allied High Command could react.

Secrecy vital

To ensure absolute secrecy, only a select few were to be told of the offensive; a different code name for the offensive was to be used at every command level, and changed every two weeks. Moreover, nothing of the offensive was to be trusted to telephone or teletype. Officers, sworn to secrecy, were to be used as couriers, their silence assured by the threat of summary execution should any leak occur. Only with such precautions, reasoned Hitler, could security be maintained.

German preparations

On 25 September Field Marshal Gerd von Rundstedt, Commander in Chief in the west, was ordered to withdraw I and II Panzer Corps from the front line, ostensibly for rest and reorganisation. In fact, they were to form the backbone of a new SS Panzer Army, the Sixth, which Hitler placed under a trusted friend from the early days of the Nazi party, SS *Oberstgruppenführer* Josef 'Sepp' Dietrich, and which was to form the main assault force in the north. The second of the assault tank formations, responsible for the attack in the centre, was to be the Fifth Panzer Army, commanded by General Hasso von Manteuffel, then facing Patton in the south, but withdrawn for reorganisation in late October. All units would be part of Army Group B, under Field Marshal Walter Model, theoretically

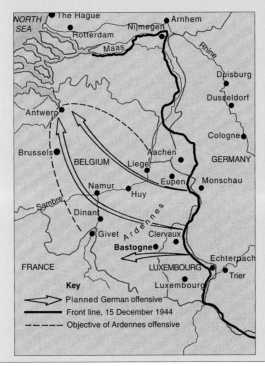

The Battle of the Bulge
101st Airborne Brigade, Bastogne, December 1944

In December 1944, 24 German divisions were thrown into a final offensive against the advancing Allied armies on the Western Front. Hitler's plan called for a breakthrough in the Ardennes, splitting the Allied armies in two, and pushing on to Antwerp. The offensive took the Allies by surprise and from 16 – 20 December the German divisions pushed forward to Stavelot, St Vith, Houffalize and Bastogne. General Eisenhower committed the 101st Airbone Divisions to the defence of Bastogne, which was situated on a vital crossroads controlling movements north-south and east-west. By 20 December Bastogne was surrounded but the 101st held out, imposing delays on the exploitation of the 'bulge' that were to prove fatal to the German offensive.

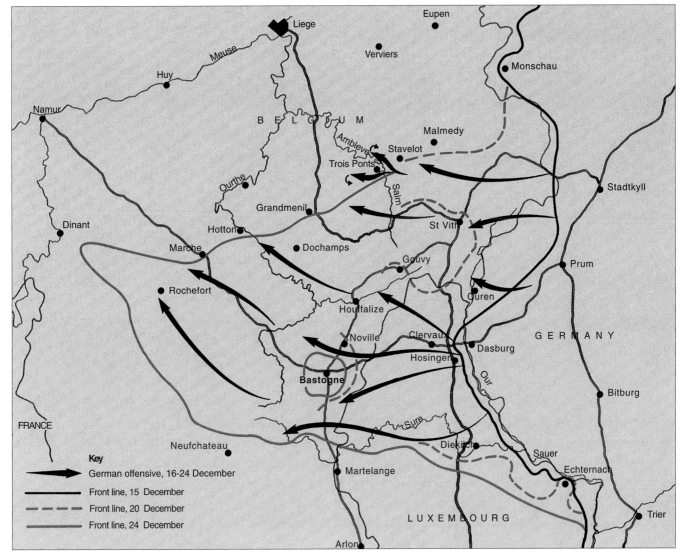

BELOW
German motorised troops race through the Ardennes forest in the early days of the German attack.

BOTTOM
This American-built bridge was captured intact by the Germans during their attack in the Ardennes, and quickly put to use.

under command of von Rundstedt, but, for the purposes of the attack, answerable directly to Hitler at OKW. A code name was now assigned to the operation – *Wacht am Rhein* (Watch on the Rhine) – which was intended to suggest a static, defensive frame of mind.

Hitler's bold plan

On 21 October Hitler briefed SS *Obersturmbannführer* Otto Skorzeny on the role he was to play. Skorzeny, who had led a daring glider assault onto the top of Gran

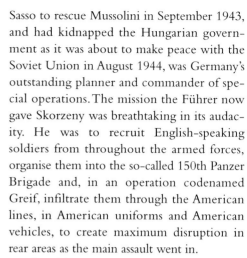

Sasso to rescue Mussolini in September 1943, and had kidnapped the Hungarian government as it was about to make peace with the Soviet Union in August 1944, was Germany's outstanding planner and commander of special operations. The mission the Führer now gave Skorzeny was breathtaking in its audacity. He was to recruit English-speaking soldiers from throughout the armed forces, organise them into the so-called 150th Panzer Brigade and, in an operation codenamed Greif, infiltrate them through the American lines, in American uniforms and American vehicles, to create maximum disruption in rear areas as the main assault went in.

The following day Hitler briefed the Chiefs of Staff to von Rundstedt and Model, and here the Führer ran into the same problems he had encountered in the spring of 1940. The minds of officers trained at a Staff College were programmed to reject anything so unsound. Model read the plan with dismay and exclaimed 'This damned thing hasn't got a leg to stand on!' Von Rundstedt shared his concern, and offered a counterplan, a more modest attack of 20 divisions on a 64km (40-mile) front. Meeting with his generals, Hitler delivered a lecture on German military history: 'Apparently you don't remember

Frederick the Great,' he said to von Rundstedt. 'At Rossbach and Leuten he defeated enemies twice his strength. How? By a bold attack ... Why don't you people study history?' The only concession he made to the concerns of his generals was to postpone the assault date, first to 10 December, and then to 16 December. This slippage allowed more time to build up supplies, but it also pushed the timing of the operation dangerously close to the end of the autumnal fogs, with their low cloud and mist, and into the first snow falls of winter with temperatures dropping below zero, which would make the Ardennes landscape look like the pictures on Swiss chocolate boxes – snow-covered evergreen trees set against a bright blue, cloudless sky.

Stealth by night

In the first two weeks of December tens of thousands of troops, and thousands of tanks and guns, moved into the Eifel Hills, the

ABOVE
Obersturmbannführer *Jochen Peiper pictured in his command car at the St Vith–Malmedy crossroads during the Ardennes offensive. It was Peiper's SS troops who were responsible for the massacres of soldiers and civilians during the armoured dash.*

LEFT
Jochen Peiper had been Himmler's adjutant before the war, and saw extensive action on the Eastern Front before the massacre at Malmedy. He was tried at Dachau for war crimes after the war.

Hitlerjugend *guarding American prisoners captured during the early stages of the German attack. The SS division had been severely mauled in Normandy, and would shortly be pulled back to Germany.*

German extension of the Ardennes, during the hours of darkness. German night-fighters flew low over the Ardennes all night long, their engines masking much of the noise that the movement of so much materiel and so many men naturally created. All movement ceased an hour before dawn, when teams of soldiers with pine branches and brooms swept away all evidence of tank and tyre tracks on the roads, so that they would not be detected by Allied aerial reconnaissance. Final orders were issued on 11 December. By this time German forces in the Ardennes stood at 23 divisions, with a further two in reserve, and of this total 10 were armoured. In the north Dietrich had under his command four panzer divisions (1st SS, 2nd SS, 9th SS and 12th SS), the 3rd Parachute Division, and four *Volksgrenadier* divisions. He fielded a total of 450 tanks and self-propelled guns. On his left Manteuffel also had four panzer divisions, the 2nd, 9th, *Panzer Lehr* and 116th, which possessed about 350 tanks and armoured fighting vehicles, the 15th Panzer Grenadier Division, and four *Volksgrenadier* divisions. To Manteuffel's left, in the south of the assault area, Seventh Army under General Erich Brandenberger consisted of the 5th Parachute Division and four *Volksgrenadier* divisions. In

addition, OKW held a reserve, two divisions and two elite brigades, which were to be released at the express orders of Hitler alone. Overall the Germans had assembled nearly 300,000 men, 1000 tanks and self-propelled guns, and 2000 heavy artillery pieces. In addition, the Luftwaffe had scraped together 1000 fighters and fighter-bombers, including about 200 Me 262 jets, which meant that in certain conditions the Germans might be able to achieve temporary local air superiority.

Surprise attack

The Americans called the Ardennes the 'Ghost Front', because the forces deployed here were largely figments of the imagination. There were, in fact, six weak divisions, amounting to about 75,000, two of which, the 28th and the 4th, had been sent to the Ardennes to recover from the blood-letting they had experienced in the Huertgen Forest, and two of which, the 99th and 106th, had recently arrived in Europe, and had been sent to the Ardennes because it was a quiet area where they could acquire some basic military skills. Over the preceeding month Allied intelligence had been picking up pieces of information which, if interpreted correctly, would have alerted SHAEF to the fact that the Germans were

**M3 Half-Track
USA**

about to launch an offensive, but which were explained away by intelligence officers who were convinced that the Wehrmacht could no longer launch a large-scale offensive. Patton's intelligence officers, for example, had reported the absence of Manteuffels' Fifth Panzer Army and its replacement by *Volksgrenadier* divisions, but this was interpreted as a symptom of a manpower crisis in Germany. At the same time Allied signals intelligence reported complaints coming from all over Germany about lack of fuel, which was taken as evidence that Germany was indeed running out of fuel, not that (admittedly limited) supplies of petrol were being stockpiled for some other purpose. At the beginning of

ABOVE
The M3 half-track was widely used by the US Army and its allies. Over 40,000 vehicles were produced, and they were a common sight in north west Europe in the last year of the war.

LEFT
A photograph from a captured German film showing an SS soldier with a wrecked and burning American half-track. The Germans had assembled a formidable force of 300,000 men for the Ardennes offensive, many of them experienced and battle-hardened troops.

November Allied intelligence even monitored the Wehrmacht's call for English-speaking soldiers to volunteer for special duty. At first intelligence analysts weren't too sure what to make of this, but eventually decided that the Germans were probably stepping up their interrogation of Allied prisoners as a means of gathering additional information.

Surprise attack

At 0400 hours on 16 December, 2000 German guns opened up on the American lines of communication, creating alarm and confusion amongst American front line units. In many places GIs, who had assumed they were on the front line, were surprised to see jeeps loaded with American soldiers – some six to a vehicle – roaring westwards with alarming information and new orders. The Germans have broken through – you are to withdraw as quickly as possible – don't demolish that bridge, we'll handle that for you – and so on. Skorzeny had hoped to infiltrate American positions with at least 2000 men in American uniforms, but in the end his Commando was only about 800 strong. And although most of them could speak English, he considered that only about a dozen could convincingly pass themselves off as Americans. Moreover, he had been able to

RIGHT
English-speaking soldiers recruited by Obersturmbannführer *Otto Skorzeny infiltrated Allied lines to capture key points and generally cause as much disruption as possible. They were shown no mercy if captured; here, one faces summary execution.*

OPPOSITE ABOVE
Heavily-armed SS troops attack across a Belgian road. The rapid capture of Allied fuel dumps to sustain the armoured drive was a key feature of the offensive; but thanks to stubborn pockets of resistance, such as Bastogne, the plan failed.

OPPOSITE BELOW
German vehicles and equipment lie camouflaged in the Ardennes forest, hiding from Allied fighter-bombers. When conditions were suitable for flying, any movement on the roads would attract an attack.

acquire relatively few vehicles (most German units had hidden their captured jeeps when they heard Skorzeny was on his way to requisition them), and so the Commandos had had to travel six or more to a jeep, something real American soldiers would never do.

Chaos spreads

Due to these difficulties, most of Skorzeny's Commandos were detected within the first three days, and many of them were executed, but by then they had created chaos. After the detection of the first couple of jeep loads, rumours flew along the communication lines through the Ardennes, multiplying the

strength of the Commandos many times. Throughout the Ardennes units established road blocks, stopping and questioning closely the occupants of each vehicle, so that a drive which should have taken 30 minutes took four hours or more, and this happened not once or twice but many thousands of times. All armies are like delicate mechanical mechanisms, and Skorzeny's Greif Commando acted like a handful of sand in the workings of a Swiss watch.

Panzer power

In the centre of the Ardennes, the tanks of Manteuffel's Fifth Panzer Army rolled over parts of the US 28th and 106th Divisions, both of which quickly lost coherence, and then headed for the road junctions of St Vith and Bastogne. German camera crews, following in the wake of the tanks, shot hours of newsreel footage showing long columns of American prisoners marching eastward,

which served to convince audiences in Germany that the tide had turned, at least for a while. In the south Brandenberger's Seventh Army hit the 109th Regiment of the 28th Division, sending it reeling back to the south west. The crucial advance was to be made in the north by Sixth SS Panzer Army, which was spearheaded by a *Kampfgruppe* under the command of *Obersturmbannführer* Jochen Peiper, a 29-year-old SS officer who had earned a formidable reputation on the Russian front. When arranging the line of march of his *Kampfgruppe*, Peiper decided that the psychological effect of Tiger tanks on the Allies was so great that he placed them at the head of the column.

For 48 hours Peiper tore through the Ardennes to Stavelot, 40km (25 miles) from his startline, leaving a trail of murdered American prisoners and Belgian civilians behind him – 19 American POWs at Honsfeld, eight POWs at Ligneuville, 86

POWs just to the south of Malmedy and approximately 100 unarmed Belgians.

Shock offensive

News of the German attack took a long time to filter out of the Ardennes. Part of the problem was that shell fire and Skorzeny's Commandos had cut telephone and telegraph lines, and radio communications in the hills and forests, particularly in wet weather, was never more than intermittent. But part of the problem was the inability of junior officers to understand the enormity of what was happening. They had got so used to the Germans being on the defensive that they assumed German activity could be nothing more than limited counter-attacks, not a full-scale counter-offensive. It was not until late in the

afternoon that news of the offensive reached Eisenhower at SHAEF Main at Versailles. Bradley had arrived a little earlier, and when told the news, dismissed it as a mere spoiling attack. But Eisenhower couldn't see the purpose of a limited offensive in the Ardennes, because there was nothing intrinsically valuable to the Germans. The only type of attack in the Ardennes which made any sense was a full scale strategic attack, designed to replicate the events of the summer of 1940.

Eisenhower astute

There is little doubt that Eisenhower's rapid and accurate assessment of the situation saved the Americans from a much larger disaster. Studying the map with Bradley, who still thought Eisenhower was over-reacting, he

ABOVE
Field Marshal Montgomery and Lieutenant General William H Simpson, commanding the US Ninth Army, survey the land that lies beyond a line of German defences. During the Ardennes operation, Simpson's men were transferred from Bradley's to Montgomery's command, much to Bradley's chagrin.

made plans to reinforce Middleton's Corps. That night he ordered Patton's 10th Armoured Division to the southern flank of the penetration, while 7th Armoured was sent to occupy the road junction at St Vith on the northern flank.

Strategic reserve committed

The following morning he committed the last of his strategic reserve, the airborne divisions, sending the 101st to Bastogne (another important road junction) along with a battle-group from 10th Armoured Division, while the 82nd Airborne was ordered to the northern edge of the penetration. Eisenhower had been at his best when deploying his reserve

ABOVE
Captured German film, showing German paratroops examining American equipment that they have taken in December 1944. However they have failed to capture what they needed most – fuel.

RIGHT
German motorcycle troops pictured during the Ardennes offensive. Units like these could move rapidly through the tight forests of the region – weather permitting.

divisions, but he handled other aspects of the battle much less effectively. With his approval, SHAEF Public Relations ordered a news blackout, which allowed rumours to flourish unchecked. In these circumstances, a not unreasonable assumption was that the American army had suffered a major disaster. Within 24 hours of the attack another rumour was circulating, that elite units of German Commandos dressed in American uniforms, and driving American vehicles, were on their way to Paris to assassinate Eisenhower. Machine gun emplacements and barbed wire entanglements quickly surrounded SHAEF HQ, and security became so intense that even Bradley and Bedell Smith had difficulty seeing the supreme commander. All this over-reaction created an atmosphere of crisis: the heavily armoured column in which security insisted Eisenhower now travel only served to reinforce the panic. Soldiers, seeing the fortifications going

up around SHAEF HQ and hearing no news of the real situation, assumed the worst.

Panic measures

The atmosphere, in part self-created, seemed to infect Eisenhower, who became deeply pessimistic. He added enormously to the sense of impending crisis by making an offer to the thousands of GIs inside the Army's prison stockades in England and Europe – any man who would pick up a rifle and go into battle could have a pardon and a clean slate. Eisenhower also issued a circular to black servicemen, almost all of whom were serving in supply services, offering them the chance to transfer to a combat unit 'without regard to color or race'. The fact that Eisenhower's circular contravened War Department policy – black soldiers could not serve in the same units as white solders because black officers and NCOs could not give orders to whites – was quickly noted and

ABOVE
Weary, battle-stained troopers of the 101st Airborne attending a church service in Bastogne on Christmas Eve. Priests of every denomination showed great personal gallantry during the battle, and did much to sustain the spirits of the men.

*Manna from heaven: C-47
transports dropping supplies
to the besieged Bastogne
garrison. From 23 to 28
December, 842 Dakotas
kept Bastogne supplied
from the air, enabling the
Americans to hold on for
a few more crucial days.*

a new circular issued allowing blacks to volunteer for segregated combat units, in which they would serve under white NCOs and officers.

An even stronger indication of the seriousness with which Eisenhower viewed the situation was his willingness to give Montgomery command of all US forces north of the Ardennes, in effect US Ninth and First Armies, leaving Bradley's Twelfth Army Group composed solely of Patton's Third Army. Bradley could not but regard this as a massive vote of no confidence in his generalship and reacted with extreme anger. He screamed down the telephone 'By God, Ike, I cannot be responsible to the American people if you do this. I resign.' Eisenhower refused to accept Bradley's resignation, gave him time to cool down, and phoned Montgomery to offer him control of US First and Ninth Armies. This was what Montgomery had been wanting since the end of August, and a man more attuned to the psychology of others would have reacted with magnaminity. Montgomery did not. Within two hours he had visited both Hodges and Simpson, striding into the HQ of the former 'like Christ come to cleanse the temple.' Insensitive as ever, Montgomery reported to Brooke that Simpson and Hodges 'seemed delighted to have someone to give them firm orders.'

German problems

In fact, even before Eisenhower's reserves arrived in the Ardennes, it was becoming clear that December 1944 was not going to see a replay of May 1940. In the latter campaign the Germans had attacked with relatively light armour following the east-west grain of the Ardennes, when the sun was shining and the ground was dry. Now the Germans were trying to swing south-north, over secondary roads which were little more than farm tracks, over ground that was sodden. Many columns, copying Peiper, had placed 68-tonne (67-ton) King Tiger tanks at their head, in order to overawe the enemy, and had succeeded in churning the roads into rivers of mud, with the powerful Tiger IIs being reduced to towing lighter vehicles through the quagmires they had created. Driving in low gear

LEFT
Men of the 101st Airborne Division recovering a case of medical supplies just dropped into Bastogne. Before the fighting was over, the American garrison suffered some 50 per cent casualties.

BELOW
Belgian refugees cross the Meuse at Dinant, fleeing the German advance. To avoid the bridge falling into enemy hands, the US Army – so keen to capture bridges intact only weeks before – had rigged it with explosives.

for hours at a time also increased fuel consumption, and within 24 hours most columns were experiencing logistic difficulties.

The main difficulty, however, came from the fact that (unlike the French in 1940) isolated American units, some as small as a squad with a bazooka or an anti-tank gun, continued to fight even when they had lost contact with higher formations. The Americans had begun to think of themselves as unbeatable, and no soldier wanted to be first to give in to an army they had chased from Normandy to the frontiers of Germany. By the second day of the offensive, rumours of Peiper's massacres were circulating on divisional radio nets, and these served as an additional motivation – one might as well die fighting because the Germans were not taking prisoners. At

US soldiers struggle to position an anti-tank gun on the German–Belgian frontier. However the mud that is making their task so difficult was also slowing down the German advance.

Echternach on the extreme southern flank of Seventh Army's advance, a single company of 4th Division's 12th Infantry Regiment held out for five days in a hat factory, seriously delaying the advance of an entire division. Peiper himself was held up outside Stavelot on the evening of 17 December for 13 hours by 13 American combat engineers, armed with a bazooka and a few mines. As his lead tank approached, it was stopped by a bazooka shot and Peiper withdrew. He was stopped again at Trois Ponts, this time by by a small task force belonging to the 51st Engineer Battalion, who blew the bridges just as Peiper's spearheads were reaching them. These delays allowed time for the 82nd Airborne Division to move up the valley of the Ambleve River and block Peiper's most direct route to the Meuse and Liège, only 27km (17 miles) to the north.

Defence takes shape

Eisenhower's prompt response on the evening of 16 December now paid dividends. The leading elements of 7th Armoured Division, commanded by Brigadier General Bruce C Clarke, arrived in St Vith before the Germans, and quickly threw together a horseshoe-shaped defence line extending for ten miles to the east of the town, largely manned by battlegroups cobbled together from retreating American soldiers. Manteuffel threw two SS panzer divisions against St Vith, but Clarke managed to hold on until 23 December, forcing the advancing Germans to use secondary routes to bypass the town, and therefore lose time. To the south, a battlegroup of 10th Armoured Division smashed into the spearhead of Manteuffel's Fifth Panzer Army east of Bastogne and delayed its advance for 24 hours, allowing the 101st Airborne to slip into Bastogne before dawn on 19 December. Brigadier General Anthony McAuliffe, temporarily in command in the absence of Maxwell Taylor, who was on leave in Washington, immediately began preparations for defence. By 20 December he had a divisional size group, composed partly of paratroopers and the tanks of 10th Armoured, but also battlegroups (for example Task Force SNAFU) constructed from the remnants of other shattered formations.

Strategically Bastogne was the most important town in the Ardennes. The main routes to Namur and Dinant on the Meuse ran through it, and unless it could be taken, the German advance could only be conducted on secondary roads, which would lead to traffic jams and logistic problems, which would result in long delays. The first German attacks came on 19 December from *Panzer Lehr* and the 26th *Volksgrenadier* Division, which managed to destroy part of US 10th Armoured in the outlying village of Longvilly, but failed to break into the town. By 21 December Bastogne was surrounded and under heavy bombardment, but the following day, when offered honourable terms of surrender, McAuliffe replied with one word - 'NUTS!' - which caused the Germans some confusion, though they soon got the general idea as the paratroopers opened fire. The German attack was remorseless, and by 23 December Bastogne's garrison had suffered 50 per cent casualties and was running low on ammunition.

Patton's counterattack

On 19 December Eisenhower had met with his army group and army commanders at Verdun. Bradley, Simpson, Devers and Hodges were all worried and despondent, but Patton had seen the German offensive as a

wonderful opportunity. In one of the most famous exchanges in American military history he said to the assembled American High Command, 'Hell, let's have the guts to let the sons of bitches go all the way to Paris. Then we'll really cut 'em off and chew 'em up.' Eisenhower had asked Patton how long it would take him to change the direction of his offensive, from east to north, to counterattack the southern flank of what was, by now, a pronounced German bulge in the Ardennes. Patton replied, 'Two days'. This was the high point of Patton's career. He later wrote in his diary, 'When I said I could attack on the 22nd, it created quite a commotion – some people seemed surprised and others pleased – however I believe it can be done.' What Patton had proposed was one of the most difficult operations of war. It meant the reorientation of his entire army from an eastward direction to the north, a 90-degree turn that would pose logistical nightmares. His staff now had to get divisions on new roads and make sure that supplies reached them from dumps which had been established for quite different operations.

Patton's III Corps, spearheaded by 4th Armoured, began attacking north at 0630 hours on 22 December, its objective the relief of Bastogne, and by dusk had made 11km (7 miles). Under the prevailing conditions this was almost miraculous, but that night Patton wrote to his wife, 'I had hoped for more but we are in the middle of a snow storm and there were a lot of demolitions. So I should be content, which of course I am not.' On the morning of Saturday 23 December, Patton wrote a prayer, in which he addressed God as the Supreme Commander. 'Sir, this is Patton talking. The past fourteen days have been straight hell. Rain, snow, more rain, more snow – and I am beginning to wonder what's going on in your headquarters. Whose side are You on anyway? ... Sir, I have never been an unreasonable man, I am not going to ask you for the impossible ... all I request is four days of clear weather.' The prayer was printed and circulated widely throughout Third Army where it did much to maintain morale, and it did seem to work, at least in the short term. Around midday on 23 December a sudden break in the cloud allowed US transport aircraft to drop 146 tonnes (144 tons) of supplies to the defenders, while US Army Air Force fighter bombers pounded German positions. By evening the sky had clouded over again,

and on Christmas Eve Manteuffel threw yet another division into the attack.

The Germans made an all-out effort to take Bastogne on Christmas Day, the weather having closed in completely. Panzers, supported by artillery, penetrated the 101st perimeter in many places, and some American units had now run out of anti-tank rounds. On 26 December the weather cleared sufficiently to permit supplies to be parachuted into Bastogne, but because the Germans now controlled many of the drop zones, it was cancelled. Instead ten gliders mainly loaded with ammunition and one carrying a surgical team and medical supplies swooped down into the heart of the American positions. Later that day the 101st discovered the reason for the frantic German attacks. Shermans of the 37th Tank Battalion, the spearhead of Third Army's 4th Armoured Division, broke through to Bastogne's southern perimeter. A relieved McAuliffe came out to shake the hand of the armoured battalion's commander, Lieutenant Colonel Creighton Abrams, who was awarded a DSC for his part in the action, and was later to command US Forces in South Vietnam.

Battle unfinished

Bastogne had had a dramatic day on 26 December, but the fighting was very far from finished. All US 4th Armoured Division held was a narrow corridor with German panzers divisions on either side, and Manteuffel now determined to break through the American corridor. This was precisely the battle Patton wanted to fight, and by New Year's Eve the fighting had sucked in elements of an additional six German divisions, including von Rundstedt's strategic reserve. The battle on the northern side of the Bulge was also becoming attritional. The US 2nd Armoured Division and British 29th Armoured Brigade crushed the westernmost German units, 2nd Panzer Division and the bulk of *Panzer Lehr*, which

ABOVE

American infantrymen of the US Third Army's 4th Armoured Division spread out as they advance over the snow-covered Belgian slopes to relieve the troops encircled at Bastogne.

RIGHT

Men of the 4th Armoured Division cover the advance of their colleagues towards Bastogne with their M1 Garand rifles.

had run out of fuel within sight of the Meuse near Dinant. On 28 December Eisenhower asked Montgomery to counter-attack into the Bulge from the north and link up with Patton, but Montgomery, expecting another German attack, delayed until 3 January.

By that time the Germans had attacked again, but not where Montgomery expected it. On New Year's Eve Hitler launched Operation Nordwind, a nine-division attack against Devers' forces in Alsace, which was intended to force Patton to pull out of the Ardennes to protect his own lines of communication. Devers fell back, and some of his units panicked, but supplied with details of German intentions by Ultra, Devers was able to hold: however, that he was going to be able to do so was not clear until the middle of January. On 1 January the Luftwaffe also launched a major offensive (its last), sending 1000 aircraft to attack Allied airfields though-out Belgium and north eastern France. The

Germans destroyed 206 Allied aircraft, mainly on the ground, damaged another 300 or so, and badly dented Allied morale. In Washington, Army Chief of Staff Marshall prepared a memorandum which addressed what, only four months earlier, had seemed unthinkable – that the Western Allies might not possess the material strength or the will to break into Nazi Germany. It was just possible, Marshall thought, that the Anglo-Americans might have to opt for a negotiated peace.

V1 and V2 attacks

In London, too, Churchill was beginning to show signs of despondency. The German V1 and V2 campaigns continued unabated, and the government was on the point of ordering the evacuation of London, where scores of people were being killed and hundreds injured each day. During the night of 3/4

January, for example, 50 V1s had been launched in an attack lasting three hours, and two nights later 13 V1s crashed down on the city. On 6 January Churchill wrote to Stalin, confessing that the 'battle in the West is very heavy and, at any time, large decisions may be called for from the Supreme Command.' He let Stalin draw his own conclusions, and, hinting heavily that all was not well, asked Stalin 'whether we can count on a major Russian offensive on the Vistula front, or elsewhere, during January'.

Churchill's letter was unfortunate, because the Battle of the Bulge had already been won, but it allowed Stalin to claim that the Soviet Vistula-Oder offensive, launched on 12 January, had saved the West from defeat. By that time 26 American divisions had moved into the Ardennes, and had begun the process of remorselessly destroying von Rundstedt's

BELOW
American soldiers inspecting a PzKpfw VI Tiger II tank which ran out of fuel on the Stavelot road in Belgium. The Germans never succeeded in their objective of capturing Allied fuel dumps intact, a major contributory cause in the offensive's failure.

forces. Advance patrols of US First Army moving from the north met patrols of Third Army coming from the south at Houffalize on 16 January, and two weeks later American troops had recaptured the positions they had occupied on 16 December. Total American losses had been heavy (over 80,000), of whom 19,000 had been killed and 15,000 captured, but the Germans had lost 100,000. The British, who lost 1400 men, had played a useful but not vital role in the battle. But this did not stop Montgomery claiming the credit. Having been given what he always wanted, effective operational control over American First and Ninth Armies, on 7 January Montgomery gave a press conference during which he made it politically impossible for any American commander ever to place American troops under his command again. Montgomery began by claiming that he had masterminded the defence. It had been an 'interesting' battle, he said, rather like El

RIGHT
Relief at last. Supply columns roll through the hard-won town of Bastogne after the siege is lifted. It took 36 hours to evacuate all 964 stretcher cases. In all, 19,000 Americans were killed in the 'Battle of the Bulge'.

OPPOSITE ABOVE
American reinforcements moving up to the front: a M8 armoured car noses its way past a US artillery train in the Ardennes forest.

OPPOSITE BELOW
Major General Maxwell Taylor, commanding general, 101st Airborne Division (left) with his deputy, Brigadier General Anthony C. McAuliffe. Taylor was in Washington when the Germans attacked in the Ardennes, and it was McAuliffe who organized the division's defence.

Alamein; indeed, 'I think possibly one of the most interesting and tricky battles I have ever handled.' Montgomery's presumption, outrageous as it was, might have been laughed off as an expression of his well-known vanity, but for what came next. The GIs were amongst the finest fighting men in the world, Montgomery said, but only when given proper leadership. The American leadership exploded in rage – Patton described Montgomery to a press conference as 'a tired little fart', and Eisenhower was heard to say that Montgomery was 'a little man, just as little on the inside as he is on the outside.' The war still had four months to run, and Allied planning would now be dominated far more by personal animosities than by abstract strategic considerations.

CHAPTER TEN

CROSSING THE RHINE

Although the Battle of the Bulge marked the end of the Wehrmacht as an offensive force, the German army fought on, and one major obstacle remained for the Allies: the Rhine.

The Battle of the Bulge had been a great shock to the Allies, but by the end of January 1945 they had recovered all of the ground that they had lost during it and were optimistic for the future. Although the Americans had suffered particularly heavy losses during the Ardennes fighting, the Germans continued their fight for survival in north west Europe demoralised, struggling for supplies and fishing an increasingly shallow pool for their manpower requirements. It was these weaknesses that General Eisenhower wished to exploit as he planned the next phase of his campaign – operations that would see the Allies planted firmly onto German soil.

Natural obstacle

However, the Germans could not be written off as a fighting force yet. Although they might have taken a blow to their morale, the German army were still motivated by a desire to defend their homeland, and as such the Allies had to anticipate a hard fight as they edged their way towards Berlin. Indeed, the next major obstacle for Eisenhower's troops to overcome was the Rhine, a natural defensive feature that could provide the enemy with exactly the sort of psychological boost that they required in order to mount a fierce resistance to an Allied attack. If the Rhine crossing

was not enough to occupy the minds of the Allied commanders in early 1945, they could always turn their thoughts towards the breaching of the defensive barrier that the Germans had built further to the west as protection – the West Wall, or Siegfried Line. These considerable obstacles, together with awful weather conditions which had led to widespread flooding in the region due for attack, meant that crossing the Rhine was going to be a complex operation. As a result, it would take time to plan and to amass the resources required for an assault.

The failure of Operation Market Garden, Field Marshal Montgomery's attempt to cross the Lower Rhine at Arnhem in September 1944 employing a narrow fronted thrust, had an impact on Eisenhower's plan for the crossing of the Rhine. For the 1945 operations that could close in on the river, there would be a broad fronted push from positions on the German border in order to keep the Allied front unified, dilute the defending forces and attain momentum, albeit relatively slow, that would not give the enemy time to reorganise themselves. For the Americans, the strategy also had the advantage of stopping the British, and Montgomery in particular, from 'stealing the show'. The Field Marshal's attempt to win the war in Europe by Christmas 1944 via Operation Market Garden had been approved

OPPOSITE
A US Army 81mm (3.18 inch) mortar team in action in the French Alps in early 1945. Sixth Army Group, a mix of American and Free French forces commanded by General Devers, had the task of advancing through this difficult terrain.

by Eisenhower, but by the early months of 1945 the US contingent in Europe outnumbered troops from Britain and her Empire or Commonwealth, and the US commanders wished to be seen as providing more to the war effort than a mere supporting cast for the Twenty-First Army Group.

Allied plans for the crossing

Eisenhower's plan was for Montgomery's troops, which included US Ninth Army under Lieutenant General William H. Simpson, to clear the way to the Rhine opposite Wesel. Operation Veritable would be launched first, and see the British XXX Corps advance from the east of Nijmegen through the forests of the Reichswald. The next phase would see the US Ninth Army push through Münchengladbach to the northeast, and link up with the British in Operation Grenade. After a consolidation period, Twenty-First Army Group would then prepare for an assault crossing of the Rhine to outflank the Ruhr (Germany's industrial heartland) from the north, and then move onto the North German Plain. If all went well, then in this good tank country, Montgomery could then move swiftly on towards Berlin.

The plan for the US Twelfth Army Group, commanded by Lieutenant General Bradley – Operation Lumberjack – was for an advance to Field Marshal Montgomery's south in an attempt to clear the approaches to the Rhine from Cologne to Koblenz. The US Third Army under Lieutenant General Patton was then to swing southeast towards Mainz and Mannheim in order to link up with Lieutenant General Devers' Sixth Army Group, who were advancing from the Saar in Operation Undertone. Bridgeheads over the Rhine would then be seized in the south, but only to divert German reserves away from Montgomery's assault and to provide a southern pincer against the Ruhr. This plan was not to the liking of either Bradley or Patton, as they wanted a larger role for the US forces. It did not take long for

Eisenhower to learn of the disquiet that his proposals had engendered, and this eventually led to a change of plan once the Rhine had been crossed.

Thus, in early 1945, the focus of Allied operations was on a rapid advance to the Rhine and preparations for an assault crossing in the early spring. But first the West Wall had to be breached. This defensive position, situated along the German border, consisted of block houses and anti-tank defences forming a formidable obstacle for any attacker. To make it even more difficult for Allied armour,

the wet weather of February 1945 water-logged the battlefield; even worse, in Ninth Army's area the Germans controlled a series of dams on the River Ruhr which, if opened, would flood the area so badly that very little would be able to move at all. Thus, although it would have been advantageous for the Allied commanders, co-ordination of the four offensive operations was something that could not be relied upon.

In the north, the areas where Operations Veritable and Grenade were to simultaneously take place, Montgomery prepared his attacks

with the sort of precision that was so characteristic of him. Such precision was warranted, for if the British were to scythe through the German defences in order to reach the Rhine, they were going to have to overcome considerable difficulties. Lieutenant General Crerar's Canadian First Army was given responsibility for Veritable, and included Lieutenant General Sir Brian Horrocks' British XXX Corps, which consisted of five divisions: 2nd and 3rd Canadian, 15th (Scottish), 51st (Highland) and 53rd (Welsh). His reserves included the Guards and 11th

ABOVE
Warrant Officer Millard Grary, a US soldier of Scottish descent, playing his bagpipes in the 'dragon's teeth' defences of the Siegfried Line. Shortly after this photograph was taken, German artillery opened fire on the piper, forcing him to stop and seek cover.

British Second Army troops, one armed with a PIAT (Projector, Infantry, Anti-Tank) weapon, advance cautiously into the village of St Joost supported by a Crocodile flamethrower tank, during the advance through Holland in January 1945.

Armoured, together with the 43rd (Wessex) and 52nd (Lowland) Divisions. This amounted to some 80,000 men and 1000 tanks. This force would, however, need all its guile and power to overcome the 12,000 men and 36 self-propelled guns of Lieutenant General Alfred Schlemm's First Parachute Army that opposed them, as the latter's in-depth defences were well prepared and carefully situated on the high ground. In terrain that favoured the defenders, the wet ground in the region (both to the north and south of XXX Corps) forced the attack onto the narrow roads through the dense forests of the Reichwald. In such terrain there were many things that could bring the Allied attack to a grinding halt.

Operation Veritable

Operation Veritable began at 0500 hours on 8 February 1945. The bombardment from 1000 guns lasted two and a half hours before being halted. The enemy's response was to return fire and, having given away their positions, they were targeted by the Allied guns and subjected to a fresh three-hour bombard-

ment. Having thus neutralised the German artillery, the infantry then moved forward under the cover of smoke. Their advance was slow, as the rain had turned the battlefield into a quagmire and put the roads out of action. In such circumstances, command and control were extremely difficult, and attaining any forward momentum was almost impossible. In conditions that resembled the hard-fought slogging matches of World War I in Flanders, the infantry struggled forward with little armoured or aerial support.

XXX Corps were to have attained their objectives in three or four days, but this proved to be a schedule that they just could not keep, and the town of Cleve did not fall until 11 February. The British failed to achieve any worthwhile momentum despite the heavy air bombardment of enemy positions and Horrocks' commitment of 43rd Division to add impetus to the advance. The traffic jams and then the German decision to open the Ruhr dam conspired to prevent all movement in Ninth Army's area, and freed German troops to oppose the Anglo-Canadian assault. By the fourth week of

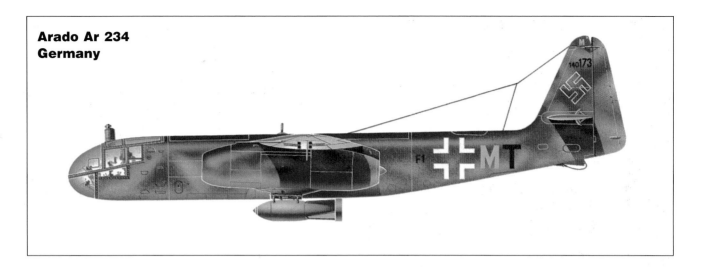

**Arado Ar 234
Germany**

February, Goch had been entered and the remaining German defenders had pulled back across the Rhine, destroying all of the bridges in the area. The British had achieved their objectives, but the affair had been far tougher than had been expected and this was an ominous sign for the fighting yet to come. Operation Grenade was meant to have opened 24 hours after Veritable, but because of the Ruhr floods it had to be postponed until 23 February. By this time the water levels had dropped, and the Americans actually encountered relatively weak German

opposition. A link up was made with the Anglo-Canadians at Geldorn on 3 March. Thus, the approaches to the Rhine from Nijmegen and Düsseldorf were clear, and this allowed Montgomery to begin the detailed planning of his Rhine crossing, scheduled for 23/24 March.

Lack of bridges

The problem for Twenty-First Army Group was that no bridges had been taken in their area of operations. On 2 March, US Intelligence reported that two bridges, one at

BELOW
*British tank crewmen take
the opportunity for a warm
meal during their advance
through Holland.*

Oberkassel and the other at Uerdingen, were still in one piece. Men from the US 83rd Infantry Division therefore disguised themselves as Germans and moved towards the first bridge. They managed to get within a few hundred metres of the structure when the bridge was blown up in their faces. Men from the US 2nd Armoured and 95th Infantry Divisions, meanwhile, sped to capture Adolf Hitler Bridge at Uerdingen. A few of the party managed to get over the crossing, but they were forced back before it too was destroyed. An assault crossing in the northern sector was therefore necessary.

Cologne taken

Bradley's attack began with Lieutenant General Hodges' First and Patton's Third Armies on 28 February. Operation Lumberjack started well, largely because the defenders had been diluted by the German need to defend against Montgomery's advance to the north. Hodges' troops advanced on the left, crossing the Ruhr once the flood had subsided and then pushing onto the Cologne Plain. Cologne itself was taken on 5/6 March after a relatively easy advance, during which the remaining pockets of German resistance had been destroyed using tanks and infantry co-operating closely together. Simultaneously, other elements of First Army moved in on Bonn, whilst 9th Armoured Division manoeuvred to the southeast and established a link-up with Patton's men at Sinzig on the Ahr River. On the evening of 6 March, 9th Armoured reached the town of Meckenheim, about 16km (10 miles) west of the Rhine, and immediately prepared to exploit the scattered nature of the opposition. At this point Brigadier General William M. Hoge's Combat Command B was ordered to close the Rhine at Remagen, shielding other elements of the division that would advance down the Ahr Valley to make contact with Patton. He divided his units into small 'task forces', with one of them, commanded by Colonel Leonard Engemann and consisting of part of 14th Tank Battalion, all of 27th Armoured Infantry Battalion and some engineer support, moving off on the morning of 7 March to seize Remagen. By the early afternoon a unit of the 27th Armoured Infantry, commanded by 2nd Lieutenant Karl Timmermann, exited the woods above the town and saw something that he did not expect – the Ludendorff railway bridge across the Rhine, still intact. In such circumstances

there was little time for a detailed reconnaissance; Engemann's men moved into the town and eventually forced a crossing after German attempts to destroy the bridge had failed. Timmermann led his men across the damaged, but still intact, bridge, and reached the east bank of the Rhine at 1600 hours.

US bridgehead

The news that a crossing of the river had been made spread quickly through the American troops and the Allied chain of command. Indeed, by nightfall on 7 March Bradley knew of the success and he responded by saying with glee, 'This'll bust 'em wide open!' Eisenhower immediately ordered a crossing over the bridge by as many troops as possible. But the crossing at Remagen was not without its disadvantages. It certainly did not fit into the Allied plan that had been gradually unfolding. Bradley, however, failed to see the problem: 'A bridge is a

OPPOSITE ABOVE
British tank men survey a German anti-tank gun that has just been knocked out. The Germans did everything possible to slow down the British advance through Holland, fighting suicidal rearguard actions.

BELOW
A gun crew of the 1st Battalion, 327th Glider Infantry Regiment, 101st Airborne Division, man a camouflaged anti-tank gun in a barn during the advance on the Western Front. Crossed gate posts have been used to camouflage the barrel.

ABOVE

US infantry from First Army advance in the company of a tank through the ruins of Cologne, with the twin spires of the cathedral visible in the background. The city never recovered from an RAF 1000-bomber raid in 1942.

RIGHT

Infantry of the 84th Division, US First Army, move into the village of Baal, Germany, under heavy sniper fire, on 24 February 1945.

bridge,' he argued, 'and mighty damn good anywhere across the Rhine.' However, the taking of the Ludendorff Bridge did not tempt Eisenhower to take his focus off Montgomery's action in the north, especially as the Remagen bridgehead led into the hills of the Westerwald, with limited opportunities for swift attack and breakthrough thereafter. Nevertheless, the taking of an intact Rhine crossing was a major psychological boost for the Allies and a serious body blow for the Germans. Having seized the bridgehead the

Americans became a new threat for the defenders, who in turn had to redeploy troops from the north to the south in order to contain the new danger. The bridge at Remagen eventually collapsed on 17 March.

Patton pushes forward

Patton's Third Army, meanwhile, endeavoured to capture its objectives in Operation Lumberjack and successfully linked up with Hodges' troops at Sinzig on 9 March. By 18 March, the west bank of the Rhine had been secured as far as Koblenz; Patton, never one to spurn an opportunity, recognised that he had attained some momentum, and immediately sent units southeast towards Mainz and Mannheim. These troops threatened to cut off German forces in the Saar that were already under attack from Lieutenant General Alexander Patch's US Seventh Army in Operation Undertone. Patton did not stop on the Rhine, however. He was angry that the focus of the attack was still in the north, and was envious of Hodges' success at Remagen, and so, on 22 March, the 11th US Infantry Regiment paddled across the river at Nierstein and Oppenheim against inconsequential opposition.

The news that Patton had crossed the river reached Montgomery just as the British were about to launch their own operations after

LEFT
Another view of First Army's advance into Cologne on 6 March 1945. Many German cities were reduced to a similar state by Allied bombers.

BELOW
Devastated Cologne pictured from the air, early in 1945, its cathedral standing amid a mass of ruin. The last of over 100 RAF raids on Cologne took place on 2 March 1945, four days before the city was captured by US forces.

immensely detailed preparations. 'Without benefit of aerial bombardments, ground smoke, artillery preparation and airborne assistance,' a US Army communiqué read, 'the Third Army at 2200 hours Thursday evening, 22 March, crossed the Rhine river.'

Allied disagreements

Such messages were designed to cause the British embarrassment, and the growing antipathy between the Allied field commanders was reflected in Patton's words about Montgomery: 'I can outfight that little fart anytime.' Eisenhower was not moved to change his plan at this stage in order to give the US troops the role that they so desired – but they were still hopeful of a revision to the Supreme Commander's intentions. The reason for their optimism was founded on the agreement that the Allied political leaders had already come to at the Yalta Conference in February 1945.

At Yalta it had been agreed that Berlin would fall within the Soviet zone of occupation once the war was over. Thus, observers decided, Eisenhower would be unlikely to want to commit his troops to the battle for a city that would then have to be handed over

Seen after the capture of a German position, a heavily-customised Sherman tank of the US 7th Armoured Division stands next to the body of a SS trooper. The Sherman's crew have used spare wheels and sandbags in an attempt to improve the tank's protection against German anti-tank guns.

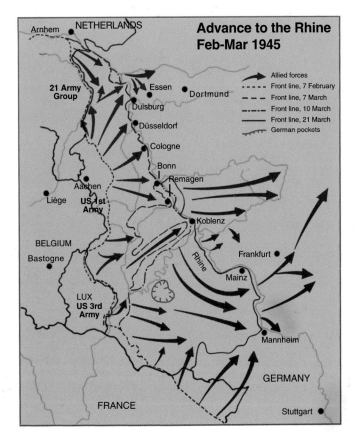

Advance to the Rhine Feb-Mar 1945

NETHERLANDS
Arnhem

21 Army Group

Essen
Dortmund
Duisburg
Düsseldorf
Cologne
Bonn
Remagen
Aachen
Liège
US 1st Army
Koblenz

BELGIUM
Bastogne

Rhine
Frankfurt
Mainz

LUX
US 3rd Army

Mannheim

GERMANY

FRANCE
Stuttgart

→ Allied forces
---- Front line, 7 February
– – – Front line, 7 March
–·–·– Front line, 10 March
——— Front line, 21 March
⌐⌐⌐⌐ German pockets

to the Soviets. This, together with the attainment of American bridgeheads at Remagen and further to the south, made it possible for great advances to be made deep into central and southern Germany where enemy defences were weak. In such circumstances, American commanders believed, it would be logical for Eisenhower to switch the emphasis of the attack to the US forces.

Belt and braces approach

Meanwhile, Montgomery, who was well aware of the feeling that was growing against him, continued his preparations to cross the Rhine – Operation Plunder. Schemes for this operation had been fermenting in Montgomery's mind ever since D-Day in June 1944, because he knew that it was a major obstacle that would eventually have to be crossed, but planning for the crossing did not begin in earnest until early March 1945. The nature of the task, together with the characteristic 'belt and braces' approach to his operations, led Montgomery to try to exploit fully growing Allied assets for the crossing. In

his desire to do everything that he could to dislocate the enemy before the infantry advanced, the collation, analysis and dissemination of intelligence was crucial, for only then, the commander of Twenty-First Army Group argued, could artillery bombardment and air strikes be effective. Montgomery was also keen to ensure that all arms co-operation, as well as inter-unit co-operation, was as close as it could possibly be for this attack. The assault was to require the infantry to create a bridgehead with artillery support, engineers to build pontoon bridges for the armour, resupply and reinforcement, airborne troops to defend against counter-attacks and aircraft to provide close air support.

RIGHT
As US troops cross the Ludendorff bridge, German prisoners are marched in the other direction.

BELOW
The Ludendorff bridge at Remagen was captured after a dramatic armoured dash by the US 9th Armoured Division, who erected this sign on the bridge to mark their achievement.

Montgomery's plan was issued by his headquarters on 9 March, with the assault scheduled to take place on the night of 23/24 March. In order to stun the enemy, neutralise their defences and create gaps in their line, a massive air and artillery bombardment was planned to precede the infantry assault. The main attack was to be carried out by Lieutenant General Sir Miles Dempsey's British Second Army, which was tasked with seizing the towns of Rees and Wesel on the Allied left. A subsidiary attack, to be conducted by Simpson's Ninth Army, was to take place simultaneously on the right, in order to split the German defenders between Wesel and Duisburg. In many respects this operation was designed in a similar way to those mounted by the Allies in the last days of World War I, but new technology enabled Montgomery to do things that his predecessors nearly 30 years before could not. Radio communication aided co-operation at all

levels, the infantry could cross the river in amphibious vehicles and landing craft, reliable tanks could be quickly deployed once the river had been spanned, and aircraft could drop airborne troops. The intention was to create a bridgehead that was 64km (40 miles) long and 16km (10 miles) deep in the first 24 hours. From this, the bulk of Twenty-First Army Group would then advance and encircle the Ruhr, before deploying in strength onto the North German Plain. The final phase of Operation Plunder was for the Canadians to cross the Rhine at Emmerich on the extreme left once the main assault had been successful, and then advance north into Holland.

Overwhelming forces

The plan, therefore, was elaborate but conservative, as it was based on the build-up of overwhelming superiority of forces to ensure victory. Montgomery's plan was probably not, on the face of it, what Patton would have chosen as his plan of action, but in Twenty-First Army Group's sector there was great need for caution, as it was here that the Germans were expecting the main assault to take place, and the British commander had little option but to devise a set-piece attack. The operation also had to be meticulously planned because of the numerous problems associated with a crossing of the Rhine in this area. The Rhine in front of Montgomery was up to 460m (1500 feet) wide, and the approaches on the western side were soaked and unfit for heavy vehicles. As a result, engineers had to be brought forward to build roads, construct hard-standings for the stockpiling of supplies and ammunition, and prepare bridging sites. By 19 March, more than 25,400 tonnes (25,000 tons) of bridging equipment had been delivered, and a number of suitable sites selected, but secrecy was all-important. Again, just like the prelude to World War I attacks, deception measures were

BELOW
After days of heavy use, the bridge at Remagen collapsed on 17 March, but by that time the Americans were well-established on the other side of the Rhine.

undertaken in order to keep details from the Germans, and special smoke generators were used to create a dense smoke barrier for 32km (20 miles) along the river.

Smokescreen

One British tank commander said of the scene, 'Long before you came to the Rhine, you saw the smokescreen. It stretched along the front without a break; a tall white cloud, two or three hundred feet [60–90m] high, curling at its top like a wave-crest caught in slow motion.'

The smoke hid a build-up of nearly one million troops, and without it the German artillery could have done an awful lot of damage.

In such circumstances there was no chance of attaining operational surprise. Awaiting the onset of the British storm were the remains of Schlemm's First Parachute Army, who had been preparing their defences for weeks. Sitting in their trenches and defensive positions the German troops had an anxious wait, made all the more difficult by the news that Schlemm had been wounded by an artillery strike against his headquarters on 22 March. Their ability to defend themselves had already been dealt a blow by the replacement of the now-retired Field Marshal von Rundstedt, the capable Commander in Chief West, with the out-of-touch Field Marshal Albrecht Kesselring on 8 March, and Schlemm's removal from the battlefield only made a bad situation worse. Allied air and artillery attacks targeted German command and control centres, and plagued their rear areas, causing German commanders immense difficulties. Heavy bombers had been hitting transportation in and around the Ruhr since February, and thwarted the movement of reinforcements and valuable supplies.

As March progressed, fighter-bombers began to attack enemy positions on the east bank of the Rhine in support of the 5500-gun artillery bombardment that sought to do as much damage to German defences and morale as possible, while also disabling their guns. Such preparation and support made the assault troops – the 15th (Scottish) and 51st (Highland) Divisions, plus 1st Commando Brigade in the British sector and the 30th and 79th Infantry Divisions in the American – full of confidence, and the belief spread that Plunder was the beginning of the end of the war in Europe.

Winston Churchill shared this confidence, and flew to Montgomery's headquarters at Venlo on 23 March with Field Marshal Sir Alan Brooke to witness the battle. While Churchill was airborne, Montgomery issued

**Gun Motor Carriage M10
USA**

his final orders for the attack and ended them with the words, 'Over the Rhine, then, let us go. And good hunting to you all on the other side.'

Opening bombardment

At 1800 hours on 23 March, 3500 field guns and 2000 anti-tank guns and rocket projectors unleashed a tremendous bombardment. Whilst the bombardment gradually gained in intensity, the assault troops moved down to the river bank and boarded a variety of amphibious craft whilst Major General Percy Hobart's special Duplex Drive (DD) tanks awaited the word to 'swim' across the Rhine. These were tense moments.

ABOVE
The M10 mounted a 76.2mm (3 inch) gun in an open-topped turret, but had relatively little armour protection to help improve its performance.

LEFT
A M18 tank destroyer of the 4th Armoured Division, US Third Army, crosses the Moselle River on a treadway bridge. The task of Patton's Third Army was to drive on to the River Weser via Frankfurt. Patton attempted to steal Montgomery's thunder by crossing the Rhine the day before Twenty-First Army Group.

Motor Machinist's Mate 2nd Class Robert Mooty of the US Navy ferries members of the US 89th Infantry Division across the Rhine at Oberwesel.

Major Martin Lindsay, commanding the 1st Battalion Gordon Highlanders in 51st (Highland) Division on the left, described it as 'a lovely night with a three-quarter moon', and remembered 'the long ghostly files of men marching up to [the Buffalo amphibious vehicles] ... a few busy figures darting here and there in the moonlight directing people to this or that Buffalo'.

Violent explosions

One of the commanders of a troop of Crocodiles (converted Churchill tanks, each equipped with a flamethrower), Andrew

Wilson, remembered the bombardment: 'East and west as far as [I] could see, the night was lit with gunfire; it flickered through the trees and flashed on the underside of the clouds. The ground shook ceaselessly, and now and again there was a violent, continuing explosion, like a pack of cards being snapped.'

Anti-climax

The weight of numbers of the attackers and the firepower that supported them made the job of crossing the Rhine far easier than it might otherwise have been; in fact the operation was something of an anti-climax, but a welcome one. At 2100 hours, the vehicles of the first assault waves, the 7th Battalion Black Watch and the 7th Battalion Argyll and Sutherland Highlanders of the 51st (Highland) Division, entered the cold waters of the Rhine. It took them two and a half minutes to reach the east bank to the west of Rees. They suffered some casualties from anti-personnel mines, but quickly pushed out, with the support of amphibious tanks, to create a bridgehead. At 2104 hours General Horrocks received the news that he had so

anxiously been waiting for: 'The Black Watch has landed safely on the far bank.' Crucially for the operation, the left flank had been secured.

The 1st Commando Brigade attacked one hour later, and carved out a bridgehead on

LEFT
US troops during the Rhine crossing. Landing craft were used where the river was at its widest, or where the Germans had flooded the area to help in its defence.

BELOW
An amphibious assault vehicle filled with troops hits the waters of the Rhine under cover of a smoke screen during the crossing of the river by General Simpson's US Ninth Army.

the extreme right of the British assault area close to the town of Wesel. Although a number of their assault boats and amphibious landing craft were hit by German artillery, their crossing also went smoothly. The commandos immediately set up a defensive perimeter on the east bank, but awaited an air strike on Wesel before they entered the town. The bombing that followed once again reflected Allied superiority at this time and a German inability to do anything about their enemy applying it. At 2230 hours, over 200 RAF Avro Lancaster and de Havilland Mosquito bombers roared over their target and dropped more than 1016 tonnes (1000 tons) of high explosives. These bombs, when coupled with the damage already done by the artillery, resulted in the total devastation of the town. As fires raged in the ruined buildings, the commandos (supported by 1st

Battalion of the Cheshire Regiment) attacked Wesel from the west. The surviving German defenders put up a stubborn fight, but the area was under Allied control, if not completely cleared of Germans.

Scottish attack

The 15th (Scottish) Division, the third of the British assaults, attacked as soon as both flanks had been secured. Their crossing was virtually unopposed. At 0200 hours on 24 March, the 8th Battalion Royal Scots and 6th Battalion Royal Scots Fusiliers were ferried across to take the village of Bislich to the west of Wesel, whilst on their left, the 10th Battalion, Highland Light Infantry and the 2nd Battalion, Argyll and Sutherland Highlanders, crossed to take Haffen and, eventually, linked up with the 51st (Highland) Division around Rees. By dawn both assaults had been

BELOW
Two British artillerymen,
Gunners O. Woods and R.F.
Jackson, provide a welcome
cup of tea for Winston
Churchill, the British Prime
Minister, who flew out from
England to watch the
crossing of the Rhine.

reinforced, and their initial objectives taken. Included in the follow-up battalions were the Canadian Highland Light Infantry, attached to 51st (Highland) Division, but overall this attack was very much a Scottish concern.

Further to the south, the Americans conducted an equally successful attack. Here the 2000-gun hurricane bombardment began at 0100 hours on 24 March, firing 65,261 artillery shells in just an hour, whilst 1500 heavy bombers launched raids on other targets. The surprise and the weight of the bombardment caused the Germans all sorts of problems and they lost all cohesion. At 0200 hours the US 30th Infantry Division were ferried across at Büderich, Wallach and Rheinburg, and here they created bridgeheads with very few casualties. An hour later, the US 79th Infantry Division landed on the east bank to their right around Walsum and Orsay. This division did encounter some problems with the current of the river in this area – indeed, one of the amphibious landing craft was turned round in mid-stream – but casualties were minimal nonetheless. Once again the preliminary bombardment had

done its job, in the words of Lieutenant Whitney O. Refvem, commanding a company of 117th Infantry Regiment, 'There was no real fight to it. The artillery had done the job for us.'

Five bridgeheads established

As the infantry consolidated their positions, the engineers moved forward to take supplies across the river and begin the time-consuming task of building pontoon bridges. By dawn on 24 March, five bridgeheads had been firmly established and, although there was still heavy fighting at Rees and Wesel, there was little to concern the attackers as the German defenders' response had been, and continued to be, weak and uncoordinated. During the day, Kesselring did manage to despatch the 116th Panzer and 15th Panzergrenadier Divisions from a very limited reserve, but this was what Montgomery had anticipated, and he had airborne troops in situ to deal with any such counter-attacks.

The airborne element of the plan was known as Operation Varsity, and involved Major General Matthew Ridgway's US

ABOVE

Men of the Cheshire Regiment, who crossed the Rhine on the afternoon of 24 March 1945 in support of the 1st Commando Brigade, landing from Buffalo amphibious vehicles on the east bank of the river.

XVIII Airborne Corps, comprised of US 17th and British 6th Airborne Divisions, dropping onto the east bank of the Rhine on the morning of 24 March to reinforce the bridgehead. The classic airborne role was to take vital objectives in advance of the ground offensive, and then for the airborne troops to wait for relief from the link-up ground troops. This had been the plan for Montgomery's Operation Market Garden in September of the previous year. However, having failed to get XXX Corps across Arnhem Bridge on that occasion, Montgomery did not want to try such a bold use of airborne troops again, and argued that their flexibility would be best served in this operation to consolidate ground already taken by the infantry. The airborne divisions were to be used to 'disrupt the hostile defence of the Rhine in the Wesel sector by seizure of key terrain ... in order to deepen rapidly the bridgehead and to facilitate further offensive operations of 2nd Army.' They were to seize and hold the high ground north of Wesel and defend the bridgehead from counter-attacks before enough troops could be concentrated in it for the advance to continue. At all costs, momentum was to be maintained.

Parachute attack

The use of airborne forces in the crossing had been mooted from the very earliest planning

RIGHT ABOVE

The crossing of the Rhine by Twenty-First Army Group took place under cover of a massive smoke screen. Observation posts were established forward of the screen, in the dangerous 100m (110 yards) between the winter dykes and the river.

RIGHT

The assault on the Rhine was backed up by the biggest artillery barrage of the war. The photograph shows a British 140mm (5.5 inch) gun – one of 1500 artillery pieces assembled by the Allies for the operation – in action during the bombardment.

CROSSING THE RHINE / 225

stages, and research was conducted into the best use of Ridgway's troops in the light of Operation Market Garden. On 7 November 1944, the first staff study for Operation Varsity was issued by the headquarters of the First Allied Airborne Army, and by 9 February 1945 Ridgway had received his first instruc-

tions for the airborne operation from Montgomery. Ridgway, responsible for the detailed planning and execution of Varsity, established an airborne corps command post to help facilitate close contact with ground force formations, and he also held a planning exercise in England which was attended by

BELOW

The LVT 4 (or Buffalo as it was known by the British) had proven its worth in the Pacific war against the Japanese, and was equally successful on the Rhine.

**LVT 4
USA**

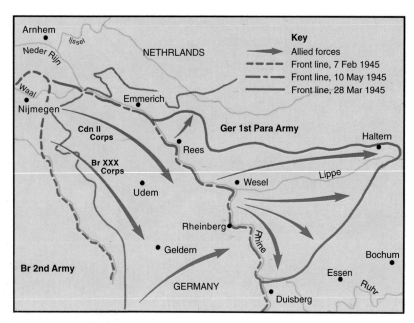

the deputy airborne corps commander, Major General Richard Gale, the two divisional airborne commanders, and the three British brigade commanders. The aim was for a study of a series of situations that might develop during the operation and how to resolve them. By 13 February the headquarters of the US XVIII Airborne Corps had begun planning for Operation Varsity, and two weeks later the first air co-ordinating conference was held at the Supreme Headquarters of the Allied Expeditionary Force. On 1 March, 17th US Airborne Division was given its tasks, and 6th British Airborne Division started its planning and training for the operation. The planning phase went as smoothly as anybody could possibly have imagined.

RIGHT
Men of the Gordon Highlanders advancing over the floodbank of the Rhine before crossing the river in the wake of the airborne and commando assault. Bridgeheads 4570m (5000 yards) deep had been established east of the Rhine by the end of the first day.

Daylight attack

To take full advantage of Allied air supremacy and overwhelming superiority in artillery, the operation was to take place in daylight. It was expected that the use of paratroops after the crossing rather than before would confuse the enemy. The advantages offered by surprise also drove the decision made for the deployment of the airborne troops in one lift, and that they were to be landed almost on top of their objectives, unlike at Arnhem. In deciding where the paratroops should land, the principles employed were that they should be within friendly artillery range, and that link-up with the ground forces should be effected on the first day of the operation. The specific airborne objectives were the Diersfordter Wald, the thickly forested high ground

overlooking Wesel and the Rhine; the roads running into the area of the landings along which counter-attacks might be focused; and the bridges over the River Issel to the east of the Wald. The river was not wide, but it did have steep banks and was a tank obstacles. It was, therefore, essential to capture and hold its bridges to secure them for the subsequent offensive operations, and to prevent the Germans from using them to reinforce the area. The British were given the task of securing the northern area and the Americans the sourthern area. Ridgway later said that the plan was 'right in all aspects' and this was the bedrock for the success of Varsity.

The British 6th Airborne Division left England aboard their transport aircraft and gliders at 0700 hours on 24 March. At

ABOVE
British troops and tanks entering Brunen, Germany, on 27 March 1945, three days after crossing the Rhine. By 1 April the Ruhr was completely encircled, and the Allied armies were advancing up to 80km (50 miles) a day.

0900 hours, the US 17th Airborne Division took off from bases in France and joined up with the British air armada over Brussels that morning – a total of over 1572 aircraft and 1326 gliders, holding over 21,000 men. Although no enemy air reaction was reported by the air forces lifting the airborne troops into battle, no chances were taken, and 2000 fighter aircraft escorted them to their destination. Air supremacy had long been attained by the Allies, and in Operation Varsity, they used it to their full advantage.

Landings begin

The airborne landings commenced at 1000 hours, and they were watched by Churchill from the west bank of the river. The landings required immense skill, as both divisions were landing in a very small area just five miles wide and six miles long, situated north and west of Wesel. As the battle for the Rhine was already in progress, and the areas designated for the airborne landings were so close to the river, it was not anticipated that air crews would have any difficulty in finding the drop zones and landing zones, but there was still some confusion. Some of the transport pilots were disorientated by the bad visibility and dropped their parachutists in the wrong area, and a number of gliders were released either too early or too late. The net result was that the German machine-gunners and anti-aircraft crews (there were 712 light and 114 heavy anti-aircraft guns in the vicinity) that had survived the attentions of the Allies thus far, began to inflict considerable casualties on both aircraft and men.

The landings took two hours to complete and more than 100 aircraft and gliders were destroyed, and 332 severely damaged. The

BELOW

British airborne troops carry out a last-minute briefing beside their Horsa glider before taking off for their pre-arranged landing zones east of the Rhine on 24 March 1945. So many glider pilots were lost in the earlier Arnhem debacle that RAF pilots had to be drafted in for this operation.

losses included Curtiss C-46 Commando transporters that were used for the first time in this operation. Those carrying the US 513th Parachute Infantry Regiment, for example, were caught in anti-aircraft fire before they reached the drop zone. In total, 22 C-46s were shot down and a further 38 badly damaged. Nevertheless, such was the weight of the airborne numbers and the flexibility of a plan that anticipated confusion and losses, that Operation Varsity was a great success. The British flew in with its two parachute brigades leading and despite accurate anti-aircraft fire, the 3rd Parachute Brigade began dropping at 1000 hours around the northwest corner of the woods. The earliest casualties were sustained because German troops held woods on the edge of the drop zone, and were in a position to fire on a number of parachutists who landed in the trees, and to rake the area with fire during the landings. The brigade cleared the woods in about an hour, and by the middle of the afternoon had made contact with the leading elements of the 15th (Scottish) Division.

Meanwhile the 5th Parachute Brigade had dropped on the north side of the Mehr–Hamminkeln Road (a mile and a half west of the 3rd Parachute Brigade) – after intense anti-aircraft fire and airburst shelling – into a drop zone that was being mortared.

These factors meant that their drop was not as accurate as it might have been, and the airborne troops on the ground often found themselves some way from their intended positions. Nevertheless, the brigade did move out towards its objectives that morning, the ground astride the road leading to Hamminkeln, and the important road and rail junctions in the gap between themselves and the 3rd Parachute Brigade. The Germans held practically all of the farms and houses in the vicinity, but they were quickly cleared, and by 1530 hours all of the objectives had been captured. Enemy shelling and mortaring was much reduced by the afternoon, and although there was a counter-attack, it was beaten off. The 6th Airlanding Brigade, the third and final brigade of the British airborne division, started to land at about 1030 hours.

Problems

The enemy's flak concentrated on the gliders and about half were damaged by the time that the troops disembarked. Accurate tactical landings were not possible, as mentioned earlier, owing to bad visibility – dust clouds caused by the bombing and shelling, smoke from crashed and blazing aircraft and smoke laid down by the enemy. Some pilots were unable to get their bearings and therefore landed in the wrong place and some crashed

German civilians enlisted to work for the Allies gaze up at the vast armada of aircraft heading for their objectives east of the Rhine. The Germans could barely comprehend the sheer scale of the Allies' resources.

badly. However, the important *coup de main* parties did land safely on their objectives, and sufficient numbers of the remainder of the brigade landed close enough to overcome the enemy in one rush.

Issel bridges taken

By 1000 hours the three bridges over the Issel had been captured intact, and the village of Hamminkeln had been secured. Considerable heavy fire from enemy anti-aircraft guns in a

ground role and mortars did continue for some time after the landings, but they were soon silenced. The only organised enemy force was in an eastern portion of the bridge-head near Ringenberg (north-east of Hamminkeln), where there appeared to be four or five tanks and some infantry. The only available battalion to deal with them were the 2nd Battalion, Oxfordshire and Buckingham-shire Light Infantry, but at the time the unit was only at half strength and therefore too weak to be of use. As a result some Typhoon fighter-bombers were called upon to assist, and they quickly succeeded in keeping the enemy quiet.

The landings of the US airborne troops were also successful, with the 507th Parachute Infantry Regiment dropping at the southern edge of Diersfordter Wald. Although some scattering of these troops during the drop did occur, once on the ground they found little enemy resistance, and took their objectives in just a few hours. The 513rd Parachute Infantry Regiment, meanwhile, was due to land to the east of the woods, but they were dropped too far to the

ABOVE
German prisoners taken in the Hamminkeln area by men of the 6th Airborne Division soon after their landings. The increasing desperation of German recruitment is shown by the wide variety of ages amongst the soldiers.

LEFT
A still from a film made by the RAF Film Unit of the airborne landings over the Rhine on 24 March 1945. This photograph shows L. Marsland Gander (wearing glasses), war correspondent of the Daily Telegraph, *who landed in a glider, with a party of airborne troops at the first rendezvous.*

north in a strongly-held German area, and had to fight their way south. Nevertheless, by mid-afternoon they too had secured their objectives. The US gliders landed accurately by the bridges over the Issel to the south east of 513rd Parachute Infantry Regiment, despite the smoke from Wesel. Once again, however, intense German flak and small arms fire caused problems, which resulted in less than one third of the gliders landing without damage. Small actions took place all over the US glider zone, but German resistance soon began to crumble. Two of the bridges over the Issel were secured intact, and they were held successfully against several enemy counter-attacks with tanks.

Allied success

Thus, by the end of the day, Twenty-First Army Group had gained a firm footing on the east bank of the Rhine, and the airborne troops had attained all of their intended objectives. The enemy had been overwhelmed, and

was not in a position to take effective action against any part of the bridgehead, or to halt Second Army's advance. Operation Varsity had been a triumph; careful appreciation of what airborne forces could achieve, together with good planning and properly allocated resources, provided the firm foundation upon which the operational success was built.

The Germans were certainly surprised by the way in which the Allied airborne troops were employed on 24 March. Major General Fiebig, the commander of the German 84th Infantry Division, was captured and interrogated by Canadian officers. Their subsequent report of their interviews with Fiebig provides an interesting insight into the German reaction to the airborne landings: 'General Fiebig claimed the Germans were not aware of our preparations for the airborne operation in support of the Rhine crossings and ... confessed that he had been badly surprised by the sudden advent of two complete divisions in this particular area, and throughout the

RIGHT
Paratroops of the 17th Division, First Allied Airborne Army, boarding a Curtiss C-46 Commando transport prior to the assault on the Rhine crossings at Wesel in March 1945. This was the first time that C-46 aircraft were used in an airborne assault.

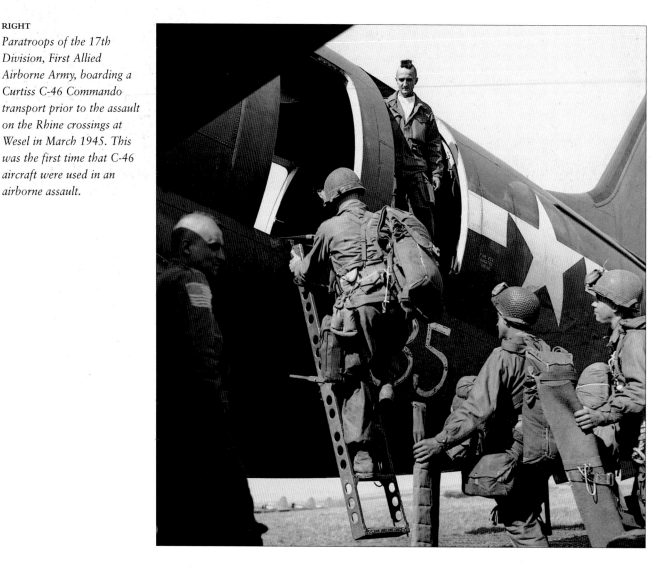

interrogation reiterated the shattering effect of such immensely superior forces on his already depleted troops.'

The fighting on the east bank of the River Rhine did not end on the afternoon of 24 March, indeed, the battle for Rees involving the 51st (Highland) Division and German paratroopers was both bloody and protracted. In it Major General Thomas Rennie, the divisional commander, was killed, and it took until 26 March for the town to be secured. Wesel also held out for a considerable period, as the 15th (Scottish) Division endeavoured to clear the ruins of the town, and small pockets of resistance took some time to overcome along the entire front. It was not until 28 March, by which time Montgomery had 20 divisions and 1000 tanks over the Rhine, that the whole area had been consolidated. In the face of such overwhelming force, this process was perhaps as inevitable as the breakout that followed it.

Strategic reassessments

The crossing of the Rhine was not as painful for Eisenhower's troops as it could so easily have been, as the American commanders in the south seized the opportunities that came their way, and made some dramatic advances. In the northern area, however, the difficulties inherent in closing to the river and then crossing it required an appropriate plan and meticulous preparation. The deft execution of that plan was one of the high points of Montgomery's period of command during the north west Europe campaign, but in its wake there were to be some major strategic reassessments, and Twenty-First Army Group were not to be able to reap the rewards of their endeavours as they would have liked.

ABOVE
Men of the US 17th Airborne Division in action in fog near Wesel, 24 March 1945. The Americans lost 46 aircraft to ground fire during the operation, and 37 more were shot down during subsequent tactical support operations.

CHAPTER ELEVEN

The Fight to the Elbe

With the Rhine crossed, there was no way back for the Reich. Most Germans now hoped that the Allies would advance quickly enough to spare them from any Russian desire for vengeance.

Once the Rhine had been crossed in March 1945, the Allies had victory in their sights and were thinking about where they would link up with the Russians. The final push into the heart of Germany was to be conducted by three Army Groups: Field Marshal Montgomery's Twenty-First Army Group consisting of the British Second, Canadian First and US Ninth Armies; Bradley's Twelfth Army Group consisting of the US First, Third and Fifteenth Armies, together with the Sixth Army Group, commanded by Lieutenant General Jacob Devers and consisting of the US Seventh Army and the First French Army – a total of 73 divisions.

Allied advantages

By this stage in the war these forces had strength in many vital areas: troop numbers; air support; supplies and, crucially, morale. The Allies were consequently confident about their future prospects, and they had good reason to be, especially when the weaknesses of their German enemy was taken into account. By late March 1945, the German armed forces were in a shambolic state. Eisenhower wrote in his memoirs, 'Militarily the thing for [Hitler] to do at that moment would have been to surrender'. Nevertheless, Germany continued to fight, motivated now by the protection of the Fatherland and in fear of what fate might befall them and their families if they did not. Hitler was certainly not going to lay down and let the Allies march into Germany without a fight. Moreover, Hitler did not care about the fate of an exhausted population of a post-war Germany when he ordered his retreating forces to destroy anything that might be of value to the advancing enemy. As a result roads, communications, railways, vehicles, bridges, factories, among many other things vital to Germany's infrastructure, were destroyed. Hitler told Albert Speer: 'If the war is lost, the nation will also perish. This fate is inevitable. There is no need to consider the basis even of a most primitive existence any longer. On the contrary, it is better to destroy even that, and to destroy it ourselves. The nation has proved itself weak, and the future belongs solely to the stronger eastern nation. Besides, those who remain after the battle are of little value; for the good have fallen.'

Hitler did not move from this view, nor from the view that his field commanders were letting him down. The mistakes made by some officers, argued Hitler, was having a detrimental affect upon troop morale, and the German High Command was compelled to initiate new awards in the hope that it would help soldiers find from within themselves

OPPOSITE
A white flag of surrender is propped up in the rubble of a German city. By the war's end, the country's infrastructure was in a very bad state, and the Allies had to provide humanitarian relief to their former enemy.

some as yet untapped source of fighting spirit. There were medals for fighting out of an encirclement and back to friendly lines, and there was even the offer of a signed photograph of von Rundstedt for acts of bravery – although few, unsurprisingly, applied for such an award. In such circumstances, the High Command was forced to use the direct threat of the firing squad in order to regain discipline. Failure to blow a bridge or withdrawing without orders were just two of a plethora of offences made punishable by death.

Thus an army that had once been so loyal and successful was, by the spring of 1945, a ramshackle outfit that had to be gripped by an iron fist of fear that squeezed relentlessly for one final effort and the last drop of blood.

Spent force

But the German army was a spent force, it could give little more. Tortuous lines of communication, few resources, very little air support and widespread demoralisation all had a damaging impact upon fighting ability. When compared directly to their opposition, the Germans were no match for them either on the ground or in the air. When Günther Blumentritt took command of the First Parachute Army in late March 1945 – a unit with a good fighting reputation – he was horrified to discover many frailties in what was supposed to be the most powerful German Army in the west. He later recalled: 'I found that there were great gaps in my front, that I had no reserves, that my artillery was weak, that I had no air support whatever and hardly any tanks. My communications and signal facilities were entirely inadequate [and]...reinforcements that still came to me were hastily trained and badly equipped.'

The attritional war that Germany had been subjected to for nearly four years had never bit so deeply as it did in the last days of the fighting on the Western Front. The Commander-in-Chief of the German forces in the West, Field Marshal Kesselring, was well aware of the difficulties that faced all three of his Army Groups. In the north were Army Group H, commanded by General Johannes Blaskowitz, consisting of First Parachute Army and Twenty-Fifth Army. In the centre were Army Group B, commanded by Field Marshal Walter Model, consisting of Fifth Panzer Army, Seventh Army and Fifteenth Army. In the south were Army Group G, commanded by General Paul Hausser, consisting of First Army and Nineteenth Army. All suffered similar weaknesses and all were readying themselves for the coming storm. Kesselring certainly had neither the quality nor the quantity of the troops that he needed. Indeed the shortage of troops was so bad that

BELOW

Combat engineers of the 83rd Division, US Ninth Army crossing the River Saale in April 1945. The Ninth Army reached the Elbe on 11 April, and the First Army took Leipzig on the 18th. Patton's Third Army, meanwhile, was pushing on through southern Germany towards Austria and Czechoslovakia.

LEFT
Men of the US 194th Glider Infantry Regiment, 17th Airborne Brigade, avail themselves of some hospitality in a captured German inn. According to the wartime caption, the front line was only 182m (200 yards) away.

the *Volkssturm* – the German Home Guard – were called upon to provide manpower to help stem the Allied tide. Even then the Germans could only manage to raise 26 full strength divisions in the west. Hitler's army was on the point of destruction and ready to exacerbate their many weaknesses were four million Allied soldiers anxious to end the war in Europe as quickly as possible.

Final mission

The push from the Rhine to the Elbe marked the climax of the war in western Europe, for Kesselring's front was about to be torn apart in a fatal blow from which Germany was unable to recover. The Allies clearly wished to inflict a total defeat upon Germany during this final phase of the war, but what were their military objectives? Up until 28 March, Eisenhower had often stated that that his strategic aim was Berlin, an objective that had certainly caught the imagination of the public on both sides of the Atlantic and the troops deployed in Europe. Even so, in the dying days of March, just as Twenty-First Army Group was beginning its advance across the north German plain towards the capital of the Fatherland, Montgomery received a telegram outlining a change in strategy. In this note the

Allied Supreme Commander stated that it was his intention to switch the main thrust away from Twenty-First Army Group and Berlin and towards Twelfth Army Group and the Elbe and Mulde rivers. The aim of the Allies now was to cut the German army in two and, ultimately, facilitate a smooth link-up with Stalin's Red Army.

The new objectives required a modicum of reorganisation, and to aid his advance Bradley regained Ninth Army from Montgomery's command, and was given access to the newly created Fifteenth Army, commanded by Lieutenant General Leonard Gerow, for defensive operations on the west bank of the Rhine. Twenty-First Army Group, meanwhile, were to protect Bradley's left flank, clear Holland, seize the north German ports, cut off Denmark and reach the Baltic before the Soviets. On Bradley's right, the Sixth Army were to protect his southern flank and drive into Germany and on into Austria. These objectives were undeniably very different from what Eisenhower had been saying since Operation Overlord. In September 1944, for example, he had written, '...clearing Berlin is the main prize...we should concentrate all our energies and resources on a rapid thrust to Berlin' – so why the change of mind?

Firstly, the political leaders of American, the Soviet Union and Britain had all agreed in July 1944 that after the war Germany was to be carved up into National Zones of Occupation. These arrangements, confirmed at Yalta in February 1945, ensured that Berlin would become an area controlled by all three powers even though it was deep inside the proposed Soviet zone. Thus, the capture of Berlin could no longer be considered a priority for the British and Americans unless it was deemed either vital strategically, or necessary in trying to keep the Soviets out of central Germany.

Berlin no longer important

The second reason for the change in strategy stemmed from Eisenhower's belief that Berlin was no longer as strategically important as it had been. The supreme commander argued that the war could be shortened more effectively if other, more critical, military objectives were seized instead. He wrote to Montgomery on 28 March: 'You will see that in none of [my plan] do I mention Berlin. So far as I am concerned, that place has become nothing but a geographical location; I have never been interested in these.'

The area that Eisenhower now wanted to capture with some urgency was the Ruhr. The Ruhr was Germany's industrial heartland and contained Model's Fifth Panzer and Fifteenth Armies. Even SHAEF believed reports that the region's industrial output had

suffered a mortal blow as the result of the Allied bombing raids, and Eisenhower's order to US Ninth and First Armies encircle it was instructive – the Allied High Command were not in the business of taking any chances at this late stage in the war.

The third reason for the strategic rethink was the perceived necessity of advancing south into the mountains of Bavaria and Austria. It was believed that in this area, some 240 miles long and 80 miles deep, the Allies would find the 'German National Redoubt', the final ideological demonstration of National Socialist resistance. SHAEF intelligence had identified SS troops, jet aircraft and, crucially, 'some of the most important ministries and personalities of the Nazi regime' moving into the area. This National Redoubt, because it was located in such difficult terrain, threatened to be an awkward fortress to clear if the Germans were given time to consolidate in the area – and the Allies did not want to expend huge casualties unless absolutely necessary. Eisenhower was therefore adamant that the Nazis were removed from the area as quickly as possible.

The fourth and final reason for the removal of Berlin from Allied strategic aims had to do with distance and numbers of troops. By the end of March, the Soviets had over two million men just 30 miles from Berlin whilst the Allies were 200 miles away, back on the Rhine. Eisenhower was also persuaded by Bradley's estimate that it would

RIGHT

Soldiers of the US Ninth Army searching the ruins of the Krupp armaments works at Essen, in the heart of the industrial Ruhr, for hidden 'Werewolf' (stay-behind fanatical Nazis) snipers, on 17 April 1945. Attacked many times by RAF Bomber Command, and repaired just as often, the Krupp factory had been totally destroyed in October 1944.

cost approximately 100,000 casualties to take Berlin, a price that was immediately regarded as too high in order to take a 'mere symbol'.

Whilst these four reasons for changing strategic priorities were confessed by Eisenhower, there was also, very probably, an unrevealed influence upon his decision to change tack. The supreme commander was under a great deal of pressure from the United States not to allow the British to capture the prestigious prize of Berlin whilst the Americans played a mere supporting role. The United States were clearly the driving force behind the western war effort, and Bradley (in particular) thought that the Americans should gain the lion's share of the glory when victory eventually came – or at least that that glory should be denied the British alone. Bradley vigorously argued that his reputation and that of the United States Army, had been tarnished when Montgomery had been given command of a large part of Twelfth Army Group at a critical phase in the Germans Ardennes offensive during December of the previous year. It is probable that Eisenhower was influenced by such comments.

New tactics

In the end, despite the British protest, Allied strategy was redirected. Twelfth Army Group was to lead an advance aimed at the Elbe and Mulde rivers, and a successful union with the Soviet forces advancing from the east. Boldness had been replaced by caution.

On 28 March, Lieutenant General Sir Miles Dempsey's British Second Army broke out of its Rhine bridgehead at Wesel on a three-corps front. By 5 April, with their right on Uelzen and their left on Bremen, the British were fast approaching the Weser River. Three days later two corps had crossed the Weser and one of them, VIII Corps, had also gained a bridgehead over the Leine River just north of Hanover. It was at this point, however, that VIII Corps ran into Panzer Training Battalion 'Grossdeutschland' and was held up. Although the Germans were generally weak in the west, they often made good use of defensive positions, and fought bravely to slow the Allied onslaught. Indeed, Montgomery used the delay on the Leine to justify his claim for more troops to aid his advance. The Twenty-First Army Group commander thought that extra manpower was vital if the Second Army had any hope of blocking a Soviet advance to the North Sea.

Assistance eventually came in two forms: Eisenhower decided that Bradley could look after his own left flank (thus freeing more British troops to concentrate on the Second Army advance), and that Dempsey could call upon US XVIII Airborne Corps to help seize a line from the Elbe to the Baltic Sea. By mid-April all three British corps were advancing well: on the left, XXX Corps were on the outskirts of Bremen; XII Corps, in the centre, were moving towards Hamburg; and VIII Corps, on the right, having snatched Lüneburg, were just short of the Elbe. The British had managed to advance some 200 miles in just three weeks.

The Canadian First Army, commanded by Lieutenant General Crerar, advanced on a two-corps front with the aim of clearing eastern Holland, the area south of the Zuider Zee and the Wilhelmshaven Peninsula. Moving out of their bridgehead on 2 April, the Canadians had reached the Twente Canal within two days. From here II Corps were to break north and north-east whilst I Corps were to attack west

ABOVE
Faces of defeat; young and old German prisoners of war pose reluctantly for the camera. Even now, Hitler was still directing the movements of phantom armies from his bunker beneath the ruins of besieged Berlin.

RIGHT

Part of the massive mopping-up operation: 10,000 German troops were taken prisoner in the Ruhr pocket by the 99th Infantry Division, US First Army.

BELOW

A paratrooper of the 82nd Airborne Division, wearing the standard American parachute uniform and armed with a .45 calibre M1 Thomson sub-machine gun, the famous 'Tommy Gun'.

across the Ijssel River. By the second week in April the Canadians were making fast progress; indeed, on 8 April, II Corps crossed the Eems River at Meppen and by the 10th had not only taken Deventer and Zwolle but were also moving towards Oldenburg in Germany.

On 12 April, a division from I Corps attacked across the Ijssel River towards Arnhem. The town that had been the focus of so many Allied hopes and so much fighting in September 1944, took just three days to overcome in April 1945. Canadian success continued when the Zuider Zee was eventually reached on 18 April, after Apeldoorn had been overrun two days earlier. By the third week of April, therefore, I Corps was looking out across the Eem and Grebbe rivers towards a starving Dutch population which desperately needed help.

The Ruhr pocket

The US Ninth and First Armies, commanded by Lieutenant General William Simpson and General Courtney Hodges respectively, began their encirclement of the Ruhr on 28 March. Field Marshal Walter Model did try to break out of by counterattacking in the north near Hamm and in the south near Siegen, but both attempts failed and on 1 April, the two American armies met at Lippstadt. Model had tied up his fortunes with Hitler's regime, and in reward had been promoted to the rank of Field Marshal at the age of 54, but he could not prevent the collapse of the German army – nobody could.

The mopping up of the Ruhr pocket was a relatively slow process due to both the terrain and the nature of the built-up industrial environment that provided plenty of hiding places for snipers. As the Americans advanced, they could see the ragged state of both the army and the civilian population in the pocket. The unceasing strategic bombing offensive had devastated three quarters of the housing in the region, and communications were hopeless. What little food and ammunition the besieged Germans had could not get to where it was most needed, and by 12 April, as the Americans reached Essen, it was impossible to transport anything anywhere at all. The critical situation in the Ruhr was certainly depressing for the Fuhrer, but was even more demoralising for those that fought there. General Kochling, the commander of LXXXI Corps, one of the encircled formations, later said of the antagonising position that his troops had been placed in: 'The continuation of resistance in the Ruhr pocket was a crime. It was Model's duty to surrender ... only the danger of reprisals against my family prevented me from taking this step myself.'

What little fighting spirit there had been in German units soon evaporated as the Americans advanced; indeed it was not uncommon for the Wehrmacht soldiers to celebrate on hearing that another town had fallen. By 14 April, the Germans were surrendering at such a rate that administering them became a problem for the Americans. On this day, the pocket had been split when a corps from Ninth Army and two from First Army met near Hagen on the Ruhr River. On 16 April, some 80,000 Germans surrendered in one 24-hour period. Two days later, a massive 325,000 Germans soldiers (including 30 general officers) were taken prisoner and all organised-armed resistance came to an end. Field Marshal Model, the man who had criticised Field Marshal Paulus for surrendering at Stalingrad in February 1943, walked out into some woods near Dusseldorf and shot himself. By this stage there was no organised front in the west. Hitler had lost all control over events and, in fact, found it very difficult to find out what was happening anywhere. The Führer's military conferences had had a tendency to meander aimlessly from the topic for a number of months. By April they were increasingly confused and, generally, a waste of time. A definite move towards a discussion of past events in these meetings was an unhelpful symptom of Hitler's inability to deal with the present. As Hitler lost touch with reality, his stock answer to many questions became 'No withdrawal'. When presented with information that suggested that certain officers had failed in their duties, Hitler would not look

into the matter but immediately order dismissal, demotion or execution. When Sepp Dietrich, the commander of Sixth SS Panzer Army and once in charge of the Fuhrer's personal bodyguard, was driven back into Vienna in the face of overwhelming force, Hitler radioed to him: 'The Führer believes that the troops have not fought as the situation demanded and orders that the SS Divisions *Adolf Hitler*, *Das Reich*, *Totenkopf*, and *Hohenstaufen*, be stripped of their arm-bands.'

Dietrich radioed back that rather than carrying out the order, he would shoot himself.

The Elbe reached

The Ninth Army continued to push east towards the Elbe River in the opening days of April. On 4 April elements of Ninth Army were on the Weser River, on 8 April they had bridged the Leine, on 10 April Hanover was seized and, remarkably, on 11 April the Elbe River was reached just south of Magdeburg. The incredible advance prompted Eisenhower into a statement about exactly where the Twelfth Army Group stop-line would be. It was decided that the line would run from Wittenberge in the north to Bayreuth in the

BELOW

German prisoners are marched to the rear on the central reservation of an autobahn near Giesen in southern Germany as vehicles of the 6th Armored Division, US Third Army, roll past them towards the Czech frontier. Patton's army entered Czechoslovakia and Austria on 4 May 1945.

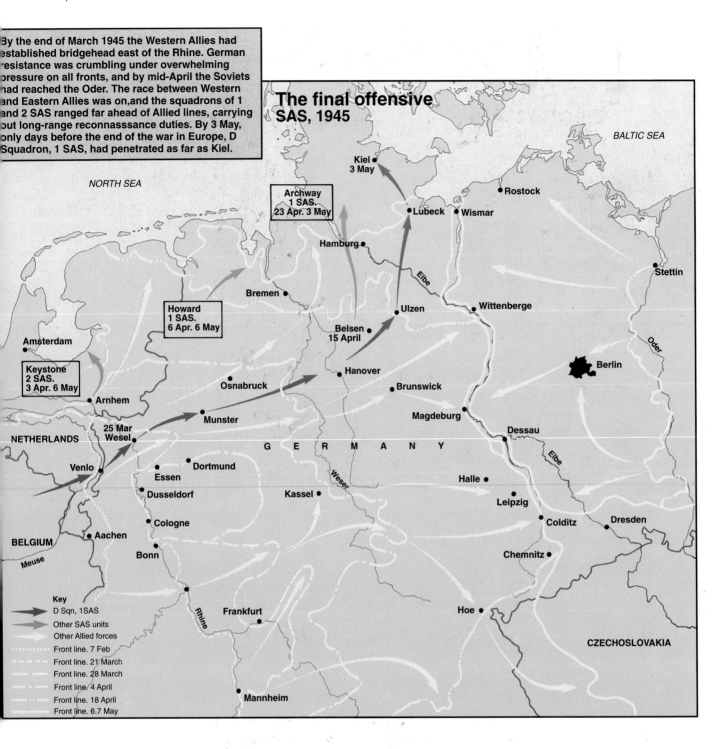

By the end of March 1945 the Western Allies had established bridgehead east of the Rhine. German resistance was crumbling under overwhelming pressure on all fronts, and by mid-April the Soviets had reached the Oder. The race between Western and Eastern Allies was on, and the squadrons of 1 and 2 SAS ranged far ahead of Allied lines, carrying out long-range reconnaissance duties. By 3 May, only days before the end of the war in Europe, D Squadron, 1 SAS, had penetrated as far as Kiel.

The final offensive
SAS, 1945

Key
- D Sqn, 1SAS
- Other SAS units
- Other Allied forces
- Front line. 7 Feb
- Front line. 21 March
- Front line. 28 March
- Front line. 4 April
- Front line. 18 April
- Front line. 6.7 May

south, connecting Dessau, Leipzig and Chemnitz on the Elbe and Mulde rivers. It was the case, therefore, that by 11 April, Ninth Army's forward element had moved as far east as Eisenhower would allow – despite the fact that Berlin was only two days away at the current rate of advance. Eisenhower was not drawn into an unthinking dash to Berlin, however, despite the pressure put on him by some commanders. In this sensitive situation the supreme commander emphasised the need to clear his flanks, to achieve a problem-free union with the Soviets and, as he wrote to the Combined

Chiefs on 15 April, 'It must be remembered that only our spearheads are up to the river; our centre of gravity is way back of there'. The decision was a wise one. Once again the watchword was 'caution' rather than 'boldness'.

The First Army also made great progress towards their eastern objectives from a very early stage. By 9 April, with Kassel and Gottingen already seized, General Hodges' troops were heading for the Harz mountains, where they co-operated with the Ninth Army in the envelopment of some 15,000 German troops. These were members of Wenck's newly

German troops. These were members of Wenck's newly formed Eleventh Army, which had only just been formed and which was supposed, in theory, to have gone to Model's assistance in the Ruhr. In practice, however, the Germans had been overwhelmed by the speed of the American advance and, as a result, on 18 April, were encircled. By this point the First Army had reached their stop line on the Mulde River at Dessau and had to call a halt to their advance.

Patton's advance

The Third Army, commanded by General George Patton, had also broken out of their bridgehead at the end of March and immediately fanned out. Some units cleared Frankfurt, others moved in to Kassel and Gotha (both eventually overrun on 4 April) whilst others still advanced towards the Thüringian Forest. By the second week in April, large areas of the forest had been cleared and by the 14th Chemnitz, Hoth and Bayreuth had been reached. Indeed, the advance was going so well that Patton asked Eisenhower for permission to push into Czechoslovakia. The supreme commander replied that he could not order such a move until the flanks of Twelfth Army Group had been cleared, but in principle he was in favour of an advance up to the line Carlsbad-Pilsen-Budejovice.

Although for the time being any push into Czechoslovakia had to be put on hold, Patton was asked to move down to the Bohemian Forest to link up with the Soviets in the

Danube Valley. This advance was to be co-ordinated with Sixth Army Group who had already begun the clearance of southern Germany. By 4 April the US 7th Army, commanded by Lieutenant General Patch, were on the outskirts of Würzburg whilst the First French, commanded by General Jean de Lattre de Tassigny, were busy in Karlsruhe. Both armies came up against stiffer opposition here than could be found elsewhere on the front. On 7 April, for example, 10th Armoured Division were forced to withdraw after an attack on Crailsheim failed due to the strength of the German defence. It seems that at this stage Hausser's troops of Army Group G were not as demoralised as those who bore the brunt of the Allied offensive further to the north. The Germans were not, of course, strong enough to halt the American advance altogether. By 8 April, Seventh Army had captured Schweinfurt and was soon on its way, via the Hohe Rhöne Mountains, to Nuremberg which was eventually reached nine days later. By this stage the French had started to engage the German Nineteenth Army in the Stuttgart-Black Forest area, and were already focusing on the Austrian border.

Roosevelt's death

With the Allies having taken over one million prisoners since the beginning of April, the German army in the west was clearly on the point of disintegration. Even though President Roosevelt had died on 12 April, the Allies remained calm and assured, whilst the Germans sank further into a state of panic and confusion. By 18 April, Hitler had little of Germany, save Bavaria, under his command. By the fourth week of April, Marshal Zhukov's lead tanks had penetrated the eastern suburbs of Berlin whilst in northern Italy, Field Marshal Alexander's offensive was progressing well. Yet whilst Hitler was still alive German commanders, possibly due to their oath of allegiance, but more probably due to the fear of retribution, would not surrender.

BELOW
Immediately after crossing the Elbe, the Gordon Highlanders began the task of clearing the nearby woods of German troops and snipers. Here, a German major and his 'command' – children between the ages of 13 and 16 – stand under guard.

In the last week of April, with the British Second Army on the Elbe, on the outskirts of Hamburg and in the vicinity of Bremen, Montgomery and Dempsey discussed the next phase of their operations. The British were to clear Bremen and the Cuxhaven Peninsula, cross the Elbe, advance up to the Danish border and, as a matter of priority, reach the Baltic before the Soviets managed to slip through to the North Sea.

Bremen crushed

At Bremen, XXX Corps commander, Lieutenant General Horrocks, decided to give the Germans a chance to surrender before he attacked. Nobody in the city, however, had the courage to take the necessary decision, and as a result the fighting lasted for five days. Once again the German people were made to suffer for Hitler's tyranny. On 25 April, medium and heavy bombers hit Bremen levelling many areas. A ground attack followed. As the British soldiers entered the devastated city, it was quite clear that the Germans were both disorientated and dispirited. The British took possession of Bremen on 27 April, and immediately turned north to face their next objective, the Cuxhaven Peninsular. Meanwhile, with Berlin finally encircled by Soviet troops on 25 April, the British had now to reach the Baltic as quickly as possible. Dempsey crossed the Elbe at Lauenburg on 28 April, and from there advanced north to Lübeck and the west to Hamburg – both capitulated on 2 May. US XVIII Airborne Corps meanwhile, joined by British Sixth Airborne Division, crossed the Elbe at Dachau and sped north for the Baltic. Wismar was reached on 2 May, just hours before the Soviets.

Stalin was never in any doubts as to Eisenhower's intentions because, on 30 April, the Allied Supreme Commander had sent him a telegram outlining his plans. The Twenty-First Army Group would hold the line from Wismar to Dömitz on the Elbe and also occupy the area up to the Kiel Canal. The Twelfth Army Group would hold their position on the Elbe and Mulde rivers although Third Army, resources allowing, would advance into Czechoslovakia. The Sixth Army Group would continue to advance deeper into southern Germany and penetrate into Austria. Eisenhower now eagerly awaited Stalin's response to these plans and continued to hold Patton's thrust into Czechoslovakia until one was received.

The Canadians, meanwhile, although not having the problem of encroaching upon territory earmarked by the Soviets, did have difficulties of their own. Whilst II Corps, firmly established across the Küsten Canal, continued to advance slowly up into the Wilhelmshaven Peninsular, I Corps awaited orders to advance over the Eem and Grebbe rivers in order to relieve the starving Dutch population – but the orders never came. Montgomery feared that the German commander in the region, General Blaskowitz and *Reichskommisar* Seyss-Inquart, would carry out their threat to open the dykes protecting the Netherlands from the damaging salt waters of the North Sea and the Zuider Zee if the Canadians continued to advance. Thus, on 30 April, Eisenhower sent his chief-of-staff, Lieutenant General Walter Bedell-Smith to talk to the two men. The Germans agreed to a truce period during which time the Allies could drop food behind their lines, but when Bedell-Smith mentioned surrender, it was clear that neither man wanted the responsibility.

In the Twelfth Army Group area, with Ninth Army firmly established along their stop line, the First Army continued to mop up the remaining pockets of resistance on their front. Halle and Leipzig were captured on 19 April, after a great deal of street fighting, and Dessau was taken on the 22nd. Two days later, Hodges' men reached their own stop line on the Mulde and, on the following day, the forward elements of 69th Division linked up

ABOVE

The historic meeting on the Elbe between American and Soviet troops, 25 April 1945. Spearheads of the US First and Ninth Armies both made contact with the Russians. The friendly atmosphere evident here would very soon be a thing of the past.

With the Allied advance into Germany came the shocking discovery of the Nazi concentration camps. Here bodies of former inmates are stacked in a common grave at Bergen-Belsen. The commandant of Belsen, Josef Kramer, was tried by the British and condemned to death.

with Marshal Konev's 58th Guards Division on the Elbe. The first link up had been successfully made, and before long Soviet and American troops were shaking hands all along the front.

Patton, meanwhile, still awaited orders from Eisenhower to move into Czechoslovakia, but while he was waiting, his Third Army continued their thrust south. On 25 April, Patton's men crossed the Danube River and on the following day, overran Regensburg before heading for Austria and Linz. Linz was finally captured on 5 May, just one day after Eisenhower received word that the Soviet High Command had agreed to his boundaries. As a result the Third Army was ordered to seize the line Carlsbad-Pilsen-Budejovice, whilst the Soviets, much to Patton's dismay, were left the rest of Czechoslovakia including Prague.

Allied advance

On Third Army's right, the US Seventh Army and French First Army were still making good progress. On 20 April, the Americans finally captured Nuremberg after a five-day battle, and the French took Stuttgart. By 22 April,

both Armies had crossed the Danube and in so doing, finally shattered General Hausser's Army Group G. Ulm was taken by the Americans on the 23rd, whilst the French were to reach Lake Constance on the Swiss border a few days later. By the end of the month, Seventh Army had moved into Dachu and Munich and the First French had entered Austria. By 3 May, the American forces were in Austria, at Innsbruck where they quickly advanced to the Brenner Pass and linked up with the US Fifth Army that had fought its way up through Italy. Other units meanwhile seized Salzburg on 4 May, and some even penetrated as far as the bombed ruins of Hitler's mountain retreat, the Berchtesgaden. German resistance had all but vanished by this point.

By the last week in April, it was clear to everyone that the war was nearly over. Indeed, it was at this time that Himmler tried to seek surrender without Hitler's approval. On 23 April, Himmler, Hitler's SS *Reichsführer*, contacted the head of the Swedish Red Cross at Lübeck, and told him that he felt at liberty to ask the Swedish Government to let the Allies know that the German Government were prepared to surrender on the Western Front. Himmler's attempts to initiate surrender failed immediately. The British Prime Minister quickly informed both the Americans and the Soviets of Himmler's overtures in accordance with a secret 1943 protocol. This protocol pledged that the American, British and Soviet Governments would consult each other if the German Government ever came forward to one of them with a surrender proposal. The British Cabinet made it quite clear in their reply to Himmler that, whilst the surrender of a front, or any army, or indeed any lower formation, by a German commander was acceptable in the field (as this was purely a tactical and military matter), the German Government could only surrender unconditionally on all fronts.

German surrender in Italy

Whilst Himmler was making his offer to the British, the Germans were finally beaten in Italy. On 29 April, as the result of the Allied offensive, General Vietinghoff signed unconditional surrender at Alexander's headquarters. The 30 days of April had not been happy ones for Field Marshal Kesselring; indeed, the month had seen the western powers take over 1.65 million prisoners including Field Marshals von Kleist, von Leeb, Weichs, List and von Rundstedt. This brought the total number of prisoners taken since June 1944 to almost three million. The German army simply could not withstand this sort of pressure for much longer.

As the German war news become worse, Hitler became withdrawn and turned away from the truth as he waited for a miracle. In mid-January Hitler had moved into the Chancellery building in Berlin, but the frequency and ferocity of the Allied air raids forced him into a bunker nearby. This incredibly strong structure, some 50 feet below ground and consisting of 18 rooms on two storeys, was Hitler's refuge until his death. The subterranean life that Hitler led during his last days was not that dissimilar to that that he had experienced in the trenches during World War I, especially when Soviet shells began to reverberate his shelter. He found solace in his Alsatian, Blondi, and a portrait of Frederick the Great which hung above the table in his study. As the news that Hitler received in his bunker got worse, he turned for comfort to the campaigns of Frederick the Great who, against the odds in 1757, defeated the invad-

ing armies of Prussia and routed them. The military conferences that were held every afternoon and at midnight, however, brought little prospect of anything other than inevitable defeat.

The bad news, the bombing and the shelling, when combined with Hitler's already poor state of health, took its toll on him. Now only sleeping between 8 am and 11 am, an exhausted Hitler seemed to age visibly with every passing day. Göring said in 1944 that Hitler had aged 15 years since the war began. The assassination attempt in July 1944 had severely damaged his hearing and shattered his nerves, but even more debilitating were the cocktail of drugs that he was addicted to by this time. Possibly already suffering from Parkinson's disease, the drugs that Hitler had injected six times a day did little to help his massive mood swings. The news that Roosevelt had died pulled him momentarily out of a deeply despondent state and into euphoria; he turned to Speer and said, excitedly, 'You never wanted to believe it...Here we have the miracle I always predicted. Who

BELOW
Two German U-boats sunk at their moorings in a north German base in May 1945. Many U-boats were destroyed by bombing in the closing months of the war, or scuttled deliberately to escape capture by the Allies in the last days of the conflict.

was right? The war isn't lost...Roosevelt is dead'. The reality of the situation, however, pushed Hitler once more into a deep malaise. Albert Speer said that Hitler had, 'reached the last station in his flight from reality, a reality which he refused to acknowledge since his youth'. The man was disintegrating before the eyes of those that knew him and disappointed those that met him for the first time. Captain Gerhardt Boldt Hitler saw for the first time during this period and said that: 'His head was slightly wobbling. His left arm hung slackly and his hand trembled a good deal. There was an indescribable flickering glow in his eyes, creating fearsome and wholly unnatural effect. His face and the parts around his eyes gave the impression of total exhaustion. All his movements were those of a senile man'. General Guderian said that Hitler 'walked awkwardly, stooped more than ever and his gestures were jerky and slow'. The Führer's decline in health mirrored that of Germany's.

The month of April saw a number of Hitler's closest colleagues leave the bunker. Among them was Göring who had been told in 1941 that in the event of Hitler's death or inability to carry out his functions, he should take over as Führer. Having left Berlin, Göring sent a telegram to Hitler asking whether the time had come for a hand over of power:

My Führer,
In view of your decision to remain at your post in the fortress of Berlin, do you agree that I take over, at once, the total leadership of the Reich, with full freedom of action at home and abroad...You know what I feel for you in the gravest hour of my life. Words fail me to express myself. May God protect you and speed you quickly here in spite of all
Your loyal
Hermann Göring

Hitler, shocked by the lack of loyalty being shown by key members of his regime, ordered Göring's arrest.

The situation in Berlin was desperate. A German officer wrote in his diary: '27th April: Continuous attack throughout the night. Increasing signs of dissolution... Hardly any communication amongst troops, except a few regular battalions equipped with radio posts. Telephone cables are shot to pieces. Physical conditions are indescribable. No rest, no relief. No regular food, hardly any bread. We get water from the tunnels and filter it. The whole large expanse of Potsdamer Platz is

BELOW
Admiral Hans von Friedeburg, the commander of the German Navy at the end of World War II, surrenders all German land, sea and air forces in Northern Germany, Holland and Denmark to Field Marshal Montgomery at Twenty-First Army Group HQ, Lüneburg Heath, on 4 May 1945.

waste ruins. Masses of damaged vehicles, half-smashed trailers of the ambulances with the wounded still in them. Dead people everywhere, many of them frightfully cut up by tanks and trucks.'

As the days passed, even Hitler's thoughts turned not to a last minute victory, but to his own death. In the early hours of the morning of 29 April, Hitler married Eva Braun in a brief ceremony in the bunker and then dictated his last will and testament. This document reveals that, to the very end, Hitler still firmly believed in a Jewish conspiracy. The last paragraph of the Political Testament said, 'Above all I charge the leaders of the nation and those under them to scrupulous observance of the laws of race and to the merciless opposition to the universal poisoner of all peoples, international Jewry'. His body had failed, but his mind had not changed. Having expelled Göring and Himmler from the Nazi Party, he then named his successors: Admiral Dönitz was to become Führer; Goebbels the Chancellor, and Bormann Party Minister.

Hitler's end

In his will, Hitler stated that after his death, his body was to be burned together with that of his new wife – he feared the same fate as the bodies of Mussolini and his mistress, which had been strung up in Milan. Eva Braun was stoical during this period, and had no other desire than to die with her husband, indeed, she was often heard complaining during the final days, 'Poor, poor Adolf, deserted by everyone, betrayed by all. Better that ten thousand others die than that he should be lost to Germany'.

Dönitz did not have to wait long before he took up his unenviable new position. On 30 April at 1530 hours, ten days after his 56th birthday, Hitler shot himself and Eva Braun took poison. The bodies were carried up into the garden, soaked in petrol and then set alight just before the Soviets reached the area. As news of Hitler's death and Dönitz's appointment reached the front, the remaining pockets of resistance began to negotiate for peace independently. Floods of German soldiers moved across the increasingly small strip of land dividing the Eastern and Western Fronts so that they could surrender to the Anglo-American forces.

On 4 May, at Montgomery's headquarters at Lüneburg Heath, Dönitz's envoys agreed to the unconditional surrender of German forces

in Holland, Denmark and North Germany with effect from 0830 hours on 5 May. The Twenty-First Army Group immediately received a tour by the effervescent Field Marshal Montgomery, who addressed his victorious troops. Montgomery said that they had been successful for four main reasons: enemy mistakes; Allied dominance; Anglo-American co-operation and the fighting abilities of the British, Canadian and American troops.

On 5 May Dönitz's representatives arrived at Eisenhower's headquarters at Rheims in France to negotiate unconditional surrender. Once again the Germans tried to stall the process, but the supreme commander demanded the surrender immediately. At 0240 hours on 7 May, Admiral von Friedeburg and

ABOVE
Refugees walk past the Brandenburg Gate after the fall of Berlin. Eisenhower, to the dismay of the British, gave the Russians a free hand in the capture of the Reich's capital. The Russians withdrew from the western sectors of the city in July 1945, when an inter-Allied government was created.

ABOVE

In a brief idyllic moment before the onset of the Cold War, a soldier of the 4th Armored Division, US Third Army, shares a cigarette with Russian troops of the 3rd Ukrainian Army, in the Strakonice district of Czechoslovakia.

General Jodl signed the surrender document with the British, Soviet and French representatives present. Operations on all fronts formally ceased at 2301 hours Central European time on 8 May.

Allied victory

The signing of these documents sealed a victory for the Allies in both a military and political sense. Militarily the Allies had achieved what their political masters had required in order to attain unconditional surrender of German – the destruction of the German armed forces both morally and physically. This victory had not been without great sacrifice for the Western Allies, indeed, between the Normandy landings and the German surrender their casualties in western Europe numbered 766,294 (which included nearly 200,000 dead). German casualties over the same period were just a little higher, but defeat had come in the wake of their sacrifice.

The fighting continued for as long as it did because of Hitler's insistence that there would be no surrender whilst he was still Führer.

The all-enveloping grip that Hitler had on the German population and armed forces should not be underestimated when trying to discover why Germany kept on fighting until May 1945.

In the final analysis, his fanatical prosecution of the war when coupled with decision making based upon an increasingly poor grip upon reality, made him a dangerous man that few had the courage to stand up to for fear of the consequences. Had Hitler died or been killed before the end of April 1945, there might have been a very strong possibility that a negotiated surrender could have been arranged; as it was, the Allies had to fight all the way into the German heartland. In such circumstances the campaign in North West Europe achieved what it needed to achieve via a strategy that exploited German weaknesses and stretched their resources to the full. Mistakes were certainly made, but Eisenhower's cautious advance with increasingly superior numbers and supplies was a credit to what was, in retrospect, the most successful coalition in history.

INDEX